COME, SEE THE PLACE

COME, SEE THE PLACE

PLACE

A Pilgrim Guide
to the
Holy Land

Ronald Brownrigg

Hodder & Stoughton
LONDON SYDNEY AUCKLAND TORONTO

All photographs have been supplied by courtesy of Inter-Church Travel and Canon Ron Brownrigg.

Various prayers and collects from the Alternative Service Book 1980 are copyright © Central Board of Finance of the Church of England and are reproduced with permission

Extracts from the Book of Common Prayer 1662, which is Crown Copyright in the United Kingdom, are reproduced by permission of Eyre & Spottiswoode, Her Majesty's Printers London

British Library Cataloguing in Publication Data

Brownrigg, Ronald
   Come, see the place: a pilgrim guide to the
   Holy Land.
   1. Palestine – Description and travel –
   Guide-books
   I. Title
   915.694'0454   DS103

   ISBN 0 340 42578 4

FOREWORD

by the Right Reverend George Appleton
formerly Anglican Archbishop in Jerusalem

I am very glad to learn that a second edition of the book *Come, See the Place* is being published, and wish that it had been available for pilgrims in the years that I was in Jerusalem.

Many pilgrims to the Holy Land have spoken to me of their need of a comprehensive guide which would not be just a Biblical and geographical description, but would suggest contemporary relevance and spiritual inspiration. This has now been provided by Ronald Brownrigg whose initial inspiration was aroused as long ago as 1943 when he was a military staff officer on Mount Zion.

Since then he has paid many visits to Jerusalem and has conducted many pilgrimages of the Holy Land, whose members will be eternally grateful for the insights he has given them. The Bible has come alive, the story of God's saving love has been firmly planted in history and authenticated in experience and conviction.

As I look at the contents of this welcome book, I remember a paragraph from Steven Runciman's monumental history of the Crusades: 'The desire to be a pilgrim is deeply rooted in human nature. To stand where those we reverence once stood, to see the very sites where they were born and toiled and died, gives us a feeling of mystic contact with them and is a practical expression of our homage. And if the great men of the world have their shrines to which their admirers come from afar, still more do men flock eagerly to those places where, they believe, the Divine has sanctified the earth.'

I believe that Canon Brownrigg's compact but exhaustive guide will help many pilgrims to stand in wonder at the many sites where the Divine has touched not only the earth, but the hearts, minds and lives of people all down the centuries. It will also help many who for one reason or another cannot accompany him on actual pilgrimage, but under his guidance may be enabled to make a pilgrimage of the spirit.

I warmly recommend you to accept the invitation of the title of this book, which is also the invitation of the angel of the Resurrection to:

'COME, SEE THE PLACE'

PILGRIMAGE PRAYERS

THE PILGRIM INTENT

For the Jew, since the time of Solomon pilgrimage to the Temple in Jerusalem was a constant, annual obligation:

> I was glad when they suggested
> we should go to the house of the Lord;
> and now at last we are standing
> in your gateways, Jerusalem.
>
> *City restored! Jerusalem,*
> *an ordered whole again:*
> *here the tribes come up,*
> *the tribes of the Lord.*
>
> They come to give thanks to the Lord,
> as he commanded Israel,
> here where the courts of justice are,
> the royal courts of David.
>
> *Pray for peace in the City of Peace.*
> *Prosperity to your houses!*
> *For peace within your city-walls.*
> *Prosperity to your palaces!*
>
> Since all here are my brothers and friends,
> I say: 'Peace be on you!'
> Since the Lord our God lives here,
> I pray for your well-being.

(from the Psalms of Ascent)

For the Muslim, the intention is a vital part of each act of obligation, whether of confession of faith, worship, almsgiving or pilgrimage:

O God, I wish to make this pilgrimage. Make it the right thing for me and accept it from me. I have intended this pilgrimage. I consecrate myself for it unto the Most High. To Him be strength and majesty.
(from Manásik al-Hajj)

So too the Christian has, down the centuries, prepared himself for pilgrimage:

> Give me my scallop-shell of quiet,
> My staff of faith to walk upon,
> My scrip of joy, immortal diet,
> My bottle of salvation,
> My gown of glory, hope's true gage;
> And then I take my pilgrimage.
>
> *(Sir Walter Raleigh 1552–1618)*

Lord Jesus Christ; you are the Way, the Truth and the Life. May we who tread in your earthly footsteps not wander from your way of Holiness. Faring forth in your blessed company, may we feel our hearts burn within us and know you face to face at our journey's end.

PRAYER FOR ISRAEL AND JERUSALEM TODAY

> O God of Abraham, Isaac, and Jacob, Grant that
> Israel of today may inherit the callings and
> blessings of Israel of old.
> May it be
>
> a God-ruled nation within itself
> a nation of priests to the world
> a blessing to all nations
> a joy to the whole earth.
>
> Revive, O Lord God,
> the gift of prophecy
> the perception of your will
> the speaking of your Word.
>
> Deepen, O Lord,
> a sense of responsibility for the world

the care for the stranger, the homeless and the poor
the consciousness of your judgement.

Let it look afresh
to its son Jesus of Nazareth
to the Church which developed from itself
to all its Semitic brethren
to the House of Islam sharing in some degree
its faith in you.
So that it may accomplish
your purpose for the world and for itself.
O Holy One of Israel
O God of all.

O Eternal Lord God, Source of all truth, Lover of
all men, we thank you for the experience of living
in this city.
Grant that we may be humble, grateful people,
     worshipping people,
          holy people.
Help us to be peace-loving people,
     who know the things that belong to peace,
     who pray and work for peace,
     who try to understand the experiences, the
     hurts, the hopes of people from whom we
     differ.
Let this city be a centre of unity for the Churches.
Let it be a place of friendship and understanding
     for men of different faiths.
Let it be truly the City of Peace, a joy of the
     whole earth and a place of blessing to all nations.
For the sake of him who wept in love over this
     city and died in love outside its walls.
Now the Everliving One, ever present with you to
heal and bless, Jesus Christ our blessed Lord
     and Saviour.

(From Archbishop George Appleton)

A PILGRIM BLESSING

May the Babe of Bethlehem be yours to tend;
May the Boy of Nazareth be yours for friend;
May the Man of Galilee his healing send;

May the Christ of Calvary his courage lend;
May the Risen Lord his presence send;
And his holy angels defend you, to the end.

A PILGRIM POEM

Begin from first, where He encradled was
In simple cratch, wrapt in a wad of hay,
Beneath the toilful ox and humble ass,
And in what rags, and in how base array,
The glory of our heavenly riches lay,
When Him the silly Shepherds came to see,
Whom greatest Princes sought on lowest knee.

From thence read on the story of His life,
His humble carriage, His unfaulty ways,
His canker'd foes, His fights, His toil, His strife,
His pains, His poverty, His sharp assays,
Through which he passed His miserable days,
Offending none, and doing good to all,
Yet being maliced both of great and small.

And look at last, how of most wretched wights
He taken was, betray'd, and false accused;
How with most scornful taunts and fell despites
He was reviled, disgraced, and foul abused;
How scourged, how crown'd, how buffeted, how bruised;
And lastly, how 'twixt robbers crucified,
With bitter wounds through hands, through feet and side!

Edmund Spenser, 1596

CONTENTS

PREFACE AND PURPOSE

This little book is the outcome of a forty-year ministry of pilgrimage leadership and training, as a war-time General Staff officer, Camp Commandant of a Services Ordinands College, Dean of St George's Jerusalem, member of the Ecumenical Institute at Tantur Bethlehem and more recently Consultant to the Holy Land and Pauline Departments at Inter-Church Travel. Having planned their earliest Holy Land itineraries in 1956, life has come full circle and, for better or for worse, that is exactly what I am doing now!

'There is no fool like an old fool' and archaeology is a fast-moving science, especially with new opportunities for excavation of hitherto inaccessible sites in the State of Israel. It is hard to keep up with Avi-Yonah, Nahman Avigad and others who publish in Israel – as well as John Wilkinson and Murphy O'Connor. I have tried not to be partisan in an assessment of Holy Places, though inevitably some sites provide more vivid illustrations than others. I would say again that identification of exact sites for the pilgrim is secondary to his personal identification and understanding of the events which he recalls.

This is primarily a pilgrim manual of information – a companion before, during and especially after pilgrimage. For some, their pilgrimage is literally the experience of a lifetime which brightens their latter years and comes alive again in every Old Testament reading, Epistle and Gospel. Any pilgrim manual inevitably reflects its writer's own personal approach and devotion. For some, mine will be biblically simplistic and outmoded. For others I know it has been helpful.

Principles do not change over the years. Prayer, with long experience in the presentation of Holy Places and the care of groups, lends a maturity which needs to be shared. Even in my limited experience I have been aware of a sort of historical succession or chain of pilgrimage inspiration. This has been passed down from the Second World War Army chaplains – like Joe Fison (Bishop of Salisbury) and Alfred Ennis another Senior Chaplain to the Forces, Jerusalem, from resident missionaries – like Eric Bishop of the Newman School in the Street of the Prophets, from Islamic scholars – like Constance Padwick and Bishop Kenneth Cragg, Aref el Aref and Pastor Nielsen, from Jewish friends – like Norman Bentwich and Rabbi Wilhelm. Such people have passed on their love and understanding of the City, the Land and the Peoples, sparking off a world of fascination, affection and intercession, of which this manual is the fruit.

I would like particularly to thank Michael Benton of Winchester for his kindly and skilful suggestions, together with much patience and time in reading the manuscript.

I do not pretend this is a simple guide book designed for a first and only holiday visit to Israel. Some of us have made the journey together six times, some sixty. Please turn to the Contents page and you will see that it provides for a 'two-centre' stay in the Holy Land: at Jerusalem *and* in Galilee, whichever you visit first. Jerusalem is rather more 'intense' than Galilee. Galilee provides either a quieter preparation, or a restful post-resurrection atmosphere. At the present moment, Inter-Church Travel brochures tend towards a scriptural 'beginning at Jerusalem', and so this manual does the same, transferring to Galilee and travelling the North from the Lake. What you do not find in the Contents, seek in the final index.

The preparatory talks attempt to do justice to all three of the great monotheistic faiths – Judaism, Christianity and Islam – whose days of obligation span the weekend: 'Yom El Juma', 'Shabbat' and 'First day of the Week': The General Information at the end is inevitably selective and could include, if space allowed, something to satisfy the particular interests of so many of us: all the natural history and wild life, all the geography and geology, all the sociology and the politics of this wonderful country.

Finally, I hope this will prove a rewarding, if in places an exacting, study course for successive visits, in body and in spirit over a lifetime, to the Land of the Lord.

RONALD BROWNRIGG

Part One:

PREPARATORY READING

THE ESSENCE OF PILGRIMAGE
– BOTH PASSIONATE AND
PENTECOSTAL

St Augustine wrote 'Believe and thou comest; love and thou art drawn. Do not conceive of long journeyings; for unto Him, who is everywhere, we come by love and not by sailing.' But Our Lord himself said 'Come and see!' (John I).

Pilgrimage has long been a natural form of piety, like prayer and almsgiving; the Jews went up to Jerusalem for their festivals – the holy people of God to the Holy City to offer sacrifice on the holy place. The Christian Church early adopted the practice of pilgrimage to the holy places: Justin Martyr, c. A.D. 100, wrote: 'If anyone wants proof for the birth of Jesus Christ, let him go to Bethlehem and see for himself both the cave in which He was born and the manger in which He was laid.' Sophronius, c. A.D. 550, wrote: 'Upon the famous floor, where the Christ God was placed, I would press my lips, my face and my forehead that I might bear away thence a blessing.' We, who make pilgrimages to the holy places, dare consciously or unconsciously to expose our souls to the action of the Holy Spirit, who sanctifies us in the knowledge, faith and love of Our Lord Jesus Christ.

The duration of most people's pilgrimage is, of necessity, limited by financial resources and the brevity of holidays, but this has always been so. For most pilgrims down the centuries, their visit to the Holy Land has been intense, involving the output of considerable physical and psychic energy and self-sacrifice. Without these elements of effort and sacrifice, a visit to the holy places will not be truly a pilgrimage. Dostoevsky said: 'When the pious pilgrim comes in sight of the goal of his journey, he climbs down, out of his vehicle and takes to the road on foot. There is then a joy mysterious and profound. We enter an unfamiliar world – a realm of joy – a thousand times less known to us and a thousand times more profound than the realm of grief and a thousand times more fruitful.'

What makes the holy places *Holy*? Such places as Calvary and the Empty Tomb? Surely, because they have been chosen and used by God, as the stage property and scenery in the drama of our redemption. St John of Damascus said: 'I venerate them, because they are the vessels of God's action. It is thus that I venerate angels and men and all matter which ministers to my salvation, in the purpose of God.'

You and I, however, would inevitably find these stage props doubly buried: firstly by masonry and rubble, for all walled cities have been closely packed building upon building through the centuries. Secondly by oriental ornament and decoration, in marble and tapestry, which we Westerners are tempted to deplore. Notwithstanding it is oriental devotion which has preserved and protected these sites for us to enjoy. Professor Leon Zander has written: 'In saluting these sacred relics of the past, which for ever bear the imprint of Christ, we unite ourselves with the spirit that rests in them. So, we absorb the grace inherent in the material things that have been chosen and exalted by the free act of God.'

As pilgrims to the holy places, we shall have to use both our imaginations and our memories, to let go some of our Western inhibitions – if we are to recall and to make real the past within the here and now. As in the Eucharist the sacred past becomes the present, so it may be on pilgrimage: we may kneel at the manger; we may in spirit lie in the manger; we may look up and reach up to touch the limestone ceiling over the manger. We may, in present reality, go up with Our Lord from Jericho to Jerusalem; we may be present with him on Calvary; we may be laid with him in the tomb; we may know him risen again.

Above all, we shall not seek to rediscover a Christ-in-the-flesh, by the lifting up of old stones, as if to seek the living among the dead. We shall, by the awakening of our awareness to the events which have taken place within those sacred surroundings, discover the presence in spirit of the living Christ, who is 'the same yesterday, today and for ever'. We shall seek to reconstruct, in our imaginations and memories, the events of his physical life, that we may more fully grasp what happened and what those happenings mean for us, as individuals, and for the whole world.

Finally, whatever God the Holy Spirit shall reveal or withhold will affect not only our own lives but those of many others. All true pilgrims are like bees, not only to be fed by the honey drawn from sweet flowers, but bound to carry back home the pollen in order to give fresh touches of life in distant places. In other words, our pilgrimage will need to be in every sense of the words both *passionate* and *pentecostal*.

> Almighty God,
> who on the day of Pentecost
> sent your Holy Spirit to the disciples
> with the wind from heaven and in tongues of flame,
> filling them with joy
>   and boldness to preach the Gospel:
> send us out in the power of the same Spirit
> to witness to your truth
> and to draw all men to the fire of your love;
> through Jesus Christ our Lord.

HOLY LAND AND PEOPLE – CREATION TO COVENANT

TRADE ROUTES

In the ancient world of 2000 B.C., the two great centres of civilisation were those of the Nile and of the two rivers, Tigris and Euphrates. Between these two centres flowed a constant stream of military and merchandise, travelling inevitably along one or other of the *two main trade routes*.

The *first*, called 'the Way of the Sea', kept to the coast of the Mediterranean until it turned east through the passes of Mount Carmel into the plain of Esdraelon. There it skirted to the north-west of the Sea of Galilee and turned east again towards Damascus.

The *second*, called 'The King's Highway', crossed the Sinai

Desert to the Gulf of Aqaba and followed the Rift Valley north-wards, passing east and west of the Dead Sea and so to Damas-cus. Both these routes passed through the little land of Canaan, which by the fourth century B.C. became known as 'Palestine', after its Philistine invaders. This land was thus a bridge between Egypt and Babylon; its people were influenced by both civilisa-tions. It was through the *people* of this small and insignificant little country, no larger than Wales, that God progressively revealed himself to mankind.

THE LAND OF THE BOOK

The Bible is the unique library and record of the religious experi-ence and convictions of these people about God and his universe. Both Old and New Testaments are pervaded by the message of God, bound together in one common interest in God and his dealings with mankind. God's showing of himself was and is the process of man's education, recorded in the Bible, and he still reveals himself both through the inspired men of each age and in the movements of historical events. This process of revelation is briefly reviewed in the prologue of St John's Gospel: 'In the beginning was the Word, and the Word was with God and the Word was God . . . And the Word became flesh and dwelt among us.' The coming of Jesus to Bethlehem was the very climax and consummation of God's self revelation *through* and *to* the people of that land. Yet they, 'The sacred school of the knowledge of God and of the spiritual life for all mankind', have rejected him. The Old Israel has given way to a new people of God, the Church of Christ: 'To as many as received Him He has given power to become the Children of God.'

GENETICS AND GENESIS

Since the beginning of time and space, this progressive revelation of God has been the motive power in creation. Through the long evolutionary process which began with the independent emerg-ence of earth from light, its cooling and condensation within atmosphere, earth reached the point where it could begin to support life upon its surface.

Marine vegetation preceded marine life in the simplest of forms which, through long-protracted mutation, developed through reptile to fowl, through mammal to man. Somewhere along this long, long journey the mind of man became able to respond to the mind of God, if at first only to be dimly aware of a power greater than himself. Through many phases of primitive religion, man ultimately came to the point of crediting the power with personality, though the impact with later civilisation set him back again. The early chapters of Genesis express, in a threefold plait of early oral tradition and editorial addition, the mythology – the 'Just-so stories' of the Land of Canaan. The tradition may go back beyond Abraham, but the editorship is possibly as late as the exile in Babylon.

Some primitive Homo sapiens, in the form of a Carmel caveman, lived, hunted and killed his fellow men as early as 300,000 B.C. and their skeletons are to be seen in the Rockefeller Museum and in the Israel Museum, Jerusalem. A highly organised and cultured life existed by 8000 B.C. in the city state of Jericho, whose walls, towers and public buildings are still visible today – as are also the mud-sculptured skulls of the city fathers of that time. However by contrast with ancient Jericho, bordering on 'the King's Highway', the sophisticated civilisations of Mesopotamia in Abraham's day were far in advance in culture, code and construction – as witness the towers or ziggurats which, like Babel, still reach up to heaven.

LAND OF THE PATRIARCHS

It was in about 1850 B.C. that God chose a single man and his family through whom to work out his plan for mankind. Yet it was not from the settled and cultured, but from the nomadic and Semitic tribes that God called Abraham out, to 'go to a country that I will show you'. And, in faith, Abraham travelled the Fertile Crescent south-west – leaving his father and part of his family at Haran – before continuing round to the land of Canaan. There, the stories of the Patriarchs are largely domestic tales of the greed of men and the tittle-tattle of their womenfolk among the tents and round the camp fires.

Standing on the Mount of Olives, one can imagine the nomad sheikh and his clan travelling south along the spine of Judea to Hebron and Beersheba. He even went down to Egypt in the time

Holy Land Frontiers

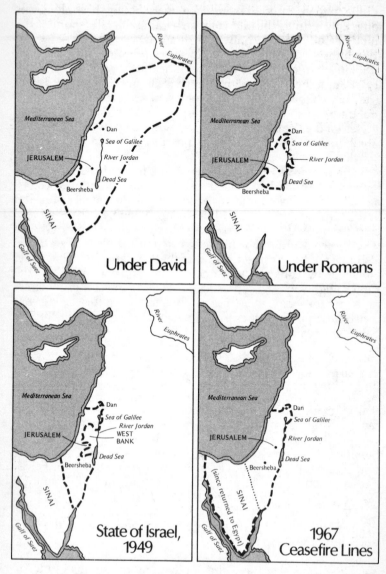

Under David

Under Romans

State of Israel, 1949

1967 Ceasefire Lines

of famine – before returning to settle at Mamre. The very first mention of Jerusalem in the Bible is the story of Melchisedek, priest-king of Salem, entertaining Abraham with bread and wine on his return from the slaughter of the kings. The city then was limited to the steep slopes of Mount Ophel. Its massive walls, sometimes sixteen feet thick, were excavated by Dr Kathleen Kenyon in 1961. Abraham and his successors are buried in the Cave of Machpelah, now to be seen below the great Mosque of Hebron – the town still called in Arabic 'El Khalil', the Friend of God.

Abraham was the father and founder of not one but two great Semitic races. Christ himself referred to Abraham as 'Your father Abraham'. Both Arabs and Jews have the same grandfather. However, the former are the children of Ishmael, son of Abraham and Hagar the bondswoman, the latter are the children of Isaac, son of Abraham and Sarah the freewoman. The Jewish writers of Genesis did not fail to cast *themselves* in the role of the children of promise and the Ishmaelites as the children cast out into the desert, of whom God made 'a great nation' also. Abraham took great pains to ensure that his son Isaac did not dilute his stock by mis-marriage. He did so by sending his trusted retainer back round the crescent to Haran, to collect for him as bride a clan cousin, Rebecca. So followed that lovely story of the watering of the camels from the well, the ring in her nose and the triumphant return. We know little of Isaac, except his blindness and debility symbolised in the miserable deception by Jacob's guile and the enraged frustration and deprivation of Esau – the uncouth man of the desert. It is well to recall the subsequent splendid reconciliation of the two brothers, despite their mutual apprehension. Nevertheless, Esau remained east of Jordan and the sons of Jacob left their names to the tribes of Israel.

Today, the Holy Land is to both Muslim and Jew the land of their twelve patriarchs springing from the call, courage, faith and obedience of Abraham. Today, to the Christian, it is the land of the early Church and twelve apostles springing from the call, courage, faith and obedience of the peasant girl Mary. For the Muslim, it is the land where God has spoken through successive prophets, of whom Jesus-ibn-Joseph is mentioned with great respect in the Quran, and of whom Muhammad is the greatest and the last. For the Jew, it is the land where God has spoken through both the Law and the Prophets, who foretold the coming of the Christ or Messiah. The Jews, however, did not and do not recognise Jesus-bar-Joseph as the Christ, whom some of them still expect to come.

For the most part, they consider Jesus to have been a good rabbi who turned against the Establishment of his day, was executed by the occupation forces and of whom little more can usefully be said. However, there are many Jews who think that the teaching of this rabbi was superb and marked a peak in the moral development of mankind. There are many who see a strange contrast between this Jew Jesus' teaching and the behaviour of his followers towards other Jews, in the medieval ghettoes, Crusader massacres and Spanish Inquisition. For the Christian, Palestine is the land where God's 'Word became flesh', where God in Christ Jesus 'became human that we might become divine'. The Christian, however, does not question God's choice of land or people for his great purpose of man's redemption, but only points to Jesus' claim, 'Before Abraham was, I am'.

PEOPLE OF THE COVENANT

The stories of the Patriarchs are largely domestic, set among shepherds' tents, concerning the greed of men and the jealousy of their women. The scene then changes with the arrival of Joseph, a son of Jacob and his favourite wife Rachel. Her traditional tomb at Bethlehem is still a focus of Jewish and Muslim pilgrimage. Joseph of the coat of many colours, as an attractive, precocious and ambitious youngster, was sold as a slave by his brothers and reached Egypt. There, despite certain disreputable adventures and with the help of his reputation for interpreting dreams, he became Grand Vizier to the Pharaoh of Egypt. After a somewhat uncomfortable reconciliation with his brothers, he invited his family down from Palestine into the fat grazing land of Goshen. There the shepherd sons of Jacob prospered into an obtrusive minority, and when the ruling dynasty changed, the new Pharaoh Rameses put the Hebrews to slave labour building pyramids and store cities. At this time, when all male children of the Hebrews were being 'exposed' at birth, in an effort to reduce their population, one – Moses 'among the bullrushes' – escaped death to be brought up in the royal palace. He grew up very conscious of the miseries of his people, ran into trouble defending slaves and fled into the Sinai Desert to become a shepherd. There he had a religious experience which convinced him that, out of a burning bush of camel-thorn, the God of his forefathers Abraham, Isaac and Jacob was calling him to return and deliver his people from Egypt.

Moses returned to Egypt and after many requests and many refusals, reversed by as many 'plagues', he led his people out of Egypt to cross the Red, or Reed Sea (the Bitter Lakes). Then the Pharaoh revised his decision to release the Israelites and pursued them. Finding themselves thus between the devil and the deep blue sea, they providentially caught the tide and left their pursuers to drown in the rising waters. The intervention of the Eternal into time and space is always timely!

The Book of Exodus is the most remarkable epic not just of an historical event, commemorated at the annual Passover or Seder Feast in every orthodox Jewish home, it is the remarkable saga of the interpretation of historical events as the acts of God, by a whole tribe inspired by their prophetic leader, Moses. They attributed their 'Dunkirk evacuation' from start to finish to the protective and saving action of their God. This interpretation was confirmed by Christ's own deliberate choice of the Passover Season for the institution of the Eucharist, as the re-enactment memorial of his own Cross and Passion, by which he redeemed his people. It was only natural that later generations of Christians should also see in the Passover and Red Sea escape some 'type' or shadow of the supper, suffering and resurrection sequence of Christ himself.

The Israelites moved into the Sinai Desert, like a Bedouin tribe on a wide front surrounded by a screen of scouts and shepherds, navigating on the pillar of cloud by day and the pillar of fire by night – possibly the volcano where Moses had had his vision of the burning bush. On their arrival, not having seen a volcano before, they were awed and appalled at the 'Holy Mount', while Moses climbed up to talk with God 'who thundered' out of the crater; Moses came down with tablets of stone, on which were inscribed the commandments or conditions of the covenant. The Israelites swore to obey his rules – God swore to care for the people of his choice. This mutual covenant was ratified by sacrifice, the blood being sprinkled upon the altar, as representing God, and upon the people, binding both parties to the covenant.

Thereafter the scattered tribe became a nation united in loyalty and obedience to their God, toughened and welded together by the discipline of the desert. The mob of slaves which rushed out of Egypt arrived at the borders of the land of their fathers, dedicated to the God of their fathers, the Patriarchs Abraham, Isaac and Jacob. It was a highly trained and toughened fighting machine, which descended from the mountains of Moab to cross the Jordan and petrify the city states of Canaan with a thousand camp fires along the valley.

Just how this nation disintegrated in the comforts of the promised land and how, though it preserved the letter of the Law, it failed more and more to keep the spirit of its covenant with God, is the story of the rest of the Old Testament. The fact remains that fourteen hundred years later, its blessings were transferred. The blessings and promises became available to the followers of Jesus, who was 'obedient unto death, even the death on the Cross', who said 'This is my blood of the New Covenant'. Whether Christians over the last two thousand years have been more faithful to the new covenant than the Jews were, in the previous two thousand years, to the old covenant, is a matter of historical opinion.

HOLY CITY AND TEMPLE – INVASION TO EXILE

WAR AND PEACE

The double-axe signs on our own Stonehenge link its origin with the Minoan civilisation in Crete. The Hebrew invasion must have just about coincided with the heyday of the House of the Axe at Knossos. Later, when this was destroyed, some Minoans emigrated to the coast of Canaan to become known as the Philistines and gave their name to their new home of Philistia or Palestine.

Invasion
Some three hundred years earlier than the landings of the Philistines, the Hebrews under Joshua invaded Canaan from the east.

They found, after their desert wanderings, a land literally flowing with milk and honey and occupied by a peaceful agricultural community centred on small, independent city states. It was not surprising that these were soon terrorised by the desert force. The scale of these cities and the size of the forces which captured them is comparatively small. Many of these so-called 'cities' were small walled towns, often standing on man-made mounds, which are known as 'tells'. These tells were formed by successive occupations of the same site with the consequent accumulations of masonry and rubble following the destructions, rebuildings and extensions outwards of successive towns. The first to fall to the Hebrew invaders was Jericho, with the strata of twenty-two different occupations within an area of, at the most, one hundred yards by three hundred. This had begun as a spring-side cave settlement and had, over perhaps tens of thousands of years, expanded into the walled city which fell to Joshua.

Occupation

The early chapters of the Book of Joshua give the impression of a complete and quick conquest, cutting the land into two halves and speedily capturing and consolidating the whole country. Some of the most exciting reading of the Old Testament is to be done following the Joshua campaign, where little imagination is needed to gain a vivid impression of the military tactics of that day. There never was, however, a complete conquest but rather a quiet occupation over a period of four hundred years. Even that occupation left many strongholds in Canaanite hands, as the first chapter of the Book of Judges implies.

There was no sudden change from a nomadic to an agricultural mode of life, but a slow, steady reversion to their previous pattern of settled life remembered by many living Hebrews. The tent was replaced by the house, the tent-circle by the walled town. The wanderers settled down to cultivate the soil and to grow olive, fig and vine. As their mode of life changed, so did their mental outlook. They became no longer nomadic tribesmen holding land and possessions in common. They became a settled peasant population jealous of personal rights and property.

Deployment

Joshua deployed the tribes all over the country and central control was soon lost. One tribe was not always willing to help its neighbour, when under attack. Every now and then, one tribe would produce a leader capable of uniting several tribes against a common enemy. Such folk were called Judges, who took the initiative against whatever enemy threatened their particular part of the country, Samson against the Philistines, Gideon against the Midianites, and others.

Gradually the Hebrews intermingled and intermarried with the Canaanites. The pagan Canaanite religion of the 'high places' was absorbed into the worship of the one God. The Hebrews no longer needed so much a God of desert and mountain, with thunder and lightning on Mount Sinai. They no longer needed so much a God of Hosts, a war-god, as a Baal to fertilise their crops; so they turned to the cults of the Canaanites. Among the creature comforts and domestic delights of a settled agricultural life, their loyalty to the covenant was diluted and the demands of Yahweh disregarded. And yet not quite, for it was the great task of the early prophets Elijah and Elisha to uphold the status and worship of the ancient God of Abraham, Isaac and Jacob against the new Baal of Canaan. This battle of the gods is finally and successfully fought out on Mount Carmel and the prophets of Baal destroyed.

PROPHETS AND KINGS

The chief value to the Christians of the Old Testament is as the record of the preparation of the land and people for the coming of the Christ. It illustrates God's purposeful and progressive plan to prepare the world for the total revelation of himself in the person of Jesus. The seed plot for this valuable seed which was to be none other than the Word of God. The soil to be prepared – was the mind of the people among whom Jesus was to be born. The chief figures in this process of spiritual education and evolution were the Hebrew prophets.

THE HOLY MAN

In the life of primitive peoples and tribes there is a person to be found all over the world – the holy man. He is the man considered to know the will of God and to speak God's message to his people. Sometimes he wanders round the country. Sometimes he works alone, sometimes in the company of others. Sometimes he is consulted on matters of war, peace and politics. Sometimes it may be an individual matter of lost property or personal health.

In giving his answers, he may cast lots or read omens from the flight of birds, the shape of clouds or the entrails of sacrificed animals. He may fall into a trance or a frenzy. He may use his native cunning or his common sense. But, whatever means he uses, there is usually some genuine spiritual sensitivity behind his pronouncements. He perceives and understands more than ordinary men. It is this power which wins him a reputation and respect, as holy. A long line of such holy men stretches far back into primitive Jewish history before Samuel, whose tomb is within a hill-top shrine visible from the Mount of Olives and on the horizon to the north. A few miles beyond is the village of Rama, where this holy man formed a guild of prophets with professional status. Many other local prophets advised their local chieftains, their compelling personality and prophetic advice often commanding respect.

Saul

About this time, a local chieftain named Saul – a man of commanding height and warlike character – won the wide acclaim of the surrounding tribes and was actually anointed by the prophet Samuel and crowned king. His capital was Gibea of Benjamin, also visible from the Mount of Olives, to the north. The exploits of Saul are probably belittled by writers of the Books of Samuel, but Saul established the monarchy successfully and conducted the war of liberation, defeating the Ammonites to the east of Jordan and the Amalekites to the south. He also broke the power of the Philistines who had infiltrated right up on to the spine of Judea. Saul's defeat and death at Gilboa were only a temporary setback in the fortunes of his people. Saul was quickly succeeded by a guerilla chieftain and one-time member of his court, David, who had married his daughter and of whom Saul had become increasingly jealous. It seems that Samuel had already transferred his allegiance to David, whom he had anointed at Bethlehem.

David

David established his headquarters at Hebron, the burial place of the Patriarchs, and suppressed all opposition with the help and ruthless efficiency of his lieutenant Joab. After seven years' rule at Hebron in the south, David realised the strategic importance of the more central fortress of Jebus, the old city of Salem, which had never been captured by the Hebrews.

The Jebusites considered it impregnable, surrounded as it was by steep valleys to north and south. The city stood on a sharp spur to the south of Mount Moriah – the traditional high place of sacrifice, where Abraham had been willing to offer his son Isaac. David standing on the Mount of Olives, would look down on this great fortress, built up on rising platforms overlooking the Kedron Valley, fortified by an overhanging scarp at the bottom with an enormous ditch at the top. It was captured through the action of Joab who, with a night patrol, entered the cave entrance of the water supply in the Kedron Valley and shinned up the water shaft or 'gutter' to emerge within the city and throw open the gates. Thereafter, David established his capital at Jebus-salem, completed the conquests begun by Saul, and consolidated and extended his borders. Having subdued Edom, Moab, Ammon and Damascus, he ruled from the borders of Egypt to the Euphrates, from the Mediterranean to the Red Sea. Only the Philistine foothills and the Phoenician coast remained outside his control.

TABERNACLE TO TEMPLE

Having captured Jerusalem, David made it both his military capital and his religious sanctuary too. He brought up the Ark of the Covenant to the city; once again Ark and Tabernacle were reunited. The evolution of the Hebrew sanctuary began from the Tabernacle at the foot of Mount Sinai, a tent surrounded by a screened courtyard, the portable sanctuary pitched night by night in the centre of the camp. Before the tent was the bronze altar of sacrifice. Within the tent were outer and inner chambers separated by a veil. Within the inner chamber was the Ark, over which was the Mercy Seat. From above the Mercy Seat, God communed with Moses. Inside the Ark were kept the two tablets of stone, upon which were inscribed the Ten Commandments; also beside the Ark was the Pot of Manna, and Aaron's rod which budded.

Mobile Shrine
Such was the Tabernacle carried from place to place through the wilderness, down into the Jordan Valley and up to Shiloh on the

spine of the country. It was from here that the Ark was carried into battle against the Philistines, captured and placed in the temples of their fishgod, Dagon, within the cities of Philistia. The superstitious Philistines soon restored the Ark which rested some years at Kiriath Jearim. It was from here that David brought the Ark up to Jerusalem.

Static Sanctuary

Towards the close of his reign David conducted a census of his population – perhaps for conscription purposes. The oriental dislike of being counted seems to have been shared by the writers of the Books of Samuel, who interpreted the events which followed as the judgment of God upon David. He was offered a choice of three punishments: defeat, famine and pestilence – and chose the last. The Angel of the Lord ravaged the country and descended upon the threshing floor with his hand outstretched to destroy the city below him. David prayed in penitence and the pestilence was stayed, for which David expressed his thanksgiving by sacrificing the oxen on the threshing floor. Most threshing floors are an expanse of flat rock. This was the early 'high place' referred to as Mount Moriah and linked with Abraham's offering of Isaac. It was therefore an appropriate place on which to erect the Tabernacle. The task and privilege of building the Temple was denied to David, though the choice of site was his and he had gathered much material in readiness for building.

Solomon's Temple

The honour of erecting the temple on the site of his father's sanctuary fell to Solomon. Solomon, unlike David, was a man of peace and politics, a great administrator and diplomat. He contracted many valuable alliances through marriage and his foreign wives occupied a vast harem overlooking the Hebrew sanctuary itself. He imposed a tyrannical tax upon his people. His communications included a network of chariot stables up and down the country. His mines and merchants, his wealth and women came second, however, in reputation to his building. The richness and variety of material at his disposal were enormous. He made vast contracts for cedar work and timber labourers with Hiram, King of Tyre, who floated the logs down the Phoenician coast to Joppa, whence they were rolled up the foothills to Jerusalem. His navy brought back gold, copper and bronze.

Solomon's Quarries

The basic material of the temple was, however, the natural limestone on which the city was built, quarried from under the temple area itself. Many folk in Mandate times will remember the endless galleries – like a white coal mine – approached from near the present Damascus Gate. The stone was and is so soft that, once a cleft is sawn, a wet plank acting as a wedge and swelling overnight will open a whole seam by the morning. Less than a hundred years ago, Solomon's quarries were rediscovered by a man who had lost his dog! Thus was solved the mystery of the reference to the stone being fashioned beneath the earth, 'that no sound of the hammer might be heard'. Indeed, the Hebrew hammers were still to be found in the quarries.

Temple Plan

The temple took seven years to build. The size of the actual central sanctuary was not so striking as the total ensemble of courtyards surrounding the tall sanctuary. These included the outer courtyard of the Gentiles, open to all, through which only Jews could pass on into the higher court of the Israelites. Within the court of the Israelites were separate enclosures for men and women, while the inner courtyard round the sanctuary itself was that of the priests. Within this court was the huge bronze laver, called the 'Sea', and before the entrance to the sanctuary was the large bronze altar corresponding to that of the Tabernacle. The sanctuary, too, like the Tabernacle was in two parts. An outer chamber, containing altars of incense, tables for shewbread and seven-branch candlesticks, led into the holy of holies in which was the Ark of the covenant. Solomon's royal palace, which took thirteen years to build, his judgment hall, his stables, and his royal apartments on the Spur of Ophel were a complex of magnificent buildings, admired by the Queen of Sheba. The whole temple area then covered some thirty-six acres.

DESTRUCTIONS BABYLONIAN AND ROMAN

Such was the appearance of the temple and its surroundings for the next four hundred years, until it was destroyed by the Babylonians under Nebuchadrezzar in about the year 600 B.C. Of the divisions of Solomon's kingdom into the two kingdoms of Israel and Judea, of the petty rivalries and alliances of their kings and capitals at Samaria and Jerusalem, there is not time to tell. The records of the Books of Chronicles and Kings are often religiously biased in their estimates of character and importance, by the orthodoxy of the king's religious policy. Omri and Ahab of Samaria, the only political giants of this period whose names survive on monuments in Egypt and Syria, receive scant recognition as 'doing more evil than their predecessors'.

The Process of Prophecy

By far the most significant factor of this period of political see-saw is the development of prophecy from the primitive to the sublime. As John the Baptist prepared the way for the Christ, so Elijah, his Old Testament counterpart, prepared the way with Elisha for the great writing prophets. Each of these in his own political or domestic situation, under the Spirit of God, through his own devotion and perception discovered fresh facets to the character of his God. It was as though each contributed piece by piece to the jigsaw of the knowledge or portrait of God. Not the least contributions were those of the prophets of the exile following the falls of the two kingdoms, particularly the philosophy of the good time coming: 'Behold the days come.' Perhaps the greatest contribution of all was messianic hope of the Deliverer, whose suffering would save his people.

Exile and Return

After seventy years of captivity, the Israelites returned with the blessing of Cyrus, King of Persia, to Jerusalem. There, despite Babylonian colonial opposition, Nehemiah restored the walls and Zerubbabel rebuilt the temple. This was a meagre building limited in extent by lack of funds. While the younger cheered its dedication, their elders who remembered the glories of the former temple of Solomon wept aloud. It was this temple which was desecrated during the stormy Greek occupation of the Seleucid King Antiochus Epiphanes, 170 B.C., and which stood throughout the Maccabean Wars. It witnessed the depressing changes from prophecy to tradition, from prophet to scribe, from sincerity to technicality, so castigated by Jesus in the Scribes and Pharisees of his time.

The Temple of Jerusalem

As described in the Mishna and by Josephus

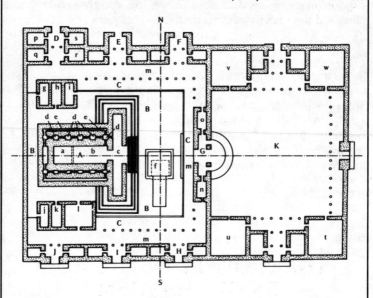

A.	The Temple.	C.	The Court of Israel.	E.	The Gate and House Abtinas.

A. The Temple.
- a. The Holy of Holies.
- b. The Holy Place.
- c. The Porch.
- d. The Little Chambers.
- e. The Ascent to the Upper Chamber.

B. The Court of the Priests.
- f. The Altar of Sacrifice.
- g. The Chamber of Salt.
- h. The Chamber of Parvah.
- i. The Chamber of the Washing.
- j. The Chamber of Wood or Palhedrin.
- k. The Chamber of the Draw Well.
- l. The Chamber Gazith, or of the Sanhedrin.

C. The Court of Israel.
- m. The Inner Cloisters
- n. The Chamber of the Vestments.
- o. The Chamber of the Pancake Maker.

The Gates of the Inner Court.
D. The House Moked.
- p. The Chamber Moked and Descent to the Bath-room.
- q. The Chamber of the Lambs.
- r. The Chamber of Shew Bread.
- s. The Chamber of the Stones of the Altar.

E. The Gate and House Abtinas.
F. The Gate and House Nitsus.
G. The Gate Nicanor.
H. The Water Gate.
I. The Gate of the Firstborn.
J. The Gate of the Kindling.
K. The Court of the Women
- t. The Chamber of the Nazarites.
- u. The Chamber of Oil.
- v. The Chamber of the Lepers.
- w. The Chamber of Wood.

Herod's Temple Built and Burnt

With the Roman occupation and the appointment of the Idumean/Edomite Herod as king, the old temple of Zerubbabel was demolished. With a munificent gesture to gain popularity, Herod erected a third temple, even larger than Solomon's but on a similar ground plan. It was in this temple that Jesus was presented as a child and 'initiated' as a Son of the Law at the age of twelve. It was here that he watched the widow and her mite, cleansed the courtyards of the money-changers and merchants, and taught daily before his arrest. It was here that he foretold the destruction and massacre which took place during the siege under Titus in the year A.D. 70 which is so graphically described by Josephus. While the prisoners of war rotted on a forest of crosses along the Mount of Olives, while the thousands of priests were slaughtered in the subterranean vaults below the temple, an enthusiastic centurion set fire to the roof timbers which collapsed upon the mass of refugees. This disastrous destruction was completed by Hadrian, following the Bar Cochbar revolt in A.D. 130, and the whole site desecrated by a pagan temple to Jupiter.

THE PROPHET IN THE HOLY LAND – JUDAISM – CHRISTIANITY AND ISLAM

CHILDREN OF ABRAHAM

The Holy Land is only a little to the north of Arabia and following the fall of Samaria in 721 B.C. and of Jerusalem in 587 B.C., it is highly likely that Jewish merchants travelled to the Arabian peninsula. There, the Ishmaelites and the descendants of Abraham, through Keturah his last wife, had journeyed long since as commercial pioneers, and had retained a memory of the God of their father Abraham.

The tribes of Arabia were really nature-worshippers, in a world peopled with spirits good and bad. Following their great dispersion in the year 70, some Jews again moved southwards and founded colonies in the towns of Arabia. In the sixth century there were three or four Jewish tribes around the city of Medina, but they kept their own religion of the one God, their Law and Prophets, to themselves. The Arabs respected the Jews for their sacred books and their prophet Moses, but it never occurred to the Arabs that they should leave their tribal customs to obey the law of Moses. It did not occur to the Jews to ask their pagan brothers to do so.

CHRISTIANITY IN ARABIA

The Christians took the gospel of Jesus to the Aramaic-speaking tribes in the north of the peninsula, but do not appear to have translated the gospel into Arabic. There is considerable evidence, however, of early Christian initiative in Arabia: five bishoprics in the province of Najtan, the attendance of Arab bishops at the Council of Nicaea in 325, three Christian kingdoms and the Arabic gospel of the Infancy. It was a Christian bishop, Quss ibn Sa'ada, who originated the Arabic script. Muhammad himself learned much from the Christian Waraqa ibn Naufal. The Arabs respected the Christians, as also having a book from the great God, whom they worshipped at the ordained times throughout the twenty-four hours. Christian tribes even fought alongside Muslims in the early days of Arab expansion.

BIRTH OF MUHAMMAD

The Quran bears witness to the strength of Hebrew traditions and the respect for the Hebrew prophets among the Arabs. The Quranic testimony to Jesus, Son of Mary, means that Jesus was an important historical figure on both sides of the Red Sea. The fact remains, however, that for nearly six hundred years after the coming of Jesus, the greater part of Arabia remained pagan, without book, without vision, without prophet, without single ruler or plan to unite the tribes. This was not from a failure of

Christian apostolic fervour, so much as from the later weakness and divisions of Christian witness all round the Mediterranean world. It was, then, in the city of Mecca that Muhammad was born to be the prophet and ruler of his people. His followers became Muslim, submitting to Allah, a brotherhood bound together by another sacred book, the Quran.

> The people of Moses and the people of Jesus were given revelations,
>   But alas! they played false with their own lights, and in their selfishness, made narrow God's universal message.
>   To them it seemed incredible that His light should illumine Arabia and reform the world.
>   But his ways are wondrous, and they are clear to those who have Faith.
>   If the People of the Book rely upon Abraham, let them study his history.
>   His posterity included both Israel and Ismail. Abraham was a righteous man of God, a Muslim, and so were his children. For God is the God of all Peoples.
>
> (Sura 2.47 and 48)

JUDAISM AND ISLAM

The chief task of the early Hebrew prophets was to combat the disloyalty and the dilution of the worship of the one, Yahweh, with the fertility cults of the many, Baalim. Following the conquest by Joshua, the nomadic Hebrew tribesmen adapted themselves to an agricultural mode of life, reverting to a settled pattern by which the tent was replaced by the house and the tent circle became the walled town. To a certain extent, the pagan Canaanite religion and worship on the high places was absorbed into the worship of Yahweh. It was the genius of the Hebrews to link their agricultural festivals with their national historical commemorations, thus sanctifying the former and celebrating the latter.

By contrast, it has been said that the genius of Islam was precisely in its gift of syncretism. Islam's veneer of monotheism, upon those of Judaism and Christianity, covers a Canaanite paganism, successfully proclaiming the oneness of God among many primitive peoples in a way which both convinces and satisfies: 'There is no god but Allah – [the God]: Muhammad is the Apostle of Allah!' As one who broke away from the primitive animism and idolatry of Arabia, Muhammad was inspired or possessed by the spirit of Abraham, who himself broke away from the idolatry of Mesopotamia. The word 'muslim', 'submitted' or 'dedicated', seemed to Muhammad a highly appropriate term for his ancestor, Abraham. Indeed, it was from the six sons by his wife Keturah (Genesis 25), that Abraham is said to have fathered the desert tribes, as well as by their cousins, the Ishmaelites.

FOLKLORE AND LOCAL TRADITIONS

Today, when the primitive features of Palestinian life are disappearing so quickly and so much folklore is being lost, the innumerable Muslim shrines in the villages, on the hills, in the valleys and fields, are not easily found. There is hardly a village which does not honour at least one local saint. The village of Anata, north of Jerusalem, possesses seven shrines, and Awarta, south of Nablus, fourteen, to mention but two villages. Today these shrines of holy Muslims are often to be found in cemeteries, surrounded by the bodies of those who valued their protection even in death. Sometimes there is no building, only a *maqam*, the site or station of an event in the life of a *wali* or saint. It may be a single tree, a large rock or a heap of stones, a watercourse, a spring or even a cistern, which local tradition over the centuries has led people to venerate. Where there is a building, it may be a rectangular shrine, with or without a tomb; it may be a simple cave. At Banias there are both. If it is a tomb, it will be likely to be covered by a *qubba*, or dome. The word suggests a pavilion, tent or tabernacle in which to shelter. The word 'cupola' comes to us from the Arabic, through the Italian. The functional use of the *qubba* is to run water off a flat roof for conservation in a hot climate; the Arabic word *qubba* means raindrop!

The rites and practices at such shrines are of an infinite variety, from the most simple prayers and offerings in money or kind, to animal sacrifice, the taking of religious vows and circumcision. The saints commemorated will in all likelihood have been good, trustworthy elders of their local community, who by their spiritual lives and devotional practices deserve respect as possible mediators between the simple people and Allah, the Holy One.

MOSQUES, SANCTUARIES, AND SHRINES

In Arabic, the word for a building for public worship, *masjid*, suggests a place of kneeling and prostration; it develops from the same root as the word for prayer-carpet. The Psalmist says: 'O come, let us worship and fall down and kneel before the Lord, our Maker.' The same word is used for the bowing, kneeling and subjection of the camel for the mounting of its rider. It is not difficult to see how the Arabic *masjid* has come through the Spanish *mesquito* to reach us as 'mosque'. The focal point within the mosque is the *mihrab*, or prayer niche, which indicates the *qibla*, or direction to be faced when praying. The last and most important holy place is the *haram*, or sanctuary, in Hebrew *herem*. The word is equivalent to the Latin *sacer* and the Greek *hieros*, implying 'consecrated to God', or 'forbidden ground'. The sacrifice of Jericho by Joshua had to be complete because Jericho was *herem*, consecrated to Yahweh. Similarly, Moses at the burning bush had to remove his shoes, for he was standing on 'holy ground'. Hence, too, the women's apartments in the Muslim household are *harim*, forbidden ground.

MECCA

It was in the city of Mecca, fifty miles from the Red Sea, that Muhammad was born, to be the prophet and ruler of his people. Mecca was already famous for a small religious sanctuary called the Kaaba (Cube) containing the 'Black Stone'. Muhammad, whose name means 'the one to be praised', was soon left an orphan to care for his uncle's flocks. He later became a business agent and camel driver and married a rich widow. They both came under the influence of a religious sect who preached a purity of worship of the one God, as did their forefather Abraham. Muhammad began to seek God in earnest and became convinced that there was only the one God, the Almighty and the Judge, and that he, Muhammad, was called to be God's messenger. He, like Moses to the Hebrews, was to be the prophet to his people.

So Muhammad descended on Mecca with his demands of purity and his warnings of judgment. The people of Mecca could not accept the demands and teachings of an apparent upstart, who demanded their obedience and loyalty. After ten years in Mecca – unable to convince the leaders of the city – he emigrated with his followers to Medina. From that year, the Muslims begin their calendar. The Arab people of Medina, together with Muhammad's followers from Mecca, formed a single unit under his leadership. He became both prophet and ruler and welded this unit into a strong brotherhood living by a strict code. In order to supply the needs of his brotherhood, he pillaged passing caravans and, as his brotherhood grew stronger, he expelled the Jewish tribes from Medina. At last he was strong enough to lead his brotherhood into Mecca and became its master.

MUSLIM

Now all the tribes began to fear him and became 'submitted' to Allah. One by one they joined his religion and promised to obey him. At his death in the year 632, he was the lord of Arabia. His followers acclaimed his friend Abu Bekr as his successor and, in their religious enthusiasm poured out of deserts into the surrounding countries, conquering all of North Africa, from the Nile to the Atlantic. These scattered races were bound together by Muhammad's own words in his sacred book. Remembering how the Law was 'sent down on' Moses and the Psalms 'on' David and the Gospel 'on' Jesus, and longing for his own people too to have a sacred book, Muhammad set down the message of God as he felt it came to him. So the Muslims became 'People of the Book', the Quran.

QURAN

To the Muslims the Quran is sacred as the very word of God given to his prophet. It is treated with great respect, learnt by heart, said every day in prayer. It is so sacred that it should not even be translated, but read by all men everywhere in Arabic – rather as the erstwhile Latin of the Mass! This belief then in the 'sacred dictation' of the Quran is both a strength and a weakness for Muslims.

The thoughts of God in the Quran are often very close to those of both Christian and Jew: God is self-existent – 'I am that I am'.

God is the Creator and Lord of the Universe – 'In the beginning, God'. God is Merciful, the Compassionate – 'I will have mercy and not sacrifice'.

Jesus

The Muslim cannot yet reconcile God's justice and wrath with God's mercy and compassion. Any theology of the Pain of God, in the redemptive suffering of Jesus Christ, is impossible. It is impossible to the Muslim that the Almighty should suffer. It is impossible to the Jew for, although he may accept the messianic vocation to suffering in the Second Book of Isaiah, he has failed to recognise Jesus as the Christ of God. To the Jews, the cross is still a stumbling block and to the Muslims quite out of character with God.

For the Muslim, 'Jesus, Son of Mary' is not the son of God, despite Quranic affirmation of the Virgin Birth. The whole ministry of Jesus as found in the Christian Gospels is, in the Quran, compressed into two muddled paragraphs! The crucifixion was not of Jesus, only his 'likeness'. Yet, the brotherhood of Islam embraces men of many lands and colours, bound together by their belief in one God and in his prophet. They are bound together in their Ramadan month of fasting and in their prayers. They are drilled like an army, instructed like a school to pray five times a day – facing Mecca, to which they must make their pilgrimage.

THE EARLY CALIPHS

Muhammad died in the year 632 and his close friend and early companion Abu Bekr was elected caliph in his place. He was a wise and true follower of his son-in-law Muhammad. Although a mild and gentle person by nature, he proved a firm and resolute ruler in Medina. But for him, Islam would have melted away in compromise with the Bedouin tribes. Successive campaigns throughout the Hejaz, Arabia, Syria and Mesopotamia extended the Muslim conquest and imperial control throughout the Middle East. The brigand spirit of the Bedouin was united with the new-born fire of Islam. The Arabs from the desert became the aristocracy of Islam.

Evolution of the
Dome of the Rock

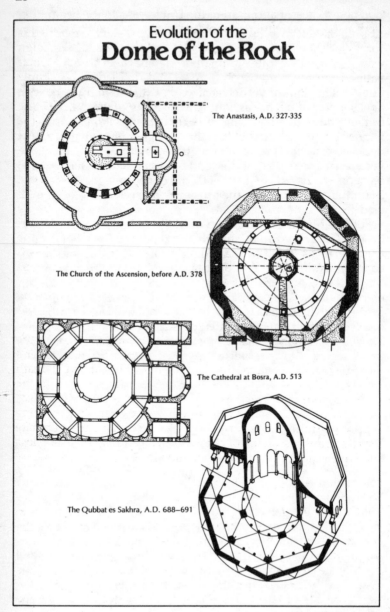

The Anastasis, A.D. 327-335

The Church of the Ascension, before A.D. 378

The Cathedral at Bosra, A.D. 513

The Qubbat es Sakhra, A.D. 688–691

Omar

Abu Bekr died in 634 having appointed the fiery Omar as his successor. The capture of Damascus and the Persian campaign were followed by the capitulation of Jerusalem in 637. Omar entered the town riding on a camel and dressed in his simple camel's hair cloak, and was received by the Patriarch Sophronius and conducted round the various places of pilgrimage. At the Muslim hour of prayer, the Patriarch Sophronius offered the Church of the Resurrection for the caliph's prayers; but Omar declined, saying kindly that his followers would only take possession of it as a place of Muslim prayer. Omar also visited the Church of the Nativity at Bethlehem, where he prayed in the south aisle facing Mecca and gave the Patriarch a written guarantee protecting the church. The generosity of Omar does not seem to have been expressed by his followers in Jerusalem, however, on his return to Medina. The Byzantine writers describe how 'the cradle of Christianity, Zion, the joy of the whole earth, was trodden under foot and utterly cut off from the sight of its devoted worshippers'.

The Muslim conquest of Egypt followed; so did the reopening of the Old Suez Canal linking the Upper Nile, Lake Timsah, and the Red Sea at Suez. This canal was originally designed by Rameses II and completed by Darius the Persian. It was the predecessor of the present canal from Suez to Port Said. After a last pilgrimage to Mecca, the Caliph Omar was stabbed to death by a slave, when leading public worship with his back to the congregation, in the year 644. His successor as third caliph was the unpopular Othman, who ruled twelve years before being murdered during an insurrection. His successor Ali's caliphate was a stormy succession of revolts in Syria and Egypt lasting less than five years before his assassination in 661.

ABDEL MELEK

Under the early caliphs, the Muslims had swarmed out of the dry deserts of Arabia, but they had been quite unable to hold the lands they had conquered. Their armies had gathered soldiers, like 'rolling snowballs'. On the basis of submission to Allah, Arabs and non-Arabs had been enlisted with promises of booty and paradise. It was inevitable that rival caliphs in Cairo and Damascus should challenge the central control from Medina. The

Bedouin chief Mu'awiyah established himself as caliph at Damascus and captured Egypt, but failed to take Constantinople. He founded the Umayyad Dynasty and reigned nearly twenty years as sole caliph in Damascus. One of the strongest caliphs, Abdel Melek, won universal recognition in 692, following campaigns in Syria, Iraq and Arabia. He issued a purely Muslim coinage, based on the Dinar (Byzantine Denarius) and proclaimed the official government and commercial language as Arabic – no longer Greek. It was Abdel Melek who built the Dome of the Rock – Qubbat es Sakhra, in the temple area or Noble Sanctuary el-Haram es Sherif, at Jerusalem.

Part Two:

JERUSALEM

WITHIN AND WITHOUT
THE WALLS

In order to understand the sites of Jewish, Christian and Muslim Holy Places in Jerusalem it is essential to have some knowledge of the hills and valleys on which the successive cities have been built, and to know something of the walls, fortresses, viaducts and highways which have enclosed, protected and connected these sites down the centuries.

VALLEYS

The chief characteristic of Jerusalem is not so much that it is a hill city, whose streets are often steps and whose transport is the ass. Its magic is in the mystery of its valleys, hills and rocks, whether it be the rock of Moriah or that of the empty tomb. A unique history is traced by these hills and valleys, of a city not three miles in perimeter, set in a triangular basin, between desert and coastline. Indeed, 'the hills stand about Jerusalem', as the Psalmist sang. The city is bounded by two valleys from north to south, the Kedron on the east and the Wadi-er-Rababi to the west from the Jaffa Gate, where it curls round the western hill to become the Valley of Hinnom. The two valleys converge below Siloam to become the Wadi-En-Nar, the 'Fire Valley', which runs down through the wilderness towards the Dead Sea. Yet a third valley bisects the city from north to south, from the Damascus Gate to the Pool of Siloam. This is the Tyropean Valley 'of the cheese-makers', once a steep gorge over which viaducts passed thirty metres high, which has been progressively filled in, so that its depression is today hardly noticeable.

HILLS

Between the first two and separated by the third valley are two hills. The eastern hill, Mount Moriah, is really on a long spur linking Bezetha, a rise within the north-east of the present Old City, with Ophel, the ridge running down to the Pool of Siloam. The western hill descends steeply to the Valley of Hinnom and overlooks the ridge of Ophel. It is on the Ophel, 'the boil', that the Jebusite city stood in the time of David. This was the original Hill of Zion, a name which may well have meant 'ridge' or 'lump', implying a fortress or citadel.

DAVID

David built his citadel on the upper part of the ridge, but probably did not extend the Jebusite walls, except perhaps to include the threshing floor of Araunah the Jebusite. Certainly the top of the ridge and Mount Moriah were included in Solomon's time, and two hundred years later, in the time of Uzziah (780–740 B.C.), the western hill was included within the city, whose north wall ran due west from the Temple. The Kedron and Hinnom valleys have always prevented further expansion on the east, south or west. Development could only take place northwards. Thus, what is now called the First Wall enclosed both the site of the Jebusite city on Ophel and the western hill. This wall contained the Pool of Siloam to the south and crossed the central Tyropean Valley to the north, along the line of what is now David Street. It was destroyed by Nebuchadrezzar and restored by Nehemiah, besides being ruined and repaired on several other occasions.

JESUS

The walls in the time of Jesus: What is called the Second Wall was rebuilt by Herod in about 30 B.C. It was this wall which was standing in the time of Jesus. To the east, south and west it seems to have more or less followed the line of the First Wall; but, as is to be expected, there was a development on the north side. Excavations at Herod's Citadel, near the present Jaffa Gate, together with excavations by Dr Kathleen Kenyon, have shown that this wall did not follow the line of the present wall, turning north-west at the Citadel. This Second Wall curved eastwards, enclosing a new suburb, before linking up with the north-west corner of the Temple Area. Josephus calls this the Second Wall and says that it started from the Gennath 'the Garden Gate', which stood in the First Wall, and that the Second Wall went northwards and eastwards as far as the Antonia fortress.

GARDEN GATE

This would have left an L-shaped depression or dart in the north-west part of this Second Wall near the Garden Gate, implying that a garden lay outside the city wall at that point. St John tells us that: 'In the place where he was crucified, there was a garden.' Furthermore, John even mentions that the tomb of Jesus was in a garden 'nearby'. And, indeed, the tomb is still to be seen in the rock of the hillside, within the Church of the Holy Sepulchre today, showing that this area must have been outside the wall; for no burials took place within the city boundary.

HEROD AGRIPPA

After the crucifixion and resurrection of Jesus in A.D. 41, Herod Agrippa built a further wall, which happened to enclose within the city the sites of both Calvary and the tomb. It is, however, unlikely that this unclean area of burial ground was soon built over. Josephus, in fact, relates that this new wall was to protect a weak place in the Second Wall, and he calls it the Third Wall. Considerable traces of the Third Wall have been found in several places, including the junction of St George's and Nablus road, north of the present city wall. It is strange to think that the site of Calvary and the tomb of Jesus were enclosed within the city within eight years of the events. And, if they were not built on, they were less likely to have been lost.

HADRIAN

When Hadrian established a Roman colony in the city following the Bar Cochbar revolt, he purposely excluded the Temple area and changed the layout of the city. Whereas the main axis of the

Jewish city had linked the Citadel and the Temple, that of Aelia Capitolina ran south from the Damascus Gate. At some time in the fourth century the old line of the wall above Kedron and Hinnom was restored. In the fifth century, the Empress Eudocia repaired it, but after the Persian invasion the line of the south wall contracted to something near that of the present south wall. The present walls include a great deal of Byzantine, Saracen and Crusader masonry, but are mainly the work of Suleiman the Magnificent, completed in 1541.

TEMPLE AREA – NOBLE SANCTUARY – DOME OF THE ROCK AND AQSA MOSQUE

JERUSALEM 'THE HOLY'

To the Muslims Jerusalem is known as 'Al Quds', 'the Holy'. Quite apart from its associations with the Old Testament figures – Abraham, David, Solomon and others whom they venerate – the Muslims cherish a strong traditional connection between Jerusalem and the Prophet Muhammad. The tradition of the Prophet's Night Journey is alluded to in the Quran thus: 'I declare the glory of Him who transported His servant by night from the Masjid al-Haram [the mosque at Mecca] to the Masjid al-Aqsa [the further mosque] at Jerusalem.' Here is meant the whole area of 'the Noble Sanctuary', not just the main building of the Aqsa which, in the Prophet's days, did not exist.

THE NIGHT JOURNEY

According to the received account, Muhammad was on this occasion mounted on the winged steed called Al-Burak – 'the Lightning' – and, with the Angel Gabriel for escort, was carried from Mecca, first to Sinai and then to Bethlehem, after which they

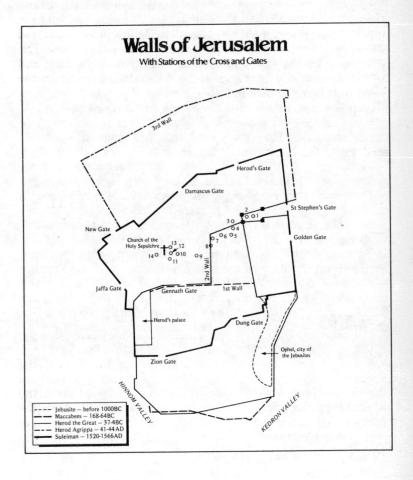

Walls of Jerusalem
With Stations of the Cross and Gates

3rd Wall

Herod's Gate

Damascus Gate

St Stephen's Gate

New Gate

Church of the
Holy Sepulchre

Golden Gate

Jaffa Gate

Gennath Gate

2nd Wall

1st Wall

Herod's palace

Dung Gate

Ophel, city of
the Jebusites

Zion Gate

HINNOM VALLEY

KEDRON VALLEY

--- Jebusite — before 1000BC
—— Maccabees — 168-64BC
—— Herod the Great — 37-4BC
--- Herod Agrippa — 41-44AD
—— Suleiman — 1520-1566AD

came to Jerusalem. 'And when we reached Bait al-Makdis, the Holy City', so runs the tradition mentioned in the Chronicle of Ibn Al Attir, 'we came to the gate of the mosque and here Jibrail caused me to dismount. And he tied up Al-Burak to a ring, to which the prophets of old had also tied their steeds.'

Entering the Haram Area by the gateway, afterwards known as the Gate of the Prophet, Muhammad and Gabriel went up to the Sacred Rock, which from ancient times had stood in the centre of Solomon's Temple; meeting there a group of prophets, Muhammad proceeded to perform his prayer-prostrations before this assembly of his predecessors – Abraham, Moses, Jesus, and other of God's apostles. From the Sacred Rock, Muhammad, accompanied by Gabriel, next ascended by a ladder of light up into heaven; here, in anticipation, he was vouchsafed a vision of the delights of Paradise. Passing through the seven heavens, Muhammad at last stood in the presence of Allah, from whom he received injunctions on the prayers his followers were to perform. Thence, after a while, he descended again to earth; and alighting from the ladder of light stood again on the Sacred Rock at Jerusalem. The return homeward was made after the same fashion – on the back of the steed Al-Burak – and the Prophet reached Mecca again before the night had waned. Such is the tradition which sanctifies Jerusalem, the Rock and the Haram, or Sanctuary area, in the sight of all Muslims. After the capitulation of Jerusalem to Omar in 635, that caliph caused a mosque to be built on what was considered to be the ancient site of the Temple of Solomon.

CALIPH OMAR

In the early days of Islam – that is, under Omar and his successors – mosques were constructed of wood and sun-dried bricks and other such perishable materials, so that of the building erected in Omar's days, probably very little remained even half a century later to be incorporated into the magnificent stone shrine erected by the orders of the Omayyad Caliph, Abdel Melek in about the year 690. It seems probable, also, that this latter caliph, when he began to rebuild the Aqsa, made use of the materials which lay to hand in the ruins of the great St Mary's Church of Justinian, discovered in the Jewish quarter in 1970.

AQSA MOSQUE WITHIN HARAM

The Chronicles make no mention of the date or fact of Abdel Melek's rebuilding of the Aqsa Mosque, and the earliest detailed description of this mosque is that given by Muqaddasi in 985, some three centuries after Abdel Melek's days. Of the Dome of the Rock, on the other hand, we possess detailed accounts in the older authorities, describing both the foundation in 691 and its general appearance. It would appear that the Arab chroniclers and the travellers who visited the Haram Area during this period were more impressed by the magnificence of the Dome of the Rock than by the main buildings of the Aqsa Mosque, of which the Dome of the Rock was in fact but an adjunct.

MOSQUE V. SHRINE

When referring to the Arab descriptions of the Haram Area at Jerusalem, an important point to remember is that the term Masjid applies not to the Aqsa alone but to the whole of the Haram Area, with the Dome of the Rock in the middle and all the other minor domes, chapels and colonnades. The Dome of the Rock (misnamed by the Franks the 'Mosque of Omar'), is not itself a mosque or place for public prayer, but merely the largest of the many cupolas in the Court of the Mosque, in this instance built to cover and do honour to the Holy Rock which lies beneath it.

In 985, during the rule of the Fatimid Caliph Al-Azziz, Muqaddasi, a native of Jerusalem, described the Aqsa thus:

> The Masjid al-Aqsa lies at the south-eastern corner of the Holy City. The stones of the foundations of the Haram Area wall, which were laid by David, are ten ells, or a little less, in length. They are chiselled, finely faced, and jointed, and of hardest material. On these Khalif 'Abd al-Malik subsequently built, using smaller but well-shaped stones, and battlements are added above. This mosque is even more beautiful than that of Damascus, for during the building of it they had for a rival and as a comparison the great Church [of the Holy Sepulchre] belonging to the Christians at Jerusalem, and they built this to be even more magnificent than that other.

CRUSADER ALTERATIONS

On 14 July 1099 the Crusaders, under Godfrey de Bouillon, captured the Holy City. The Haram Area was given over to the Knights of the recently established Order of the Temple, who derived their name from the Dome of the Rock, which the Crusaders imagined to be the Temple of the days of Christ and named Templum Domini. The Aqsa Mosque, on the other hand, was known as the Palatium (Palace of the Crusader Kings of Jerusalem) or Templum Solomonis. The Templars made considerable alterations to the Aqsa Mosque and the adjoining portions of the Haram Area, but left the Dome of the Rock untouched. On the west of the Aqsa, along the south wall of the Haram Area, they built their armoury. In the substructures of the south-east angle of the Haram Area, to the west of the Cradle of Jesus, they stabled their horses, using probably either the ancient 'Triple Gate' or the 'Single Gate' as an exit from these vaults. The Latins considered the Aqsa Mosque to hold a very secondary place, while the Dome of the Rock was in their eyes the true Templum Domini; hence the Knights Templars felt no compunction in remodelling probably the whole building, when they turned part of the Aqsa into a church for the Order, and established their mainguard and armoury in the outlying quarters of this great Mosque. ·

SALADIN'S RESTORATION

After Saladin's reconquest of the Holy City in 1187, the whole of the Haram Area and its various buildings underwent a complete restoration. The account given in the Chronicle of Ibn Al Attir of what was done in the Aqsa Mosque is as follows:

> When Saladin had taken possession of the city and driven out the infidels, he commanded that the buildings should be put back to their ancient usage. Now the Templars had built to the west of the Aqsa a building for their habitation, and constructed there all that they needed of granaries, and also latrines, with other such places, and they had even enclosed a part of the Aqsa in their new building. Saladin commanded that all this should be set back to its former state, and he ordered that the Masjid should be cleansed, as also the Rock, from all the filth and the impurities that were there. All this was executed as he commanded.

Over the Great Mihrab, in the Aqsa Mosque, could still be read the inscription set here by Saladin after this restoration was completed:

> In the name of Allah the Compassionate, the Merciful! Hath ordered the repair of this holy Mihrab, and the restoration of the Aqsa Mosque – which was founded in piety – the servant of Allah, and His regent, Yusuf ibn Ayyub Abu-l Mudhaffar, the victorious king, Salah ad-Dunya wa'ad-Din [Saladin], after that Allah had conquered [the City] by his hand during the month of the year 583. And he asked of Allah to inspire him with thankfulness for this favour, and to make him a partaker of the remission [of sins], through His mercy and forgiveness.

AQSA TODAY

The Mosque we see today was entirely renovated between 1938 and 1943. During this period all the long walls and arcades were demolished to the foundations, with the exception of the two western aisles and the arcades flanking the dome. The nave and eastern aisles were reconstructed on arches carried by monolithic marble columns. The upper part of the north wall was also reconstructed and the whole refaced. The central doors and porch were also repaired. The work was supervised by the Director of the Department for the Preservation of Arab Monuments, in the Egyptian government, which presented the magnificent gilded ceiling. At the southern end of the Mosque are the only surviving Fatimid mosaics and construction in Jerusalem. Here is also a fine rose window and mihrab in the place of the Forty Martyrs, but the very beautiful pulpit and mihrab installed by order of Saladin have recently been destroyed by an eccentric Australian visitor. Perhaps the most impressive sight of all, however, is that of some four thousand men, line after line in perfect order and action, covering every square metre of carpet in this vast mosque – the brotherhood of Islam at worship.

DOME OF THE ROCK

In remarkable contrast with the little that is known of the early architectural history of the Aqsa Mosque, is the very full account

Jerusalem: Dome of the Rock

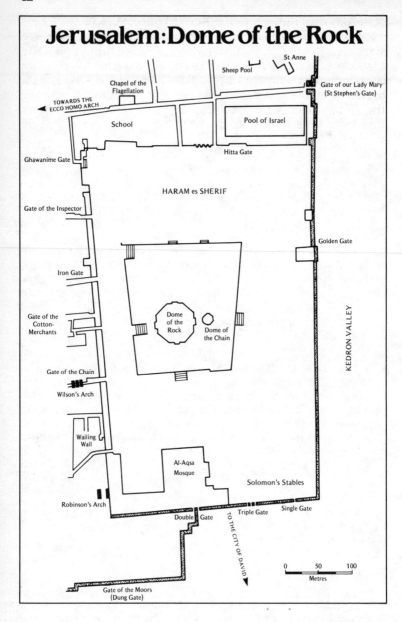

St Anne

Sheep Pool

Chapel of the Flagellation

Gate of our Lady Mary (St Stephen's Gate)

TOWARDS THE ECCO HOMO ARCH

School

Pool of Israel

Ghawanime Gate

Hitta Gate

HARAM es SHERIF

Gate of the Inspector

Golden Gate

Iron Gate

Dome of the Rock

Dome of the Chain

Gate of the Cotton-Merchants

KEDRON VALLEY

Gate of the Chain

Wilson's Arch

Wailing Wall

Al-Aqsa Mosque

Solomon's Stables

Robinson's Arch

Double Gate

Triple Gate

Single Gate

TO THE CITY OF DAVID

0   50   100
Metres

Gate of the Moors (Dung Gate)

of the date and the historical incidents connected with the foundation of the Dome over the Sacred Rock. The edifice as it now
stands is substantially identical with that which the Caliph Abdel
Melek erected in the year 691. The cupola, it is true, has on many
occasions been shattered by earthquakes, and the walls have
been damaged and repaired, but the octagonal ground plan and
the system of concentric colonnades have remained unaltered
through all the restorations; even down to the number of the
windows; the Dome of the Rock, as described in 903 by Ibn
al-Fakih, is almost exactly similar to the Dome of the Rock of the
present day.

The Dome of the Rock for Muslims ranks in sanctity only after
the Ka'ba in Mecca, according to Muslim tradition erected by
Abraham and Ishmael, and the Tomb of the Prophet in Medina.

Shrine Within the Sanctuary

One of the early accounts shows the setting of the Dome of the
Rock within the Haram or Sanctuary Area. In 978 Ibn Haukal abu
Istakhti writes:

> The Holy City is nearly as large as Ar-Ramlah [the capital of the
> province of Filastin]. It is a city perched high on the hills, and you
> have to go up to it from all sides. There is here a mosque, a greater
> than which does not exist in all Islam. The Main-building [which is
> the Aqsa Mosque] occupies the south-eastern angle of the mosque
> [Area, or Noble Sanctuary], and covers about half the breadth of the
> same. The remainder of the Haram Area is left free, and is nowhere
> built over, except in the part around the Rock. At this place there has
> been raised a stone [terrace] like a platform, of great unhewn blocks,
> in the centre of which, covering the Rock, is a magnificent Dome.
> The Rock itself is about breast-high above the ground, its length and
> breadth being almost equal, that is to say, some ten ells and odd, by
> the same across. You may descend below it by steps, as though
> going down to a cellar, passing through a door measuring some five
> ells by ten. The chamber below the Rock is neither square nor round,
> and is above a man's stature in height.

The Dome Structure

A hundred years later in 985, Muqaddasi of Jerusalem writes:

> The Cupola of the Dome is built in three sections: the inner is of
> ornamental panels. Next come iron beams interlaced, set in free, so
> that the wind may not cause the Cupola to shift; and the third casing
> is of wood, on which are fixed the outer plates. Up through the

middle of the Cupola goes a passage-way, by which a workman may ascend to the pinnacle for aught that may be wanting, or in order to repair the structure. At the dawn, when the light of the sun first strikes on the Cupola, and the Drum reflects his rays, then is this edifice a marvellous sight to behold, and one such that in all Islam I have never seen the equal; neither have I heard tell of aught built in pagan times that could rival in grace this Dome of the Rock.

DOME OF THE CHAIN

A few paces east of the Dome of the Rock stands a small cupola, supported on pillars but without any enclosing wall, except at the Qibla point, south, where two of the pillars have a piece of wall, forming the Mihrab, which was built up in between them. This is called Qubbat as-Silsilah – 'the Dome of the Chain'. As early as 913 it is mentioned by Ibn Abd Rabbih as 'the Dome where, during the times of the children of Israel, there hung down the chain that gave judgment [of truth and lying] between them'. Yakut, describing this Dome, mentions that it was here that was 'hung the chain which allowed itself to be grasped by him who spoke the truth, but could not be touched by him who gave false witness, until he had renounced his craft, and repented him of his sin'.

An obvious association with this site is the judgment of Solomon, when 'he came to Jerusalem, and stood before the ark of the covenant of the Lord . . . then came there two women . . . and all Israel heard of the judgment . . . and they feared the king.' 1 Kings 3:15–28. The Dome of the Chain was in fact, less of a lie detector than the architect's model for the Dome of the Rock!

BETHANY TO BETHPHAGE, OVER THE MOUNT OF OLIVES – PALM SUNDAY WALK

15 STADIA FROM JERUSALEM

Bethany must always have been the last stop on the way from Jericho up to Jerusalem. Bethphage is the hamlet on the track from Bethany up to the highest point on the Mount of Olives – the village of Tor. The shortest route from the Temple Area left the city by a gate on the site of the present Hadrianic 'Golden' Gate, crossed the Kedron to Gethsemane and then divided into two tracks. These run up the Mount of Olives, crossing the ridge on two separate saddles, but link up again at Bethphage, before descending to Bethany on the main road.

OLD TESTAMENT AND NEW TESTAMENT BETHANY

Today, the modern and growing Arab township of Bethany called in Arabic El Azariah (home of Lazarus) nestles under the Mount of Olives, facing across the wilderness to the Jordan Valley. Here in the time of Nehemiah (11:32) was the locality of Beth Ananyah, inhabited after the exile by Benjaminites. From a sharp turn in the Jericho road, a small spur rises up the hillside towards Jerusalem. Excavations in the early 1950s revealed that the first-century village was located on that spur.

Galilean Suburb
The ossuaries, or bone boxes, excavated here and at Bethphage bore Galilean names, indicating that this end of the Mount of Olives was, in Jesus' time, a Galilean suburb. This would account perhaps for Jesus' choice of Bethany as his home-from-home in Jerusalem. It could account for the Angel's address at the Ascension 'Ye men of Galilee, why stand ye gazing up into heaven', reflected in the title of the Greek Patriarch's residence 'Virii Galilaei'. It would also imply that the voice which challenged:

'What are you doing loosing that donkey?' and the voice which answered: 'The Lord has need of him' were both in the Galilean brogue, so obvious in Peter's denial at the High Priest's Palace!

Byzantine Church

The traditional site of the home of Mary, Martha and Lazarus was at the bottom of the spur, on which was built a church in the fourth century, which was described by the Dalmatian priest, Jerome, and the Spanish nun, Egeria. This church was destroyed by earthquake and rebuilt in the sixth century. The Byzantines called the village Lazarium, the tomb of Lazarus, and the apse of their church is still to be seen behind the altar of the present church.

Crusader Abbey Convent

In the year 1143 Queen Melisande (Millicent) built an abbey and a Benedictine nunnery from the proceeds of produce from her Jericho estates; she established her own sister Yvette as abbess. This convent was destroyed during the Turkish occupation, but the vaulted Crusader refectory ceiling, the intriguing oil press (whose pressure-screw is the carved trunk of a palm tree), the Crusader towers, walls and mosaics indicate the vastness of the twelfth-century abbey-convent complex.

Modern Church

The new church of St Lazarus, by its austerity of design and cupola, gives the appearance of a cemetery chapel. The technique of the architect Barluzzi is to make his buildings expressive of the events which they commemorate. The same theme is maintained within, though the interior is enlivened by four large mosaic lunettes, together with explanatory texts from the Gospels beneath them.

The two side altars are in the form of sarcophagi with sculptured medallions of Mary and Martha, while that of the central altar depicts two angels indicating the tomb of Lazarus. The whole church is bright with light and, within the cupola, a single all-seeing eye is surrounded by forty-eight panels illuminated with doves, flames and flowers. The gospel story is told in the mosaic lunettes high upon the four sides: on the left, Jesus is with the family at Bethany; in the centre, Jesus says 'I am the Resurrection and the Life'; on the right, Jesus raises Lazarus; over the entrance, Jesus dines with Simon the Leper at Bethany.

BETHPHAGE

On that evening of Jesus' arrival from Jericho, he had supper with his friends and disciples. The next day, traditionally called Palm Sunday, he sent two of his disciples ahead into the next village to collect the donkey on which he was to ride into Jerusalem, in purposeful fulfilment of the prophecy of Zechariah. Today, a track leads up the slope of the Mount of Olives to the hamlet of Bethphage – meaning 'House of Figs'. Jesus had told his disciples that they would find the donkey tied up at the crossroads. Now as then, the junction of tracks from Bethany and Jerusalem is overlooked by the tell, or mound, of ancient Bethphage. At this junction today stands the Franciscan convent built in the last century over the medieval foundations of a Crusader chapel or tower. The squared stones of the apse indicate considerable strength of construction.

Donkey Shrine
It is probable that the focus of this shrine, if not its *raison d'être*, was a rock associated with the finding or mounting of the donkey. This rock or stele was in Crusader times painted to illustrate the story of Palm Sunday. In 1950 the Italian artist Vagarini restored the illustrations of the Raising of Lazarus, the arrival of the donkey, and the procession of palms. It is from this convent that the Latin procession starts every Palm Sunday and, passing over the Mount of Olives, enters the city at St Stephen's Gate. The Anglican procession starts from Bethany and disperses from the top of the Mount of Olives overlooking the city.

THE MOUNT OF OLIVES

The route of the first Palm Sunday procession must be a matter of conjecture. Either it followed the present road south of the Russian convent property, or it skirted it to the north. Either it crossed the northern saddle of the Mount of Olives and descended that track down into the Kedron, or it crossed the southern saddle and descended the track passing the Pater Noster church and the shrine of the Dominus Flevit. Both these tracks join at Gethsemane before crossing the Valley of the Kedron.

PATER NOSTER

The southernmost track from the crest of the Mount of Olives, down into the Kedron, soon passes the Church of the Pater Noster. There are two traditions concerning this site, linking it with Jesus' teaching of the Apostles' Creed before their final dispersal from Jerusalem. In St Luke's Gospel the teaching of the Lord's Prayer immediately follows a visit to Mary and Martha at Bethany, but there is no question of this being on Jesus' Palm Sunday entry into Jerusalem. The Lord's Prayer tradition is Byzantine, going back to the seventh century at least, if not to Constantinian times. Certainly a church on this site was destroyed in the seventh century and a new church built in the twelfth. The present church was built in 1869 by the Princess of Auvergne, a cousin of Napoleon III. Attached to it is a convent of Carmelite nuns, and a cloister adorned with thirty-five or more frames of the Lord's Prayer in as many languages.

DOMINUS FLEVIT

Halfway down the track into the Kedron Valley is the traditional site where Jesus wept over the city, as he foresaw the catastrophe which was to take place within the lifetime of many who now came out of the city to greet him. 'If only you had known, on this great day, the way that leads to peace! But no; it is hidden from your sight. For a time will come upon you, when your enemies will set up siege-works against you; they will encircle you and hem you in at every point; they will bring you to the ground, you and your children within your walls, and not leave you one stone standing upon another, because you did not recognise God's moment when it came.'

On this site today is the striking little church of 'Dominus Flevit', built in 1955 by Barluzzi. When the Franciscans were excavating an ancient cemetery, they found traces of a hitherto unknown fifth-century church. This they rebuilt, preserving the original mosaics in situ and shaping the roof like a tear. Instead of facing east, the church faces west; through a plate-glass window it commands a truly magnificent view across the whole city of Jerusalem.

HOLY WEEK

For the next three days Jesus was to go into the city, evading arrest, surrounded by the crowds of Passover pilgrims as he taught in the Temple, before returning at dusk to the shelter of the quiet village home at Bethany.

> Almighty and everlasting God,
> who in your tender love towards mankind
>   sent your Son our Saviour Jesus Christ
> to take upon him our flesh
> and to suffer death upon the cross:
> grant that we may follow the example
>   of his patience and humility,
> and also be made partakers of his resurrection;
> through Jesus Christ our Lord.

A PALM SUNDAY PROGRESS

BETHANY TO BETHPHAGE IN SILENCE, LITANY AND SCRIPTURE:

1. *Within the Franciscan church,* on the site of the village home of Mary, Martha and Lazarus: John 11:1–44 – read in parts and groups by all members of the party, the leader reading the narrative.

By your infinite love and holy sadness,
    Jesus, save us.
By your calling Lazarus, whom you loved, from the sleep of
    death,
    Jesu, save us.
By your entire knowledge of the Father's will,
    Jesu, have mercy upon us.

Because you wept in compassionate love,
    We thank you, Lord.

Because you have raised us from death to life,
    We glorify you, Lord.
Because you have shown us the Glory of God,
    We worship you, Lord.

VISIT BYZANTINE AND CRUSADER REMAINS

Apses, mosaics, refectory and olive presses.
2. *Within the Crusader castle ruins* at the top of the spur and facing the road to Jericho: Mark 10: 32–4, 46–52.

By your infinite love and resolute courage,
    Jesu, have mercy upon us.
By your setting your face steadfastly to go up to Jerusalem,
    Jesu, save us.
By your standing still at the call of a beggar,
    Jesu, have pity upon us.

Because you accepted the sufferings that awaited you,
    Jesus, Son of David, we worship you.
Because you invited your Apostles to drink your cup,
    Jesus, Son of David, we thank you.
Because, when you have opened our eyes, we may rise up and follow.
Jesus, Son of David, we praise you.

3. *Overlooking the village of Bethany*, from the track to Bethphage: Luke 19: 28; John 12: 1–2,9.

By your infinite love and your seeking here solitude and rest,
    Jesu, have mercy upon us.
By your lowly dwelling in this quiet village,
    Jesu, save us.
By your acceptance here of active and of passive devotion,
    Jesu, have pity upon us.

Because you said the weary and heavy laden may rest in you,
    We thank you, Lord.
Because you have gone to prepare a rest for the people of God,
    We praise you, Lord.

Because you chose particular friends for your consolation and
   companionship,
      We worship you, Lord.

4. *Overlooking the Wilderness*, on the track to Bethphage: Mark
   11: 2–3.

   By your infinite love and unfaltering footsteps,
      Jesu, have mercy upon us.
   By your passing with the multitude, along this road,
      Jesu, save us.
   By your acceptance of the worship of your Father's Creation,
      Jesu, have pity upon us.

   Because you go before, that we may follow your footsteps,
      We thank you, Lord.
   Because you cover us under the shadow of your wings,
      We praise you, Lord.
   Because Patriarchs and Prophets went before you, and Saints
      and Martyrs follow on,
      We worship you, Lord.

5. *Overlooking the crossroads*, from the fig orchards above
   Bethphage: Mark 11: 4; Luke 19: 35–8.
   Followed by the Palm Sunday liturgy, up in the orchard, or
   down in the convent garden of Bethphage.

VISIT CHURCH AND ROLLING STONE TOMB

Only continue, if time, transport and energy permit, to a final
stand.

6. *Overlooking the city of Jerusalem*, from the Dominus flevit: Luke
   19: 41–4; Mark 11: 11; Luke 21: 37.

   By your infinite love and righteousness,
      Jesu, have mercy upon us.
   By your weeping at the sight of the beautiful City,
      Jesu, have pity upon us.
   By your knowledge of the days to come,
      Jesu, save us.

Because, if we follow you, you will lead us to peace,
  We thank you, Lord.
Because you chose this hill for your great purpose,
  We glorify you, Lord.
Because from the Mountain of your Church, we gaze towards
  the new Jerusalem,
  We worship you, Lord.

UPPER ROOM TO GETHSEMANE – MAUNDY THURSDAY NIGHT WALK

A corporate act of silent pilgrimage along a token route, adaptable by groups or individuals, but necessitating reconnaissance by phone or in person. (Syrian convent: 283304, Franciscan Gethsemane 283264.) Suitable *either* just before the Passion sequence of 'Arrest and Trials', *or* as a final devotion before leaving Jerusalem.

A suggested timetable might be:

Transport from hotel to Jaffa Gate	– 5.15 p.m.
Walk to Syrian Church of John Mark	– 5.30 p.m.
Devotion in Syrian church (see 1 below)	– 5.45 p.m.
Progress through Jewish Quarter to near Zion Gate	– 6.00 p.m.
Turn east and continue to High Wall corner	– 6.15 p.m.
Continue east and exit at Dung Gate	– 6.30 p.m.
Cross Kedron diagonally, below City Wall	– 7.00 p.m.
Climb, via floodlit tombs, to Russian Garden	– 7.30 p.m.
Descend to arrive at Franciscan entrance	– 8.00 p.m.
Devotion within church, until	– 8.30 p.m.
Return, walking or by transport, to supper	– 8.45 p.m.

At each station, except the first and last, the sequence may be:

Readings – Litany (see below) one section – Versicle and Response

V. Lord, you are the Light of the World. He that follows you walks not in darkness.

R. But shall have the Light of Life for Ever.

1. Within the church of John Mark
A sixth-century inscription reads 'This is the house of Mary, Mother of John, called Mark. Proclaimed a church by the holy apostles, under the name of the Virgin Mary, Mother of God, after the ascension of our Lord Jesus Christ into heaven. Renewed after the destruction of Jerusalem by Titus, in the year 73 A.D.'

Both this Syrian church and the Crusader Cenacle on the Western Hill commemorate the Upper Room, successively the scene of the Last Supper, Resurrection appearances and Pentecost, at once the synagogue and headquarters of the apostolic Christian Church.

Greetings to the Syrians, whose priest will be glad to read the Institution of the Eucharist – perhaps Matt. 26: 20–31 or the Feet Washing, John 13: 1–15. Following your own Reading and Meditation, the first section of Litany and the hymn 'Go to dark Gethsemane' are suitable. The devotion may close with the versicle and response above and a dismissal.

2. City Wall near Zion Gate
Mat. 26: 31–35, Luke 22: 31–32, Psalm 73: 23–36
Litany – Section 2 – Versicle and response

3. Corner of Wall, overlooking Siloam
John 15: 1–6, Psalm 143: 8,9,6,10
Litany, Section 3 – Versicle and response

4. Outside Dung Gate
John 14: 1–9, 16: 28–32, Isaiah 40: 6–8
Litany, Section 4 – Versicle and response

5. Top of Ophel spur, below wall corner
John 17: 24, 15: 21–22, Isaiah 63: 8–9
Litany, Section 5 – Versicle and response

6. Tombs in Kedron Ravine
John 16: 12–13, 14: 26, 14: 18–20, Psalm 43: 3–4
Litany, Section 6 – Versicle and response

7. Russian Garden, near church, beneath the olives
John 18: 1–2, Luke 22: 40, Isaiah 64: 6–9
Litany, Sections 7 and 8 – Versicle and response

8. Within Franciscan Church, kneeling round Rock of Agony

Agony reading	– Mark 14: 32–49
Hymn	– 'When I survey'
Psalm reading	– Psalm 116: 8–13
Hymn	– 'O Sacred head'
Prophets reading	– Isaiah 53: 4–5
Hymn	– 'Praise to the Holiest'

Perhaps closing with the Seven Words from the Cross, a blessing from Hebrews 1: 1–3, and silence.

The Veneration of the 'Rock of Agony' may best take place during the hymns (Bethlehem C page 113 para. 2 refers).

Additional prayers, if desired:

THANKSGIVING FOR THE HOLY COMMUNION
Almighty and heavenly Father,
we thank you that in this wonderful sacrament
you have given us the memorial
   of the passion of your Son Jesus Christ.
Grant us so to reverence
the sacred mysteries of his body and blood,
that we may know within ourselves
and show forth in our lives the fruits of his redemption;
who is alive and reigns with you and the Holy Spirit,
one God, now and for ever.

Almighty Father,
whose Son Jesus Christ has taught us
that what we do for the least of our brethren
   we do also for him:
give us the will to be the servant of others
   as he was the servant of all,
who gave up his life and died for us,
yet is alive and reigns with you and the Holy Spirit,
one God, now and for ever.

FOR THE UNITY OF THE CHURCH
Heavenly Father,
whose Son our Lord Jesus Christ said to his apostles,
Peace I leave with you, my peace I give to you:
regard not our sins but the faith of your Church,
and grant it that peace and unity
   which is agreeable to your will;
through Jesus Christ our Lord.

Father, Son, and Holy Spirit,
holy and undivided Trinity,
three persons in one God:
inspire your whole Church, founded upon this faith,
to witness to the perfect unity of your love,
one God, now and for ever.

Heavenly Father,
you have called us
in the Body of your Son Jesus Christ
to continue his work of reconciliation
and reveal you to mankind.
Forgive us the sins which tear us apart;
give us the courage to overcome our fears
and to seek that unity
which is your gift and your will;
through Jesus Christ our Lord.

MAUNDY THURSDAY NIGHT WALK LITANY

1. By your infinite Love, even to the end,
    Jesus, enkindle our love.
    By your ardent desire to eat this Passover before you suffered,
    Jesus, strengthen our faith.
    By your preparing your Apostles for heavenly mysteries,
    Jesus, wash and prepare us.

2. Because you come in to sup with us and we with you,
    Jesu, our Bridegroom, we worship you.
    Because you consecrated a new and living way into the Holiest,
    Jesu, our Leader, we follow you,
    Because you abide with us and we in you,
    Jesu, our Beloved, we adore you.

3. Because you have overcome the world,
    Jesu, the Truth, we adore you.
    Because you have gone to prepare a place for us,
    Jesu, the Way, we adore you.
    Because you have chosen us, even though we have not chosen you,
    Jesu, the Life, we adore you.

4. By your Infinite Love and perpetual Intercession,
    Jesu, have mercy upon us.
    By your going forth with your disciples over the Brook Kedron,
    Jesu, save us.
    By your words of warning to your disciples,
    Jesu, have pity upon us.

5. By your Infinite Love and by the darkness of the way,
   Jesu, have mercy upon us.
   By the great purpose of your final approach to this Garden,
   Jesu, save us.
   By your choice of the shadow of the olive trees for the agony of your
       last surrender,
   Jesu, have pity upon us.

6. By your Infinite Love and your realisation here of all sin,
   Jesu, have mercy upon us.
   By your agony and bloody sweat,
   Jesu, save us.
   By your complete obedience to the Father's Will,
   Jesu, have pity upon us.

7. Because you were made sin for us,
   We thank you, Lord,
   Because you were crushed with guilt that was ours,
   We thank you Lord.
   Because you have trodden alone the wine-press of the wrath of God,
   We worship you Lord.

8. To all who are bowed down by the weight of their sin,
   Show yourself as the Sin Bearer, Blessed Lord.
   To all those who look on your sufferings carelessly or unmoved,
   Show yourself in your agony, Blessed Lord.
   To all those who enter this Garden in body or spirit, Grant
       everlasting life, Blessed Lord.

THE PASSION OF JESUS – ARREST AND TRIAL BEFORE CAIAPHAS

We may follow the events of his Passion on the stage of history, round the Holy Places of Jerusalem. But the exact identification of places is secondary to our own personal identification with the people and events. For the Passion of Jesus, the Pain of God, is a continuing process, as we continue to be the instruments of his suffering.

GETHSEMANE

Rendezvous

Gethsemane is on the lower slopes of the Mount of Olives facing the Gateway up into the Temple. It was at a junction of tracks leading over the Mount of Olives – a regular meeting point and resting place of Jesus with his disciples, before they entered the city together – or dispersed from the city to their separate lodgings. Luke indeed indicates that, on occasion, they used to spend the night there actually on the hillside. So it was not surprising that Judas could specify the best place for the arrest 'There was a garden there,' says John, 'and he and his disciples went into it.' The place was known to Judas, his betrayer, because Jesus often met there with his disciples. The 'Garden' implied that it was an orchard of olives encircled by a wall which probably enclosed both the present Russian and Franciscan properties.

Prayer and Arrest

In the year 390 the Spanish nun, Egeria, records in her pilgrimage diary that, at the Maundy Thursday night service the congregation came to 'the place where the Lord had prayed – as written in the Gospel: "He withdrew away from them a stone's cast."' Here (she says) was an elegant church in which was read the passage 'Watch and pray that ye enter not into temptation'. Then, all went down to the Gethsemane – 'Gat Shimon' means 'olive press' – where was read the actual arrest of Jesus.

Church

Later pilgrims confirmed this sequence involving the *two* places of the Prayer and of the Arrest – the first being a church and the second a cave. Today the place of the Prayer and Agony is marked by the magnificent modern Church of All Nations, built on the ground plan of the fourth-century church and including sections of the fourth/fifth-century mosaics. The focal point of the earlier and present churches is part of a rock terrace, one among many on the rising hillside, which has always symbolised the rock on which Jesus prayed in his agony of apprehension and decision: 'Nevertheless not my will, but thine, be done.'

Cave

The second place is still a cave of considerable size (some fifty by thirty feet), whose function was to contain the actual oil-press for the olive orchard. The cave would provide shelter for a sizeable group of people, as Luke implies. Although the cave is now furnished as a chapel I think you will find it a vivid illustration of the events. Similarly, the modern mosaics within the alabaster gloom of the church bring home the awfulness of the Agony. 'Jesus went forward a little and fell to the ground and prayed "Abba, Father, all things are possible to thee . . ."' and his sweat became as it were great drops of blood falling down to the ground. 'And while Jesus spake, lo Judas one of the twelve came – and with him the crowd. Now he that betrayed him had given them a sign: "Whomsoever I shall kiss That is he. Take him"' Jesus said 'Betrayest thou the Son of Man with a kiss?' and 'You seek Jesus of Nazareth? I am he!' The troop arrived with its captain and officers. They took him and bound him and led him away to the House of Caiaphas the High Priest.

HIGH PRIEST'S PALACE

From the Garden of Gethsemane, prisoner and escort returned to the Western Hill, passing down the Kedron Valley, under those monumental tombs, to enter by the Valley Gate at the bottom of Ophel. From there, passing the pool of Siloam, they mounted the ancient stairway to the palace of Caiaphas, where the scribes and the elders were assembled and waiting. John adds a visit to Annas, who sent him back to Caiaphas. There are two separate traditional sites connected with Annas and Caiaphas; the former, of only medieval tradition, has never been fully excavated; the House of Caiaphas has a long history and appears on the Madeba mosaic of the city. It has been thoroughly excavated, as late as 1930, by the Assumptionist Father Bernadine.

St Peter's Church

The excavations at the Church of the Cock-Crowing, if fully understood, provide perhaps the most vivid visual aid and convincing sequence of illustrations of any single Jewish site of the time of Jesus. The Pilgrim of Bordeaux in 333 commented on the ruins of the palace: 'In the same valley above Siloam, you go up to Mount Zion and see the spot where the House of Caiaphas stood.' In 348 Bishop Cyril of Jerusalem recorded the site. In 457 the Empress Eudocia built on the ruins a fine basilica dedicated to St Peter. In 530 the Emperor Theodosius went from the Last

Supper Room to the House of Caiaphas, 'which is now St Peter's Church', he said. About the same time, the author of the Jerusalem Breviary wrote: 'Where St Peter denied the Lord, there is a great basilica dedicated to him.' The Frankish monk – Bernard the Wise, in 840 added more detail: 'From the cenacle, due east – and south of the Temple Area is St Peter's church.' The English Crusader, Saelwolf, in 1102 wrote: 'On the slope of Mount Zion is the Church of St Peter of the Crowing-of-the-Cock.' A twelfth-century monk, Epiphanius, adds: 'And to the right of St Peter's, at three arrow-shots, is the pool of Siloam.'

Four Levels

The present church includes four different levels, built as it is on an almost sheer hillside. Nowadays there is a convenient observation point commanding a bird's-eye view of the City of David (on Ophel) and the Central Valley (once a steep gorge) from the Dung Gate to the Pool of Siloam, and round into the Ravine of Gehenna and Aceldama. From here one can imagine the Babylonian siege in the time of Jeremiah, or the Byzantine city in the time of Eudocia. Perhaps the most impressive man-made feature of both cities, and still to be seen, is the magnificent rock-hewn staircase ascending the Western Hill from the Valley Gate. It was by this route that prisoner and escort reached the High Priest's Palace.

Store

The ruins today still include all the paraphernalia which one would expect to find: vast storage chambers, a complete set of weights and measures on a huge scale, corn stores with staircase entrances, oil stores lined with plaster and with round bottle necks; one door lintel inscribed 'Corban offering'. In fact it is a complete treasury for the Temple Dues.

Courtroom

Do not be put off by the taste of the interior decoration. The mosaic over the high altar is a useful illustration of the rock-hewn courtroom immediately below the church. The prisoner stands on a raised platform or dock in the centre and with his back to the wall, chained by the wrists to an escort on either side of him. Down on the second or courtroom level one can see the galleries and staircases around the court, and imagine Peter warming himself at the brazier and denying his Master. And what else

could he do? For the charge was the blasphemy of claiming
Messiahship and he, Peter, at Caesarea Philippi, had answered
'You are the Christ' in the presence of the twelve. Once identified
as one of the twelve, he could have been subpoenaed as the
second witness to give evidence to convict his Master. Indeed it
was shortage of evidence and the necessary two witnesses which
provoked Caiaphas himself to cross-examine the prisoner.

In most old English courtrooms, from the Mansion House
downwards, the staircase down into the cells descends from the
centre of the court. So at the High Priest's Palace – once the
prisoner is condemned – he can be let down from the centre of the
Court into a bottle-necked condemned cell. Here the story of the
rescue of Jeremiah during the Babylonian siege by Ebed-Melech
the Ethiopian is vividly illustrated. Emaciated by the siege and
imprisonment he needed rags from the storehouse to protect him
from the rope and, once drawn up out of the mire of the dungeon,
he still remained in the court (Jeremiah 38).

Guardroom

Descending again to the third level there is a complete guardroom
with staples for prisoners' chains all round the walls. A small
window acts as a peephole down into the condemned cell, but
cannot be used unless the guard stands up on a stone block. This
block was left projecting from the floor for this purpose when the
rock-hewn guardroom was originally excavated. Here too is the
whipping block where, tied up by the wrists by leather thongs
threaded through the stone staples, and anchored by a belt
stapled to the block on each side, the prisoner was suspended,
taut and helpless. At his feet, carved in the rock, were two bowls –
one for salt, to disinfect, if aggravate, his wounds and one for
vinegar to revive him. Here the apostles received the legal
number of forty stripes save one, thirteen on each side from the
back and thirteen on the chest from the front; they were commanded not to preach Christ, yet returned daily to the Temple.

Condemned Cell

Down on the very bottom level is the condemned cell which
originally had only two openings – the bottle-neck and the
peephole. There are still to be seen the carved and coloured
crosses of Byzantine pilgrims venerating the brief stay of their
Lord. Here he might have spent what was left of the night,

expressing his thoughts and prayers in psalms – perhaps the 88th:

My God, I call for help all day; I weep to you all night.
May my prayer reach you; hear my cries for help for
My soul is troubled; My life is on the brink of Sheol.
I am numbered among those who go down to the Pit, a man bereft of strength . . .
You have plunged me to the bottom of the Pit, to its darkest, deepest place . . .
In prison and unable to escape, my eyes are worn out with suffering . . .
Wretched, slowly dying since my youth, I bore your terrors – now I am exhausted . . .
You have turned my friends and neighbours against me, now darkness is my one companion left.

(Jerusalem Bible)

Whatever the timing or legality of that trial, it was early in the morning when escort and prisoner – brutally garrotted (as the Dominican scholar Vincent describes) – set out for the Praetorium, where the Procurator Pontius Pilate had been warned to expect him. It was the morning of the first Good Friday.

DAYLIGHT VISIT TO THE GARDEN OF GETHSEMANE

1. *Within the Church of the Tomb of the B.V. Mary*
Tomb shell and ambulatory; Joint ownership of tomb; Muslim-Mihrab
2. *Within cave of olive press*
Double significance of sites of agony and arrest
Luke 21: 37–38
3. *Junction of tracks over saddles of Mount of Olives*
Position of rendezvous and of cave lodging (Luke 21: 37); Bethany/Bethphage; the Galilean Suburb 'Ye men of Galilee'
John 18: 1
4. *Within Franciscan Garden*
Extent of Garden, Kedron and Mount of Olives. Age of olive trees.

5. *Within Church of All Nations*
Plan of Fifth-century church; of 1927 church; Central mosaic, Rock of Agony today
Luke 22: 44
6. *North Mosaic – Arrival of Judas*
Traditional kiss of greeting, disciple to rabbi
John 18: 3; Mark 14: 41; Matt. 26: 47
7. *South Mosaic – The surrender*
The falling to the ground; who were the police at the arrest?
John 18: 4–6; Matt. 26: 57; John 18: 14

HIGH PRIEST'S PALACE, WESTERN HILL, ST PETER OF THE COCK-CROWING

1. *Observation Point above church*
Valley of Gehenna, Field of Blood; Convent and Tombs of Aceldama
Matt. 27: 3–10
2. *Balcony of church*
Stone staircase, storage chambers, donkey mill; Function of palace, Trespass offerings, Weights and measures
Lev. 5: 14–19
3. *Back of church interior*
Trial scene on mosaic; The Verdict; Time and legality of trial
Mark 14: 55ff.
4. *Courtroom*
Rock stairs, dock, corners, galleries; Match with altar mosaic; Peter, the potential witness and his denial.
Matt. 26: 69ff.
5. *Courtroom*
Bottle-neck of condemned cell; mocking by Sanhedrin or soldiery
Jer. 38: 1–13
6. *Guardroom*
Light niche and staples; block for sentry to stand on
Luke 22: 63–65
7. *Whipping block*
Staples in block, rock bowls at feet, 39 lashes; Apostolic floggings – Peter, John, Paul
2 Cor. 11: 24

8. Within condemned cell
Pilgrim crosses, Byzantine stairs, Bottle-neck, Jesus cf. Jeremiah.
Psalm 88; Lord's Prayer

CONTINUATION OF THE PASSION OF JESUS – PILATE

PONTIUS PILATE'S PRAETORIUM

North Wall Fortresses
There were two great fortresses protecting the North Wall (what
Josephus called the second wall) of the city: at the west corner
Herod's Garden Palace, now called the Citadel, at the east corner
the Antonia Fortress. The Roman procurators normally resided in
Caesarea, a vast military barracks and seaport – a mixture of
Portsmouth and Aldershot. When visiting Jerusalem, they usual-
ly stayed in either of these two palace/fortresses, selecting which
one according to the political situation of the moment. The
Citadel dominated and controlled the Upper City. The Antonia
dominated and overlooked the Temple Area. At the time of
Passover, the Antonia, being closer to the sparking point of riot in
the Temple Area, was likely to prove the better headquarters and
was actually the vast fortress, crammed with garrison troops.
Herod's Palace, though more sumptuous and comfortable, could
be cut off by riots from the Temple. Subsequent procurators
discovered this and had to despatch reinforcements singly, only
lightly armed and in plain clothes, in order to penetrate the
rioting crowds and road blocks.

Which was the Praetorium?
It is still not 100 per cent certain to which of these two fortresses
Jesus was taken that morning. The Greek word used in the
Gospels, 'Praetorium', refers to the mobile judgment seat of the
Praetor or Procurator, rather than to a specific place. The tribunal,
or place of judgment, could be established merely by posting his

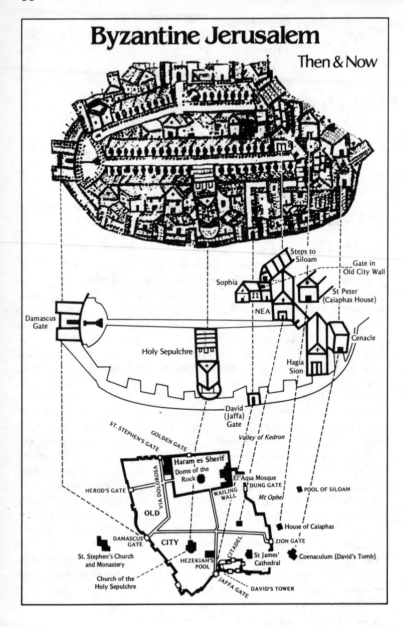

Byzantine Jerusalem

Then & Now

Steps to Siloam

Gate in Old City Wall

Sophia

St Peter (Caiaphas House)

NEA

Damascus Gate

Cenacle

Holy Sepulchre

Hagia Sion

David (Jaffa) Gate

ST. STEPHEN'S GATE

GOLDEN GATE

Valley of Kedron

Haram es Sherif

Dome of the Rock

El'Aqsa Mosque

VIA DOLOROSA

HEROD'S GATE

DUNG GATE

WAILING WALL

Mt Ophel

POOL OF SILOAM

OLD

House of Caiaphas

DAMASCUS GATE

CITY

ZION GATE

St Stephen's Church and Monastery

HEZEKIAH'S POOL

CITADEL

St James' Cathedral

Coenaculum (David's Tomb)

Church of the Holy Sepulchre

JAFFA GATE

DAVID'S TOWER

tribune outside the door of any building with his shield and lance or pennant, rather like the royal standard or admiral's pennant. The judge traditionally sits on his woolsack, the Procurator delivered judgment from his curial chair.

Both the fortresses have their weaknesses in illustrating the gospel story. The Citadel/Palace had no *'gabbatha'*, or pavement. The Antonia had no gallery from which Pilate might have addressed the crowd. Christian tradition however early chose to locate the Praetorium (seat of the Procurator) at the Antonia. In the Middle Ages, the devotional Via Dolorosa began from the Antonia site. Some forty years ago, Père Vincent's excavations revealed the massive scale and features of the Antonia.

Whereas Herod's Palace with its gardens, aviaries and fountains was protected by three independent towers, the Antonia was a gigantic quadrilateral cut almost entirely out of the rocky hill, 170 yards long by nearly 100 yards wide.

Antonia Plan

The Antonia Fortress was well protected by powerful corner towers, as much as 110 feet high and completely commanding the entire Temple Area. Within this vast perimeter were all the installations of a palace and a completely self-sufficient military camp. From the catwalks linking the towers, sentries soon observed any disturbance in the Temple courtyards and were quick to turn out the guard, which could be down in the Temple cloisters in a matter of moments. This was just as well for the Apostle Paul, who was being lynched by the crowd, until rescued by the guard and 'carried up the steps of the castle, for the violence of the people' (Acts 21 and 22). The outstanding feature was without doubt the central open courtyard, or parade ground, of 2500 square metres. It served many purposes: (1) It gathered water which was channelled into massive cisterns, which had to provide for the legions of troops, sometimes besieged there for months at a time. (2) It served as a meeting place between delegations from the city and the administrative and military representatives of the Roman occupation forces. (3) With its vast pavement, polished by countless parades and surrounded by tall cloisters, it was the heart of the fortress whose activity it regulated. Nowhere in Jerusalem is there more impressive and explicit evidence – nor more appropriate a setting for the place where Pilate pronounced the sentence which sent Jesus on his way to Calvary.

ARRIVAL OF PRISONER

So in the early morning of that Friday, the eve of the Fifteenth Nisan in the year 30, leaving the High Priest's Palace, prisoner and escort set out followed by the crowd. They crossed the viaducts from the Western Hill to the Temple cloister, left the city by the Fish Gate and went along under the rampart of the north wall to appear before the great double gate of the Antonia. The gate was outside the city wall, as though fearing less from without than from within, and with good reason. Prisoner and escort proceeded through one side of the double gate (there was one-way traffic) and emerged on the pavement. The water runnels still lead down into the cavernous vaulted cisterns and the cistern tops, set in the pavement, still bear the marks of locks and chains. The counter-weights and pulley are still visible. Meanwhile, the crowds gather and cram into the gateway, rather than risk the defilement of entering a pagan fortress before the Passover Festival.

PILATE TAKES HIS SEAT

St John says that 'Pilate sat down in the judgment seat in a place that is called the Pavement, in the Hebrew Gabbatha.' The two eastern square towers accommodated the troops. The two near (or western) towers were primarily defensive and contained the administrative offices. The chariot-way runs straight through the gateway across the pavement and down a ramp into the stables under the square towers. In the centre of the fortress there is a small tower to the right of the chariot-way, with a separate staircase from the pavement. That tower housed the Procurator's private apartments and his curial chair would be set at the top of his private staircase. Preliminary interrogation revealed that Jesus, as a Galilean, could be passed to Herod for judgment. Once more the prisoner, securely bound, and escort retrace their route to the Garden Palace. Luke's description of the mocking and making fun by Herod's court is very vague, but conceals a vicious and humiliating degradation. The carnival atmosphere of the Herod scene in *Jesus Christ Superstar* was full of oriental burlesque and sordid sexuality. When goodness was the sport of spite, the 'mocking' involved cruel, if not actually physical, horseplay. I suppose the Herod fiasco must have taken up a very nasty hour, before his return to Pilate in the 'gorgeous robe'.

THE TRIAL AND SENTENCE

Mark's Account

There are three rather different accounts of the trial: Mark's version is probably the earliest. This account reflects the undeniable fact that Jesus was convicted by Roman authority, represented by Pilate. Morally the Jewish Sanhedrin and Caiaphas were responsible, but the form and execution of the punishment were Roman. The charge was changed from blasphemy to treason. To Pilate, the case must have appeared similar to that of Barabbas, another agitator but with a record of violence. Though Pilate offers to release Jesus, the crowd demands the release of Barabbas and the crucifixion of Jesus. Jesus silently refuses to refute the charge. Pilate succumbs to Jewish pressure and sets the normal crucifixion process in motion. He condemns the prisoner to scourging and execution. The writer is not really concerned with the personalities responsible, but only with the purposeful progress of Jesus through his Passion.

Luke's Version

Luke's version is noticeably different. Writing to the Roman aristocrat Theophilus he tries to show that Rome, represented by Pilate, is responsible for neither the conviction nor the crucifixion of Jesus. The charge of treason is very specific and cannot be disregarded by Pilate but, after cross-examination, Pilate is convinced of the prisoner's innocence. He announces his intention to acquit no less than three times, but is shouted down again and again, until forced to convict. There is no scourging, only an inevitable surrender to pressure.

John's Record

John's account, though only published at the end of the first century, after the death of all those concerned, is completely fresh and independent of all other accounts. How John secured the record of the case before Pilate is a mystery. Perhaps he, John, was there and overheard, but his account is beyond the art of fiction and carries the hallmark of truth and topographical accura-

cy. Irritated by clumsy attempts to steam-roller him into convict-
ing, Pilate takes Jesus up the stairs into his own private apartments and is surprised at the quiet dignity of this unconvincing
rebel. 'Are you the King of the Jews? What have you done?' and
gets the real answer: 'My Kingdom does not belong to your kind
of world!' 'So you are a King?' 'That's why I came into this world!'
However exasperated Pilate may have been, he was convinced
both of the sincerity and harmlessness of his prisoner. He was
aware of the fraud and manipulation of Caiaphas – and offered to
exercise the usual Passover amnesty, but he had forgotten Barabbas. 'Not this man, but Barabbas.'

Scourging

Seeing he had to do something to conciliate the crowd in order to
avoid the death sentence, Pilate had the prisoner scourged –
probably in view of the people, in order to evoke their sympathy.
Scourging was the first prescribed preliminary to every crucifixion and the Turin shroud illustrates the whole process with
horrific clarity. The scourge or *'flagrum'* was a short knout on the
end of which were a number of leather throngs, in the case of the
shroud victim, three thongs. These were each studded with a pair
of heavy crude pellets or spiked balls about two inches apart,
leaving double puncture-type wounds, shaped like dumb-bells.
Thus each lash of the scourge produced six wounds on the body,
multiplying the number of strokes. The scourges were applied
from the shoulders down to the calves of the legs, by two soldiers,
converging from each side. In the case of the shroud, the number
of strokes was excessive, more than 120, and the suspension of
the prisoner over a pillar designed for the purpose ensured
accuracy.

Mocking

It was after the scourging, according to John, that the soldiers
took the prisoner to their guardroom. There they had the opportunity to vent their detestation upon this representative (who
called himself 'King') of the hated Jewish race. Just how they did
so is well illustrated by carvings in the pavement at the foot of the
troops' stairways. Among a variety of knuckle-boards and hop-
scotch designs covering several flagstones, there are the following signs: the 'B' for Basilicus, meaning 'King', described by
Plautus as derived from the Saturnalia, in which a burlesque king
is chosen, mockingly honoured and saluted, before being killed.

So, in the crucifixion squad, each soldier would adopt as his stake one of the condemned prisoners. The winner in the game of bones would crown his own 'stake' with a crown of thorns in a mocking guardroom ceremony. The king, thus crowned, would receive his soldier's homage, his swagger-stick as sceptre and his military cloak as a royal robe. All the guardroom would hail him 'Basilicus Judaiorum!' This indeed gives meaning to the Gospel account of the mocking.

The crown of thorns is illustrated on the shroud as a form of barbed cap thrust over the whole of the top of the head and leaving deep triangular punctures. This would accord with a clump of camel-thorn taken from the brazier-fuel, rather than a narrow circlet of thorns. Military and guardroom morals are very different on and off parade. When the guard are dismissed and fall out to become gaolers – then blind efficiency can give place to blind brutality. Remember that it was after a scourging that the hate of ignorant soldiery, with absolutely no understanding for any foreign faith or culture, was unleashed on a prisoner virtually paralysed by pain and fear. Then, what might have been trivial comedy was transformed into the macabre bestiality of the circus.

Ecce Homo
When the prisoner was returned to Pilate in a condition to draw pity from the crowd, Pilate presented him, with the words 'Ecce Homo!' – 'Behold the Man!' – or more contemptuously perhaps, 'See, here the fellow is!' He had, however, underestimated the determination and cunning of Caiaphas, as he must have realised when the crowd still demanded the death penalty. In his frustration and annoyance, Pilate once again attempted to pass the buck: 'Take him yourselves and crucify him, for I find no crime in him.' This finally stung the Sanhedrin into stating their real case against the prisoner, for which they had themselves convicted him – blasphemy. 'The Jews answered him, "We have a law, and by that law he ought to die, because he has made himself the Son of God." When Pilate heard these words, he was the more afraid.' (John 19: 7,8)

Interrogation
Once again entering the Praetorium, Pilate attempted to re-examine the prisoner. His sudden fear may have been due to his growing apprehension that his prisoner was perhaps out of the

ordinary. The sceptic had become perplexed and superstitious, he wished to test the prisoner's claim to divine origin: 'Where are you from?' But the prisoner remained silent. When Pilate reminded him of his procuratorial power of life and death, the prisoner calmly rejected both Pilate's authority and indeed Pilate's significance in the situation. 'Jesus answered him, "You would have no power over me unless it had been given you from above; therefore he who delivered me to you has the greater sin."' (John 19: 11). The real issue was between the prisoner and Caiaphas, in whose hands Pilate was merely a tool.

The truth of this was clearly shown within the next and final moments of this so-called trial. Pilate, more than ever convinced of the prisoner's innocence and harmlessness, once again went out to the crowd. But before he could even speak the Jews 'yelled' (the literal translation): '"If you release this man, you are not Caesar's friend; every one who makes himself a King sets himself against Caesar." When Pilate heard these words, he brought Jesus out and sat down on the judgment seat at a place called The Pavement, and in Hebrew, Gabbatha. Now it was the day of Preparation of the Passover; it was about the sixth hour. He said to the Jews, "Behold your King!" They cried out, "Away with him, away with him, crucify him!" Pilate said to them, "Shall I crucify your King?" The chief priests answered, "We have no King but Caesar."' (John 19: 12–15).

Condemnation

Outmanoeuvred by a people whom he had not even begun to understand, his already precarious reputation in Rome dangerously threatened, deafened by the clamorous bloodlust of the crowd, Pilate's resistance collapsed. He signed the death warrant and handed the prisoner over for crucifixion. Perhaps he gained some revenge by his choice of words in the title nailed to the cross of Jesus in Hebrew, Latin and Greek: 'Jesus of Nazareth, the King of the Jews.'

The three prisoners, Jesus and two bandits or guerillas, with their escort, were formed up on the Pavement. The procession passed out of the fortress through the great double gate with its two guardrooms on to each chariot-way. The prisoners carried their huge cross-beams along the road to the traditional 'Place of the Skull', or Execution Hill.

PROCURATOR'S PRAETORIUM (TRADITIONAL), ANTONIA FORTRESS, SISTERS OF SION

1. *Government school (Omariya)*
Windows down into Temple Area; Position of Fortress in relation to Temple; Plan and purpose of fortress – sentry cat-walk.
Acts 21: 27–32

2. *Chapel of Flagellation*
Character portrayals (i) Barabbas – Jesus of Nazareth, cf. Jesus Barabbas (window south)
Matt. 27: 12–18, 21b
(ii) Pilate – cf. Pontius the Pikeman (window north)
Matt. 27: 22–26

3. *Ground floor or basement – Model room in convent*
 (i) North wall plan; position of both fortresses; purpose of fortress location
John 18: 28–29
(ii) Fortress model; 2 curtain towers, 2 barrack towers, Procurator's quarters; Purpose of Gabbatha

4. *Pavement level*
Cistern water supply (visit cistern if time); Cistern top and water runnel; Block and tackle, counter-weight, chain marks, locking top
John 19: 23b–24

5. *Pavement near games*
Illuminated photo; Soldiers' gambling boards; The game of 'King' – 'crown and sword', barrackroom horseplay
Matt. 27: 27–29

6. *Striated chariot-way and wall mosaic*
Position of Pilate's personal apartments, chariot garage etc.; Pilate's personal interrogation – John's source; scourging method
John 18: 33–40

7. *Shopping – Exit info Street – Re-Enter to Convent Chapel*

8. *Sitting in back of chapel*
Note altar arches, which are Hadrianic, cf. vast, rock-hewn, first-century double gateway in which you are sitting, ten foot up within the north gate!
John 19: 15–17

9. Within northern guardrooms
Look across gateway; pattern in *each* gateway the same: guard-room with chimney, pavement, chariot-way, wall; Roman one-way traffic: in one gateway, out the other.
NB: The key of the 'Corps de Garde' may be obtained at the Convent entrance.

> Almighty God,
>   whose most dear Son went not up to joy
>   but first he suffered pain,
> and entered not into glory before he was crucified:
> mercifully grant that we, walking in the way of the cross,
> may find it none other than the way of life and peace;
> through Jesus Christ our Lord.

WAY OF THE CROSS, DEVOTIONS FROM CONDEMNATION TO RESURRECTION, ANTONIA TO TOMB

NB: Historically the stations have varied. The present ones approximate the fifteenth-century Franciscan route. Most are found in the Gospel, some in legend. Falls are linked with gateways in and out of the city. Station vi (Veronica) needs explanation: the story tells of her in the crowd, running forward to wipe his brow with her headdress. Taking back the cloth she is left with the true likeness (*vera icon*) of his face. Thought historically unlikely, the story challenges with an opportunity of prayer to face the countenance of God. The street scenery of each station can evoke penitence and love, both for the individual and for a group. Keep silence – do not be worried by distractions.

NO./STATION	EVENT/TITLE	TEXTS	THOUGHT
Rooftop view – from topmost balustrade	Orientation of Via Dolorosa		Puzzle out north wall, fortresses, Calvary, Judgment Gate
I Either under Arch *or* in School courtyard	Jesus is condemned	Matt. 27: 24–26	Knowing Jesus to be innocent, Pilate calculates the need to avoid Roman reprimand and to save face. Political compromise
II Convent Gateway above Antonia Gateway	Jesus is made to carry his cross	Isa. 53: 3 Mk. 15: 20	Give us courage to face rejection (rather than compromise) at the cost of carrying our cross for Jesus
III Polish Chapel corner, site of Fish Gate?	Jesus falls under the cross	Isa. 53: 4 Heb. 2: 6–9	A mural depicts the hosts of Angels in utter amazement looking down on the fallen figure of Jesus above the altar

NO./STATION	EVENT/TITLE	TEXTS	THOUGHT
IV Plaque above doorway opposite café	Jesus meets his mother	Isa. 54: 6–7 Luke 2: 34–35	Remember the Wise Man's gift of Myrrh and Simeon's prophecy of the sword. This is the moment – though Mary was always losing and finding him – aren't we too?
V Plaque above doorway in corner	Simon of Cyrene made to carry the cross	Luke 9: 23 Mark 15: 21	Mark must have known Simon's sons, Alexander and Rufus in Rome! Was Simon converted by carrying the Cross? Are we?
VI Within Chapel of Little Sisters of Charles Foucauld	Veronica wipes the face of Jesus	Isa. 53: 2 2 Cor. 4: 5–6	'Veronica' means 'true likeness'. The single icon in chapel. The compassionate presence and silent witness of the Little Sisters who wipe the faces of the poor in Jerusalem today.

NO./STATION	EVENT/TITLE	TEXTS	THOUGHT
VII Plaque above door corner of *suq*	Jesus falls the second time	Isa. 53: 5	The noise and the crowds were there in Jerusalem on *that* eve of Passover. 'Is it nothing to you all ye who pass by?'
VIII Wall plaque up Francis Street	Jesus speaks to the women of Jerusalem	Luke 23: 27–28 and 31	The Women's Guild of Sympathy at the Judgment Gate offer drugged wine. He refuses. Do we avoid or face our problems?
IX Within Russian excavations, basement	Jesus falls the third time	Isa. 53: 6 Heb. 2: 17–18	The stumble on the threshold of the Judgment Gate, leading out to Calvary. Note the Russian icon of the 'Crowned Christ' on wall.
X Within Russian excavations, chapel	Jesus stripped of his garments	Isa. 63: 2 John 19: 23–24 Ps. 22: 18	As the athlete takes off his track-suit before the contest, so Jesus is left with nothing. Look at Russian pictures in silence.

NO./STATION	EVENT/TITLE	TEXTS	THOUGHT
XI Holy sepulchre in *Latin* Calvary	Jesus nailed to the cross	Mark 15: 22 Luke 23: 34	The courage to submit to the control and cruelty of others. Abraham's sacrifice of Isaac prefigures God's sacrifice of Jesus (see mosaic). Pray for all whose work it is to inflict pain.
XII Greek Calvary KNEELING	Jesus dies on the Cross	John 19: 30 Agnus Dei O Saviour of the World . . .	With arms outstretched for all mankind, he gives his life. The power and wisdom of God died for man, but the so-called foolishness and weakness of God is wiser and stronger than man.
XIII Stone of anointing	Jesus is taken down from the cross	Luke 23: 50–53 John 19: 39	Only a Crusader tradition site, between Calvary and Tomb, but still deeply reverenced by all, as they enter the Church. Mural.

NO./STATION	EVENT/TITLE	TEXTS	THOUGHT
XIV Within tomb *or* as group in Chapel of Apparition	Jesus laid within the sepulchre	John 19: 41	We are buried with Christ by baptism into his death, but raised with Christ to walk in newness of life, his risen life.
XV Chapel of St Helena	Jesus risen from the dead	Mark 16: 1–9 Easter anthems	The pilgrimage of the women to the tomb had become a weekly Liturgical devotion of the Christian community in Jerusalem, on the first day of the week, by the time Mark wrote?

V/ THE LORD IS RISEN
R/ HE IS RISEN INDEED. ALLELUIA!

> Almighty Father,
> look with mercy on this your family
> for which our Lord Jesus Christ
>   was content to be betrayed
>   and given up into the hands of wicked men
>   and to suffer death upon the cross;
> who is alive and glorified
>   with you and the Holy Spirit,
> one God, now and for ever.

> Almighty God,
> who in the passion of your blessed Son
> made an instrument of shameful death
> to be for us the means of life:

grant us so to glory in the cross of Christ
that we may gladly suffer for his sake;
who is alive and reigns with you and the Holy Spirit
one God, now and for ever.

Merciful God,
who made all men and hate nothing
   that you have made:
you desire not the death of a sinner
but rather that he should be converted and live.
Have mercy upon your ancient people the Jews,
and upon all who have not known you,
or who deny the faith of Christ crucified;
take from them all ignorance, hardness of heart,
   and contempt for your word,
and so fetch them home to your fold
that they may be made one flock under one shepherd;
through Jesus Christ our Lord.

Grant, Lord,
that we who are baptised into the death
   of your Son our Saviour Jesus Christ
may continually put to death our evil desires
   and be buried with him;
that through the grave and gate of death
we may pass to our joyful resurrection;
through his merits, who died and was buried
   and rose again for us,
your Son Jesus Christ our Lord.

CHURCH OF THE HOLY SEPULCHRE AND RESURRECTION – STAGE PROPERTY OF MAN'S REDEMPTION

GARDEN

'Now in the place where he was crucified there was a garden, and in the garden a new tomb where no one had ever been laid. So because of the Jewish Day of Preparation, as the tomb was close at hand, they laid Jesus there.' John 19: 41–42. The Passion of Our Lord is fully described: 'nigh to the city – outside the gate'. The first followers of Our Lord must have known exactly where the events took place.

OUTSIDE THE WALL

If the sepulchre was in a garden, the tomb was that of a very well-known member of the Sanhedrin, Joseph of Arimathea. He had hewn it out of the rock himself. This garden was presumably his own private property. Even when Herod Agrippa, in extending the city, enclosed it within the walls, the garden would not have been built on. Because it had been a burial place, it was unclean land. If it had remained in Christian hands, how easy it would have been to point out to future generations where these great events had happened! There is a natural instinct in all men to remember the sites of great historical happenings; surely, this site would have been preserved by early Christians. They would point out to their children the sacred places so carefully described in the Gospels (see also page 88).

FIRST REVOLT

In A.D. 66 began the revolt of the Jews against the power of Rome, which ended in the destruction of Jerusalem, under Titus, in the year A.D. 70. From the crucifixion to A.D. 70 was forty years at most, too short a time for anyone to believe that these sacred places could be 'lost'. We come now to a sad period in the history of Jerusalem, from A.D. 70 to 135, a period of sixty-five years. The city was traditionally sacked and razed to the ground. But conquerors tend to exaggerate the damage they inflict upon their enemies. At any rate, repopulation and reconstruction began at once, on a modest scale. Although the city had lost all its old splendour, life began to return to normal. The battle-scarred city rose like a phoenix from its ashes.

The Christian community in the city, however small, continued to exist, for we have records of every single bishop of Jerusalem during this period. Although Titus is said to have destroyed the city, the sites of the crucifixion and resurrection, never having been built over, must have been comparatively unaffected by the rubble of destruction. There they remained for the faithful to see. The bishops of Jerusalem must have pointed them out. And it may safely be said that the tradition of these holy places continued, during these unhappy years.

HADRIAN

Once again, revolt broke out in the year 135, under Bar Cochba. Once again, the city suffered defeat and demolition. Hadrian captured and entirely rebuilt it, on the lines of a Roman colonial city. He renamed it Aelia Capitolina. He again moved the city northwards and even excluded the Temple Area! He constructed a main road north and south, through the city. Halfway along this were the forum and the capitol. He exiled the Jewish inhabitants of the city. Considering the Christian religion a Jewish sect, he tried to erase or desecrate the Christian sites. Hadrian built a great concrete terrace over the two sites of the crucifixion and resurrection. On this he erected a statue of Jupiter over Calvary and a temple of Venus over the tomb. (This part of the terrace is still to be seen in the Russian excavations.) Hadrian's action however had exactly the reverse result to what he had planned. For, under the providence of God, that mass of concrete served to mark indelibly the site of our redemption.

GENTILE CHURCH

For the next two hundred years, Aelia Capitolina remained a Roman colony. Christians of Jewish faith were exiled, but Christians of Graeco-Roman origin were allowed to stay. The Church in Jerusalem grew and prospered as a Gentile Church, but kept in communion with the exiled Judaeo-Christians outside. We have again a record of all the Graeco-Roman bishops of Aelia. There begins at this time a record of pilgrimage and of interest in the holy places, although they were still hidden and covered by Hadrian's concrete. In the time of Constantine in the fourth century, Christianity was not only well established, but there is good reason to believe that the exact location of the holy places was known from a tradition going back to apostolic times.

CONSTANTINE

On his conversion to Christianity, the Emperor Constantine decided 'To make that most blessed spot, the place of the Resurrection, visible to all and given over to veneration'. Those were the words of the historian Eusebius of Caesarea, who gives a very clear account of the finding of the tomb. He shows that the holy places specifically desecrated were indelibly marked by Hadrian's statue and temple.

Perhaps Constantine, like us, was surprised to find these sites inside the then city walls. If he had just intended to found a place of pilgrimage in honour of Christ, would not he have chosen a site outside the walls? Macarius was bishop of Jerusalem at that time and pointed out the sites to Constantine, within the city. Then began the destruction of one emperor's temple of the imperial state religion by another emperor, and this for the sole purpose of erecting the central shrine of Christendom! In a letter to Bishop Macarius, Constantine wrote: 'No words can express how good the Saviour has been to us. That the monument of his Holy Passion, hidden for so many years, has now been at last restored to the faithful is indeed a miracle. My great wish is, after freeing the site of impious idols, to adorn it with splendid buildings.'

Excavation

Constantine planned to make these holy places an object of Christian pilgrimage and devotion. So he set about the task in this order: (1) demolition of pagan shrines, (2) excavation of concrete podium, (3) discovery of the knoll of Calvary and of the tomb below, (4) levelling off to form a floor level for his church, (5) excavation into the hillside to build a rotunda for the Anastasis, a circular ambulatory round the tomb of Christ.

(a) He left the shell of the tomb in a circular space, or rotunda.

(b) He left a symbolic cuboid of the rock of Calvary.

(i) Of the shell of the tomb Eusebius wrote: 'Is it not astonishing to see this rock standing isolated in the middle of a levelled space and with a cave inside it?'

(ii) Of the cuboid rock, he describes how the token 'mound' stood with a single cross on top – in an open colonnaded court.

BASILICA WITHIN THE CITY

The cathedral or 'Martyrium' was beyond this open court. It was entered through an atrium or courtyard, from the open street, which ran at right angles to the axis of the church (east to west). We can see in the Madeba Mosaic the magnificent setting of the basilica, within the Byzantine city: to the north was the Damascus Gate, at which there was a single colossal column. Indeed the Arabic name for the Damascus Gate is still 'Bab-el-Amoud', Gate of the Column. From this column ran a colonnaded street, all through the city, to the great façade of the basilica. This façade included part of the city wall from the time of Christ, adapted and faced with white marble – against which there was an imposing line of black basalt columns. The three entrances into the basilica are still to be seen behind the Arab market, or *suq* – one in a café, one in a Russian convent, one under the Coptic convent. The crypt of the Constantinian basilica, also still to be seen today, was the cistern in which were found three crosses. One of these was 'identified' as the true cross.

Dome of the Rock, Qubbat es Sakhra, within the Noble Sanctuary, Jerusalem, built by Abdel Melek at the end of the 7th century. pp 28, 36, 41 ff.

Magnificent façade of coloured tiles from early 16th century.

Luxuriously carved and decorated ceiling within the cupola.

A Barmitzvah boy at the Western wall undergoing his initiation to participate in synagogue worship. p64.

The Old City of Jerusalem from the north-east, rises above the valleys of Hinnom, Jehoshaphat and Kedron. p33.

Left: The Franciscan Garden of Gethsemane today, then part of a walled olive grove. pp52 ff.

Below left: The Russian Church of St Mary Magdalene within Gethsemane, higher up the Mount of Olives.

Below right: The Franciscan Church of All Nations in Gethsemane, on the ground plan of its Byzantine predecessor.

The Church of the 'Cock-crowing' on a possible site of the House of Caiaphas, known as 'St Peter in Gallicantu'. p58.

Below: Stone staircase, probably pre-Christ, from the Valley Gate in Kedron up the Western Hill past the High Priest's palace. pp58 ff.

Striated chariot way across the pavement, between gate and garage.

Roman soldiers' gaming board carved on the Gabbatha, showing 'B' for 'basilicus' or king and the crown of thorns. pp62 ff.

Empty Garden Tomb interior 'outside the wall' of Jerusalem. pp84 ff.

Rolling stone and tomb at Franciscan Convent, Bethphage. p86.

Edicule, or model, of the Tomb of Christ within the Church of the Holy Sepulchre. p86.

Above: The nave of the Church of the Nativity, Bethlehem, perhaps the oldest standing church in Christendom. pp108 ff.

Right: The silver star on the traditional place of the birth, donated by an Ottoman Sultan in the 19th century. p117.

Above: Palestinian ewe and lambs. Note the fat tail to retain nourishment through the dry season. pp114 ff.

Below: Refugee cave-family at Bethlehem, after the 1947/8 Arab-Jewish war. p116.

Above: Bethlehem shepherd boy rests on his staff, surrounded by his flock. pp114 ff.

Below: Within the cave-grotto of the Nativity, below the chancel, are the shrines of the birth on the left and the manger on the right. p116.

Church of the Holy Sepulchre & Resurrection

Sections and Ground Plans

Holy Sepulchre [A] [B] Calvary C W

At the time of the Crucifixion

Temple of Venus
Statue of Jupiter
Podium built by Hadrian
Holy Sepulchre [A] [B] Calvary C W

At the time of Hadrian

The anastasis or rotunda — Courtyard — Basilica to the East of the Holy places
[A] [B] C W
Holy Sepulchre

At the time of Constantine

[A] W C B

4th Century (Constantine)

A C W B

12th Century

A Shell of Tomb
B Rock of Calvary
C Cistern of finding of Cross
W Wall of City and Basilica facade

CRUSADER CHURCH TODAY

The present Crusader church, telescoped somewhat for security and defensive purposes, does not include most of the Constantinian cathedral nor its crypt – but this lies underground outside. As we penetrate the dark and dingy Crusader passages we shall come upon the little chapel of Adam – immediately under Calvary. There we shall see part of the cuboid rock which rises up into the Chapel of Calvary above.

Here, Père Couasnon, able to excavate for the first time in eight hundred years, found that the rock was still fourteen feet wide by fourteen feet long – with a height of at least thirty feet! It is not for nothing that the endless stream of pilgrims – some with bare feet – some with dripping swords – some who see it all through the range-finder of their cameras – flows past the rock and the tomb.

'For in that Christ died – He died unto sin once – and in that He liveth, He liveth unto God. As in Adam all die – even so in Christ shall all be made alive.'

THE GARDEN TOMB

PIETY

General Gordon, hero of Khartoum, became convinced in 1883 of the identity of the small hill behind the present Old City bus station, as the site of Golgotha. From a window in what became the Bertha Spafford Vester Baby Home, he distinguished the features of a 'Skull Hill', which he read as a ring contour on a map of Jerusalem, tracing the body too within other contours due southwards. Below his Golgotha and set into the cliff face is a fine two-roomed first-century tomb which has suffered some Byzantine 'tooling'. This tomb, set in a beautiful garden, cannot claim sixteen centuries of tradition, as can the Holy Sepulchre. Because it stands outside the existing walled city, in the setting of a well-cared-for garden, with opportunity for quiet prayer near a

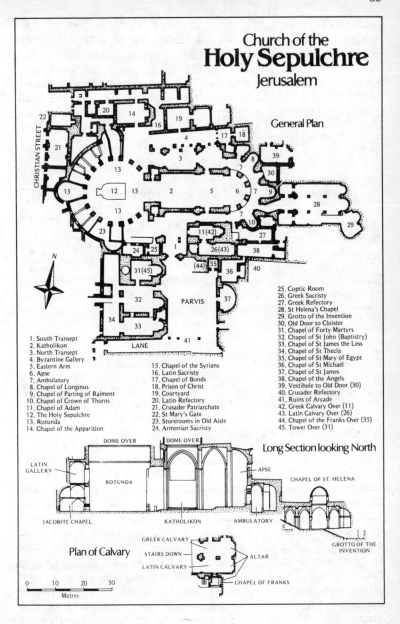

Church of the Holy Sepulchre
Jerusalem

General Plan

CHRISTIAN STREET

1. South Transept
2. Katholikon
3. North Transept
4. Byzantine Gallery
5. Eastern Arm
6. Apse
7. Ambulatory
8. Chapel of Longinus
9. Chapel of Parting of Raiment
10. Chapel of Crown of Thorns
11. Chapel of Adam
12. The Holy Sepulchre
13. Rotunda
14. Chapel of the Apparition

15. Chapel of the Syrians
16. Latin Sacristy
17. Chapel of Bonds
18. Prison of Christ
19. Courtyard
20. Latin Refectory
21. Crusader Patriarchate
22. St Mary's Gate
23. Storerooms in Old Aisle
24. Armenian Sacristy

25. Coptic Room
26. Greek Sacristy
27. Greek Refectory
28. St Helena's Chapel
29. Grotto of the Invention
30. Old Door to Cloister
31. Chapel of Forty Martyrs
32. Chapel of St John (Baptistry)
33. Chapel of St James the Less
34. Chapel of St Thecla
35. Chapel of St Mary of Egypt
36. Chapel of St Michael
37. Chapel of St James
38. Chapel of the Angels
39. Vestibule to Old Door (30)
40. Crusader Refectory
41. Ruins of Arcade
42. Greek Calvary Over (11)
43. Latin Calvary Over (26)
44. Chapel of the Franks Over (35)
45. Tower Over (31)

PARVIS

LANE

Long Section looking North

LATIN GALLERY
DOME OVER
DOME OVER
APSE
CHAPEL OF ST. HELENA
ROTUNDA
JACOBITE CHAPEL
KATHOLIKON
AMBULATORY
GROTTO OF THE INVENTION

Plan of Calvary

GREEK CALVARY
STAIRS DOWN
LATIN CALVARY
ALTAR
CHAPEL OF FRANKS

0   10   20   30
Metres

superb illustration of the Resurrection story, it has inspired millions of the more Protestant Christians, to whom the Holy Sepulchre is a less attractive, though more probable site.

ILLUSTRATION

It has already been said in general that the exact location is secondary to our personal identification with the people and events linked with a site. How best to use the illustration will depend upon the nature of the group or individual pilgrims concerned.

To read and meditate and live the Easter proclamation in Mark 15: 46–16: 8, as presented on the next pages, may be helpful, as may also be the acting out by members of the group and with a narrator, of the events of John 20: 1–18.

Then, whatever the reading, having placed within the tomb some linen (or white cassock) and a separate napkin (or scarf), allow the pilgrims to see and think for themselves. There is plenty of space for a communion facing the tomb. There is a 9 a.m. service every Sunday and a sunrise service every (Western calendar) Easter dawn.

ROLLING STONES

There is a very simple, small rolling-stone tomb in the garden of the Franciscan convent at Bethphage. The stone can easily be moved and the tomb opened. In addition, it is conveniently near to the Palm Sunday Walk route.

In the northern part of the city, east of St George's Close, in Saladin Street, are the so-called Tombs of the Kings. These were in reality the burial vault of the family of Queen Helena of Adiabene on the Tigris. When a widow, she settled together with her son Izates, in Jerusalem in the year A.D. 45. She became a proselyte to Judaism and was renowned for the generosity with which she helped to relieve the victims of a famine, mentioned incidentally in the Acts of the Apostles (Acts 11: 28). The bodies of Helena, Izates, and some twenty of his sons were buried here. A broad staircase leads down into a courtyard thirty metres square, cut out of the rock. A large vestibule leads to the thirty-one tombs, through a low doorway which still has a fine example of a rolling stone.

RESURRECTION TRADITIONS
– GALILEE AND JERUSALEM –
LITURGY OF THE EMPTY
TOMB IN THE GARDEN

TWO TRADITIONS

The 'Jerusalem and Emmaus' tradition is discussed on page 104. The 'Galilee' tradition is directly linked with the empty tomb. However distant from Jerusalem that single, vital and vivid Lakeside appearance in John 21, the Apostolic Church accepted it, but developed the Jerusalem tradition as paramount. It is as though the Galilean tradition was based on history and the Jerusalem one on theology, because both the Apostolic Church and Proclamation of Resurrection 'had' to set out from Jerusalem! (Acts 1:8).

GALILEE REFERENCES

1. On the way out to Gethsemane, Jesus had warned: 'You will all fall away, for it is written, "I will strike the shepherd and the sheep will be scattered." But after I am raised up, I will go before you to Galilee.' (Mark 14: 27–28).
2. In exactly the same context (John 16: 32): 'The hour is coming, indeed it has come, when you will be scattered, every man to his home.' For all but Judas Iscariot, that meant Galilee.
3. Later, in Gethsemane at his arrest, Jesus asks: 'Let these men go'. . . and they fled for their lives; where could they go but home to Galilee? (John 18: 8).
4. Matthew's angel in the Tomb proclaims: 'He is going before you to Galilee' (28: 7). Jesus himself hails them: 'Go and tell my brethren to go to Galilee' (28: 10). The Apostolic Commission and promise are given on a mountain in Galilee (28:16).
5. John's final Lakeside scene of recognition and encouragement ends appropriately with the personal commission and destiny of Peter and John, by their beloved Galilee.

EARLIEST PROCLAMATION

The key and earliest passage (except for 1 Corinthians 15: 5) is in the final verses of Mark's Gospel (15: 46–16: 8) in the Jerusalem Bible: 'Joseph of Arimathea bought a shroud, took Jesus down from the cross, wrapped him in the shroud and laid him in a tomb hewn out of the rock. He then rolled a stone against the entrance to the tomb. Mary of Magdala and Mary the mother of Jesus were watching and *took note of where he was laid*.'

When the sabbath was over, Mary Magdalene, the other Mary and Salome brought spices with which to go and anoint him. Very early on the first day of the week, they went to the tomb, just as the sun was rising. They had been saying: 'Who will roll us away the stone from the tomb?' But when they looked they could see that the stone – a very big one – had already been rolled back.

They stooped in, and saw a youth sitting on the right, in a white robe. They were astonished, but he said to them:

> There is no need for alarm.
> You are looking for Jesus of Nazareth the crucified one.
> He was raised. He is not here.
> Look at the place where they laid him!

LITURGY AND LOCALITY

Here is the most primitive Easter proclamation. *Every word binds it to the PLACE where it happened* – to the scene of the narrative and the walk of the women: The crucified is risen! The burial place is empty! Whether the message of 'young man' or 'angel', it was certainly the confession of faith of that first Christian community in Jerusalem. 'Look at the place' is an invitation to all who today share, in pilgrimage, the walk of the women to the tomb. The date, the occasion, the time and place are specific. Does not this proclamation describe *what had already become* a Liturgical Celebration, as the Jerusalem community walked to the Tomb, at dawn each Sunday morning, to relive in Liturgy the Easter Resurrection of the 'Crucified One'?

The Armenian excavations far below the Church of the Holy Sepulchre reveal the ancient quarry from which rises a rejected pillar of unused shale, whose top was the place of the crucifixion. Less than fifty metres away was the empty tomb in the rising hillside. Between the base of the mound and the edge of the quarry were found, less than ten years ago, not only the quarry tools but evidence of a first century Christian place of worship: first century walling and a metre-long drawing of the earliest symbol of the Christian congregation in Jerusalem. This is a detailed portrayal of a ship (Latin 'navis' – our 'nave') clearly visible on perpendicular rock walling.

Here, we are told, the early Jerusalem community met every first day of the week, at dawn, to rehearse and relive in pilgrimage the events of that very first Easter morning. The message of the 'young man in white' at the tomb (Mark 28: 6) sums up the Easter faith and proclamation of that very first Christian congregation:

> 'Don't be frightened. You are looking for Jesus, the crucified one. He has risen, he is not here. Come, see the place where he lay. Go and tell his followers.'

> Lord of all life and power,
> who through the mighty resurrection of your Son
> overcame the old order of sin and death
> to make all things new in him:
> grant that we, being dead to sin
> and alive to you in Jesus Christ,
> may reign with him in glory.

THE MOUNT OF OLIVES
SITES LINKED WITH BOTH
ASCENSION AND RETURN

PARAMOUNT PRE-CHRISTIAN SHRINE

The Mount of Olives is the natural starting point among those Holy Places sanctified by the apostolic tradition and linked with the lives of Mary, the Mother of Jesus, and the Apostles. St Luke tells us, in both his Gospel and in the Acts of the Apostles, that it was here that Jesus took leave of his followers and commissioned them, his Apostles to the world. It is not surprising, therefore, that many Christian pilgrims today begin and end their visit to Jerusalem with a glimpse of the magnificent panorama of the Holy City from the Mount of Olives. Indeed, the very first goal of all early Christian pilgrimages was the Mount of Olives. To

Graeco-Roman Christian pilgrims, the Jewish Temple destroyed in the year 70 was not of primary interest. The sites of the crucifixion and of the resurrection had been desecrated and covered by the pagan shrines to Venus and Jupiter, erected at the order of the Emperor Hadrian. The sites of the Upper Room on the western hill, and of the Ascension on the Mount of Olives, were more easily approached and venerated.

The fourth-century historian and bishop of Caesarea, Eusebius, wrote: 'All believers in Christ flock together from all quarters of the earth, not, as of old, to behold the beauty of Jerusalem, but that they may abide there and both hear the story of Jerusalem and also worship at the Mount of Olives over against Jerusalem, whither the glory of the Lord removed itself, leaving the earlier city. There also, according to the published record, the feet of Our Lord and Saviour, who was Himself the Word and through it took upon Himself human form, stood upon the Mount of Olives near the cave which is now pointed out there.'

CONSTANTINIAN BASILICAS

The pre-Constantinian Christian paid this honour to the Mount of Olives because Jerusalem, Aelia Capitolina, was not a holy, but a pagan and desecrated city. After the building of the Basilica of the Sepulchre and the Resurrection, all was changed and the Mount of Olives no longer had the place of honour. Yet it was still a popular place of pilgrimage.

Emperor Constantine, in the course of the fourth century, fulfilling the wishes of his mother St Helena, enshrined the Christian Holy Places of Palestine within three magnificent basilicas: the grotto where Christ was born, in the basilica at Bethlehem; Calvary and the Tomb of Christ, in the basilica of the Holy Sepulchre in Jerusalem; the cave where Christ foretold the end of the world and his return, in the basilica of Eleona on Mount Olivet, close to the scene of the ascension.

We have traced elsewhere the history of both the basilica at Bethlehem and that of the Holy Sepulchre. The Eleona basilica was destroyed by the Persians in 614, partly restored by the Crusaders in the twelfth century, and thereafter lost until the early years of this century. The Gospel of St Matthew describes

Jesus revealing his vision of the end of the world to his Apostles, on the Mount of Olives, on the Tuesday in Holy Week.

When he was sitting on the Mount of Olives, the disciples came to speak to him privately. '"Tell us, when will this be, and what will be the sign of your coming and of the close of the age?" And Jesus answered them: "Then will appear the sign of the Son of Man in heaven and then all the tribes of the earth will mourn, and they will see the Son of man coming on the clouds of heaven with power and great glory; and he will send out his angels with a loud trumpet call, and they will gather his elect from the four winds, from one end of heaven to the other."' (Matt. 24: 3–4, 30–31).

ELEONA OVER THE CAVE OF TEACHING

As the Gospels mention the summit of the Mount of Olives as the place where Jesus gave these teachings, the first generations of Christians held for certain that it was in the natural cave we find there still. It is, therefore, obvious why Constantine chose this site to build the third great basilica in the Holy Land: the Eleona, so called from a colloquial Greek word for 'Olive', over the traditional cave mentioned by Eusebius.

Today, Brunot describes the scale of this Constantinian basilica, which resembled those at Bethlehem and Calvary in that it enclosed atrium, nave, choir and cave-crypt:

> Going up Mount Olivet, on coming from Gethsemane, the fourth century pilgrim reached an imposing staircase leading to a vast platform; there rising eastwards, was the basilica. As at Bethlehem and the Anastasis here was a fine atrium, approximately thirty metres by twenty-five metres, with covered galleries along the sides and a large underground cistern in the middle. Three doors gave access to the church. This measured thirty metres long and twenty metres wide inside; with walls one and a half metres thick at the base and as much as two metres in the apse. It surrounded and enshrined the memorable cave which, like that of Bethlehem, lay beneath the choir, reached from the north by steps which the excavators found intact. Altogether the building had an overall length of seventy metres and covered an area of seventeen hundred square metres. Knowing how gorgeously decorated were both the basilicas of the Nativity and the Anastasis, we can imagine what this third one must have been. Eusebius tells us that 'the Emperor had adorned it with his usual lavishness, decking it in resplendent ornamentation'.

HOLY WEEK LITURGIES

Brunot further describes the magnificent liturgy within this basilica:

> On Tuesday in Holy Week, the Christian community in Jerusalem gathered there to commemorate the mystery of the second Coming of the Lord. The bishop entered the holy grotto, carrying the gospels, and read out the Master's eschatological discourse. They returned in the evening of Maundy Thursday to read again the last Words of Jesus, and to commemorate the ascension which had taken place close by. Again during the octaves of Easter and that of the Epiphany they reassembled, in order to call to mind those manifestations of Christ which foreshadowed his last manifestation.

The early Maundy Thursday processions to the Garden of Gethsemane, to the Cave of the Arrest and the Rock of the Agony, began from the Eleona basilica.

It was in 1910 that the White Fathers, excavating on a property purchased by the Princesse de la Tour d'Auvergne in 1868, revealed the entire foundations of the Byzantine basilica. In 1920 the foundation stone of a new basilica, on the same foundations, was laid by the French Cardinal Dubois. Under the supervision of Père Vincent, plans were drawn up, for as close a reproduction of the first basilica as possible.

SHRINE OF ASCENSION

In 380, Egeria differentiated clearly between the 'Church in Eleona' and the shrine 'on the Hill', where solemn services were also held. According to another pilgrim, Peter the Iberian, a round open courtyard had been built on the very hill-top by a Roman lady called Pomenia in about 378, on the traditional site of the ascension of Jesus. Arculf describes it as 'having in its circuit three vaulted porticos roofed over', as cloisters surrounding an open space. The Crusaders built, over the ruins of the Byzantine shrine, an octagon whose remains still encircle the site. Within the Crusader court an edicule was built to enclose a rock in the very centre of the octagon which was long linked with the place of Ascension.

In 1187, the Muslims transformed the shrine of the ascension of

Jesus. Today, Christians are allowed to celebrate within the courtyard and there are Greek, Latin, Armenian, Coptic and Syrian altars round the walls, besides a small central domed shrine.

COVERED WITH CONVENTS

The Mount of Olives was, so far as is known, not built upon in the time of Jesus. In Byzantine times it became the site of many monasteries and nunneries. Melania built two convents for the religious to pray night and day 'in the Church of the Ascension and in the cave where the Lord had talked with his disciples about the end of the world'; that is the crypt of the Eleona basilica. By 570, the pilgrim Placenza saw the mountain covered with convents, all of which were destroyed by the Persians in 614, when 1207 Christians were killed. Modestus restored the hill-top shrine of the Ascension in the seventh century and convents were rebuilt around it.

TODAY

Many branches of the Christian Church now own properties near the crest of the Mount of Olives. Both the Greek and Latin patriarchates look down on the city from different points along the ridge. The Latin Carmelite convent and Church of the Pater Noster together with the Franciscan site of 'Dominus Flevit' have already been mentioned in the Palm Sunday sequence on pp. 49 and 50. One of the most imposing properties is the Russian compound, east of the Byzantine site of the Ascension. The Russian tower of six storeys can be seen from the Dead Sea and sometimes from the Mountains of Gilead. There are two fine churches within this compound, one of which encloses a Byzantine mosaic and an ancient Armenian inscription. To the north-west of the Russian compound is the 'Vineyard of the Hunter'. Here are the Greek patriarchate, and the chapel of Viri Galilaei which is supposed to mark the spot on which the two men in white apparel stood and told the Apostles, as 'men of Galilee', that they would see Jesus descending again, in his day of glory, from the clouds into which he had just ascended (Acts 1: 1). This accords well with the archaeological evidence for Bethany and Bethphage being a Galilean suburb of the city.

Almighty God,
as we believe your only-begotten Son our Lord Jesus Christ
to have ascended into the heavens,
so may we also in heart and mind thither ascend
and with him continually dwell;
who is alive and reigns with you and the Holy Spirit,
one God, now and for ever.

Eternal God, the King of Glory,
you have exalted your only Son
with great triumph to your kingdom in heaven.
Leave us not comfortless,
but send your Holy Spirit to strengthen us
and exalt us to the place
where Christ is gone before,
and where with you and the Holy Spirit
he is worshipped and glorified,
now and for ever.

Almighty God,
who
taught the hearts of your faithful people
by sending to them the light of your Holy Spirit:
grant us by the same Spirit
    to have a right judgment in all things,
and evermore to rejoice in his holy comfort;
through the merits of Christ Jesus our Saviour,
who is alive and reigns with you in the unity of the Spirit,
one God, now and for ever.

SITES LINKED WITH MARY, THE MOTHER OF JESUS

CHURCH OF ST ANNE AND POOL(S) OF BETHESDA

The history of the Church of St Anne is closely linked with that of the Pool of Bethesda. The church is traditionally built over the home of Joachim and Anna, the parents of Mary the Mother of Jesus. Both in Aramaic and Hebrew the word 'Bethesda' means

'House of Effusion' which is also the meaning of the word 'Anna'. A large Byzantine basilica appears on the Madeba mosaic at the site of the present church.

St John (John 5: 2) says that the Pool was by the Sheep Gate or Pool (Nehemiah 3: 1). Some suggest that the Greek word for Sheep Gate is itself the corruption of an Aramaic word for 'baths'. Of many suggested sites for the Pool of Bethesda, that under the present church of St Anne is most interesting. Excavations show that twin pools, separated by and surrounded by cloisters, were built over by a large church, about A.D. 530. Both pools and church fell into ruins following the Persian invasion of 614, but were restored by the Crusaders, who shortened and covered in the pools, building a church of 'St Mary in the Sheep Market' over the top. Both pools and church were destroyed and lost, until discovered by the French after the Crimean War. The neighbouring Crusader church of St Anne was offered to and declined by Queen Victoria, in favour of the island of Cyprus!

The present Crusader church of St Anne, one of the most beautiful Crusader churches, though showing signs of some reconstruction, survived the Saracen occupation. It was requisitioned by order of Saladin for a Muslim school of theology. It was restored by the French and in 1878 handed over to the care of the White Fathers of Cardinal Lavigerie. They continue the excavation to this day. Beneath their Crusader church are a series of crypt-caves, recalling the house and living conditions of the family of Mary, the Mother of Jesus. (Luke 1: 26–38; John 5: 1–16.)

THE TOMB OF MARY IN THE KEDRON RAVINE

East of the viaduct on which the Jericho road crosses the Kedron is an ancient church, now almost buried by the accumulation of centuries of rubble in the bottom of the ravine. A fourth-century tradition records how the body of Mary, the Mother of Jesus, was brought here from the house of St John on Mount Zion, for burial. A slightly later tradition records how from here she was assumed soul and body into heaven, three days after burial. As in the case of the Holy Sepulchre, her rock tomb was excavated and its shell left standing within a basilica, about the year A.D. 440.

It is perhaps this basilica which is also to be seen on the Madeba mosaic, outside the eastern wall, in the Kedron.

The present church in the form of a Latin cross has a Crusader porch, the gift of Millicent, queen of Fulke, and wife of the eighth king of Jerusalem. She was also buried here in 1161. The Franciscans were entrusted with the care of this shrine until 1757, when it was ceded to the Eastern Churches. Today the Tomb of Mary is a tiny rock chamber surrounded by Armenian, Greek and Syrian altars – besides also a Muslim prayer niche in honour of Mary, the Mother of Jesus.

THE ABBEY OF THE DORMITION ON MOUNT ZION

The great modern church and convent of the Dormition stands on the traditional site of the house of St John, where Mary the Mother of Jesus 'fell asleep'. The German emperor Wilhelm II laid the foundation stone, on his visit to Jerusalem in 1898, and the consecration took place ten years later.

Beneath the magnificent Romanesque tower, dome and choir, where the German Benedictines at their offices are a constant inspiration, is the dark 'Crypt of Mary's Sleep'. Here the statue of the Virgin recumbent is looked down upon by the heroines of the Old Testament. Sing: Magnificat.

> Almighty God,
> who chose the blessed Virgin Mary
>   to be the mother of your only Son:
> grant that we who are redeemed by his blood
> may share with her
> in the glory of your eternal kingdom;
> through Jesus Christ our Lord,
> who is alive and reigns with you and the Holy Spirit,
> one God, now and for ever.

THE NEW CITY
LIMITED SELECTION OF
INTERESTING VISITS

SYNAGOGUES:	Heikhal Sholomo 58 King George St Chief Rabbinate (Melech George) Yeshurun King George St (Within the Jewish Quarter: Hanavi, Emtzai, Hurva, Istanbul, Ramban, Ben Zakkai) Attendance at service – by arrangement with the Secretary – service usually sunset Friday and mid-morning Saturday	*Sun–Thur: 10–1 and 4–7*
HADASSA HOSPITAL	Chagall windows of 12 Tribes Medical Centre	*Sun–Fri: 9–12 Sun–Thur: 1.30–4*
HEBREW UNIVERSITY	Conducted tours arranged	*Sun–Fri: 9–11*
KNESSET	Ruppin St; guided tours	*Sun–Fri: 8–2.30*
ISRAEL MUSEUM	Ruppin St; including Shrine of Book	*Sun, Mon, Wed, Thurs: 10–5. Tues: 4–10*
MOUNT HERTZL	Hertzl Boulevard	*Mon–Fri: 8–5*
YAD VASHEM MONASTERY OF THE CROSS	Holocaust Museum, Mt Hertzl Boulevard Ben Zvi	*Sun–Thur: 9–5 Mon–Fri: 8–12*
SECOND TEMPLE MODEL	HolyLand Hotel, Jerusalem West Beit Vegan	*Sun–Fri: 8–5*
BIBLICAL ZOO	10 Brandeis Street	*Sun–Thurs: 8–4*
SON ET LUMIÈRE	Jewish Quarter	*Check times with Government Tourist Office*
MINISTRY OF TOURISM	King George Ave	
CATHEDRALS, CHURCHES	Russian – Bar Kochba Square Ethiopian – Mea Shearim Scottish – St Andrew's	

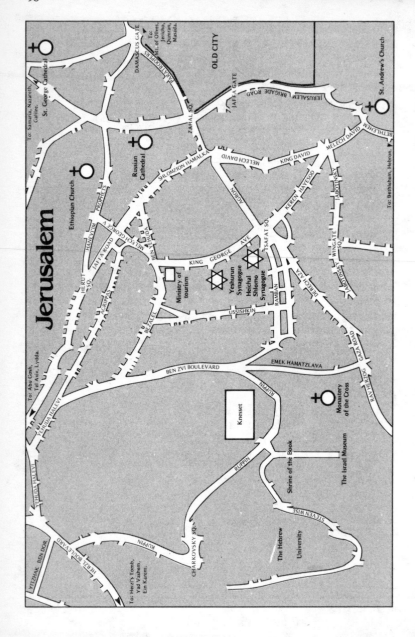

Part Three:

FROM JERUSALEM

WALKS AROUND JERUSALEM

SAUL AND DAVID SEQUENCE – north of Shufat on Ramallah Road

1 *Gibea (Tel El Ful)*
   a) The anointing of Saul by Samuel, at Gibea: I Sam. 9: 1–6, 11–20; 10: 1.
   b) Looking towards Rama, where Samuel's prophetic School was: 'was Saul also among the prophets?': 1 Sam. 10: 9–16.
2 *Mispah (Tel-An-Nazbeh)*
   The rallying point of the tribes and crowning of Saul as King: 1 Sam. 10: 23–6; 11: 12–15.
3 *Walking down the Gorge, between Michmash and Geba (Jeba)*
   a) The Philistine advance: 1 Sam. 13: 5–7.
   b) The foray of Jonathan and his armour bearer: 1 Sam. 14: 1–15.
   c) The defeat and pursuit of the Philistines down to the Shepelah: 1 Sam. 14: 16–32.
   (*Intermission* to read the rise of David: his slaying of the Philistine champion Goliath in the Vale of Elah and Saul's consequent jealousy, David's betrothal to Michal and further successes against the Philistines. 1 Sam. 17: 20 ff.)
4 *Rama (Ar-Ram)*
   a) David flees for his life to Samuel in Rama: 1 Sam. 19: 18 ff. Saul follows.
   b) David and Jonathan meet, perhaps near Gibea, to make a pact of friendship – the story of the boy and the arrows: 1 Sam. 20: 1–5, 24–42.
5 *Nob (Issawiya – north end of Scopus)*
   David flees to Nob, on his way to the caves of Adullam – the story of the shewbread and Doeg's slaughter of the priests of Nob: 1 Sam. 21: 1–9; 22: 1–2, 17–23.

PROPHETS AND KINGS IN KEDRON a
walking sequence in Jerusalem

1 *The Tombs of the Prophets*
  In the Kedron Valley there are three monumental tombs, which must have been well known to Our Lord. In fact he will have passed them both on his way out with his disciples, over Kedron to Gethsemane, and on his way back under arrest to the High Priest's Palace in the upper city. The tombs are respectively:

  a) *The Teapot Tomb* by Crusader tradition 'Absalom's Pillar', but now known to be Maccabean.

  b) *The Pyramid Tomb* until A.D. 333 accepted as that of Isaiah, but since a change of tradition now considered to be that of Zedekiah.

  c) *The Columned Mausoleum* thought to be the tomb of the Apostle James the Just: Matt. 23: 29–35.

2 *The Bridge over Kedron, below the 'pinnacle of the temple'*
  The masonry of the bridge is of the Roman period. The corner or 'wing' of the temple, linked with the temptations, is above. Here, by tradition, James the Just was thrown off the corner of the temple and clubbed to death by a fuller, below: Matt. 4: 5–7.

3 *The spring Gihon – meaning 'gusher'*
  In Old Testament times, an intermittent spring gushed out into the Kedron here. During David's siege of Jebus, the Canaanite city up above, on Mount Ophel, Joab his lieutenant entered the spring outlet and climbed up the water shaft or 'gutter' into the city itself: 2 Sam. 5: 6–9; 1 Chr. 11: 4–9.

  Three hundred years later, Hezekiah extended this water conduit to bring the water within the city and incidentally stopped the flow out into the Kedron. Consequently the Assyrians later besieging the city found the spring outlet blocked at Gihon, the one-time Upper Pool: 2 Chr. 32: 3, 4; 2 Chr. 32: 30; 2 Kings 20: 20; 2 Chr. 33: 14.

  N.B. In the late spring or summer a party will much enjoy a walk through the conduit, with torches and bathing suits!

4 *The Pool of Siloam*
  This is the pool into which the conduit leads. As the walls of the city ran down the scarp of Ophel and then circled up round the upper city, the pool was within the city of Hezekiah: Isa. 22: 9, 11.

5 *The King's Pool, now called the Red Pool*
This is in fact today a vegetable garden at the very bottom end of Ophel. It was the original pool of Siloam, filled by the original surface channel from Gihon, before the making of Hezekiah's conduit and the 'new' pool of Siloam. Nearby was the Valley or Fountain Gate, mentioned by Nehemiah on his tour of the walls.

Even as late as the time of Christ the Tyropean Valley between the upper and lower cities was bridged with viaducts and far too steep for carts and riders. No wonder Nehemiah could not get his horse through the fallen masonry by the King's Pool or garden: Isa. 7: 3–14; 2 Kgs 25: 4; Neh. 2: 14.

Tradition relates the execution of Isaiah, at the King's Pool, sawn in half by order of Manasseh, the son of Hezekiah: Heb. 11: 37 perhaps refers.

6 *En-Rogel – Job's Well*
This was the Fullers' Fountain, a little south of the King's Pool and further down the lower Kedron – the Wadi-En-Nar – the Fire Valley, perhaps so-called from Manasseh's time. The fullers' basins are still visible in the nearby rock terraces, just a few yards east of the well: Josh. 15: 7–8; 18: 16; 2 Chr. 33: 6.

7 *Aceldama*
Round in the Valley of Hinnom, we find a small Orthodox convent on the site of the Field of Blood, bought with the 'thirty pieces of silver'. Nearby are tombs 'to bury strangers in', later used as a burial vault by the Knights of St John: Zech. 11: 12–13; Matt. 27: 3–10; Acts 1: 18, 20.

RECENT REVELATIONS IN THE OLD CITY

The reconstruction of the Jewish Quarter has unearthed several important sites (examined in more detail on page 255):
1 *The Cardo*
A thousand-foot Roman/Byzantine roadway, eight feet below the Street of the Jews, which bisects the south of the Old City from the Street of the Chain to the southern wall. Floodlit shafts reveal city walls from the First Temple period 1000–586 B.C., and vaulted Crusader shopping arcades.

2 *Nea Church*
Massive sixth-century church, the ruins of which have been discovered within the southern wall, west of the Dung Gate.
3 *Broad Wall*
Built on bedrock, thick walling of the seventh century B.C. Western boundary of the pre-exilic city, said to prove the early expansion of the city on to the Western Hill.
4 *Israelite Tower*
Probably part of the Broad Wall defences, slightly to the north.
5 *Burnt House*
Excavated area above the Western Wall Courtyard illustrating the burning of Jerusalem by the Romans in A.D. 70.
6 *Citadel excavation*
The courtyard dig is completed. A new museum and son et lumière show are now open there.

WALLS OF JERUSALEM

Now negotiable from the Damascus to the Dung Gate, in daylight!

QUARTERS OF JERUSALEM

Jewish, Muslim, Christian and Armenian, reward your exploration.

EMMAUS

'JERUSALEM' TRADITION

Luke alone limits the resurrection appearances to the neighbourhood of Jerusalem, cramming the whole resurrection story into one incredible Easter Day:

The dawn discovery of the empty tomb, reported by the women, disregarded as idle gossip by the men, except for Peter who went, wondered and was 'amazed'. The story of the road to Emmaus, the evening meal, the return to the Upper Room, to find the Twelve still up and saying Jesus had appeared to Peter. As they were speaking, Jesus was among them, giving them his 'Shalom', showing them his scars and eating before them. Finally, he commissioned and blessed them, then – leading them out to Bethany – left them to return with joy to Jerusalem.

Only in Jerusalem, only on Easter Day, the events of forty days conflated into twenty-four hours do not encourage us to assess the sites of Emmaus as within or without easy walking distance of Jerusalem!

VARYING MANUSCRIPTS

Major manuscripts, including Sinaiaticus, give the distance from Jerusalem as *sixty* stadia or furlongs. Minor manuscripts, especially Palestinian ones, give the distance as *160*. It is just possible to interpret the figure as referring to the double journey *there and back*, of sixty stadia.

VARYING TRADITIONAL SITES

Amwas

A Constantinian tradition favoured a site *160* furlongs from Jerusalem, which still retained the name Amwas in an Arab village, destroyed as recently as 1967. This Emmaus is mentioned in 1 Maccabees twice and in Josephus several times, finally as the camp of the Fifth Legion at the siege of Jerusalem, A.D. 70. It became a Roman city called Nicopolis in the third century and was identified by Jerome as the site of the events of Luke 24 as early as the year 386. The site includes today a very large fifth-century Byzantine church, within which was built a smaller Crusader church. A Byzantine baptistery is within a sixth-century church, alongside.

Abu Gosh

A Crusader tradition favoured a site, sixty furlongs from Jerusalem down on the road to Joppa, and called Abu Gosh today, after a notorious local robber-chief in the eighteenth century. This site was clearly a Roman staging-post on the road to Jerusalem. The Crusaders built what is still the most beautiful and complete of all their churches over the Roman water supply and inserted in the wall of their church a stone commemorating the stay of a detachment of the Legio Fretensis, the Tenth Legion. The Roman well and a ninth-century Arab caravan-serai, below the traditional site of Kiriath Jearim – resting place of the Ark on its return from Philistia (1 Sam. 6: 21 ff.) may well have seemed an appropriate site, sixty furlongs down the coast road.

Qubeibe

Later on, in the fifteenth century, there was probably a road-route diversion, resulting in the decline and disrepair of Abu Gosh coinciding with the rise of an alternative site, with no specific tradition, but near another twelfth-century church! So, once again, pilgrim convenience triumphed over archaeological accuracy. What was a pilgrim staging-post, sixty furlongs out on Jerusalem–Jaffa main road, has become a very charming and attractive, but quite improbable site of Emmaus!

Qalunieh

Finally, Josephus mentions another 'Emmaus' in which Titus settled a colony of 800 veterans of the Jewish War, after the sack of Jerusalem. Hence the name Colonia. Those who wish to interpret Luke's 'coming and going' from Jerusalem as literally within one evening, may wish to favour this thirty-furlongs Emmaus – less than four miles' walk from the city. And who is to say that they are wrong?

EIN KAREM OF
JOHN THE BAPTIST
SCENE OF THE VISITATION

Before the birth of Jesus, Mary his mother made a journey through the hill country of Samaria and Judaea, to visit her cousin Elizabeth, the mother of John the Baptist, in a village four kilometres west of Jerusalem. Together, they exchanged news of their coming first-born children, before Mary returned to Nazareth. When the time came, the two boys were born within three months of each other, in towns within sight of each other. Joseph and Mary had come to Bethlehem for the census; the home of the priest Zacharias and Elizabeth was below Mount Orah in Ein Karem, the 'Gracious Spring'.

It was in the time of the Crusader pilgrim Daniel, in 1106, that the birthplace of John was located, within the village, in a cave that is now shown within the Franciscan Church of St John. On the other side of the valley is the Franciscan Church of the Visitation, within the crypt of which is shown the spring which according to a medieval tradition appeared at the meeting place of Mary with Elizabeth. This is the spring which gives a name to the town today. In the wall of the crypt is a hollowed rock in which, according to another medieval legend, the child John was concealed at the time of the Massacre of the Innocents at the order of Herod. An apse of the Crusader Church of the Visitation is to be seen in the upper church today, whose walls are covered in gay mural paintings.

The Russian Convent of Elizabeth, surrounded by little whitewashed cottages, rises among the trees on the slopes of Mount Orah, above the Church of the Visitation. On the Feast of the Visitation, the Russian nuns from the Garden of Gethsemane used (until 1947) to bring ikons representing Mary, to meet their sisters of Ein Karem with ikons representing Elizabeth. At the village well, called Mary's Spring, they would touch ikons together in a kiss of greeting before carrying them in procession up the flower-strewn steps to the Convent of Elizabeth.

Church of Visitation: Luke 1: 39–56, 'Magnificat'
Church of St John: Luke 1: 57–80, 'Benedictus'
The Village fountain.

> Almighty God,
> by whose grace Elizabeth rejoiced with Mary
> and hailed her as the mother of the Lord:
> fill us with your grace
> that we may acclaim her Son as our Saviour
> and rejoice to be called his brethren;
> through Jesus Christ our Lord.

> Almighty God,
> whose servant John the Baptist
> was wonderfully born to fulfil your purpose
> by preparing the way for the advent of your Son:

lead us to repent according to his preaching
and after his example
constantly to speak the truth, boldly rebuke vice,
and patiently suffer for the truth's sake;
through Jesus Christ our Lord.

BETHLEHEM – BIRTH OF JESUS

FIRST CENTURY

In the time of Jesus, the little town of Bethlehem was reached by a track which left the main road from Jerusalem to the south, at the fifth milestone. Withdrawn from the main line of traffic, the town served as a market for the small farmers and nomads on the fringe of the Judaean Wilderness. By the end of the first century, the tradition of a cave associated with the birth of Jesus was so strong that in the year 135, Hadrian felt it merited desecration – along with the sites of the Crucifixion and Resurrection in Jerusalem. Hadrian's monumental desecrations only served to mark indelibly all three sites for Constantinian excavation some 200 years later.

IDENTIFICATION OF CAVE

At Bethlehem Hadrian had planted a grove of trees sacred to Adonis, completely surrounding the cave of the Nativity. Neither St Luke nor St Matthew mentions a cave (nor any hill of crucifixion), but by the year 155, Justin Martyn born in Nablus writes: 'Should anyone desire proof for the birth of Jesus in Bethlehem . . . let him consider that, in harmony with the gospel story of his birth, a cave is shown in Bethlehem where he was born and a manger in the cave where he lay wrapped in swaddling clothes.' Origen, in 215, confirmed the cave tradition: 'They still show the cave . . . and this is well known in the district, even among strangers to the faith.' At the end of the third century Eusebius, Bishop of Caesarea, writes: 'The inhabitants of Bethlehem bear witness of the story that has come down to them from their fathers, and they confirm the truth of it and point out the cave, in which the Virgin brought forth and laid her child.'

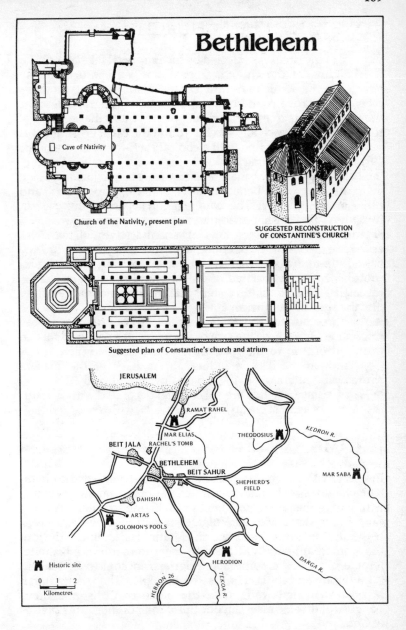

Bethlehem

Church of the Nativity, present plan

Cave of Nativity

SUGGESTED RECONSTRUCTION
OF CONSTANTINE'S CHURCH

Suggested plan of Constantine's church and atrium

JERUSALEM

RAMAT RAHEL

MAR ELIAS

BEIT JALA   RACHEL'S TOMB

THEODOSIUS

KEDRON R.

BETHLEHEM

BEIT SAHUR

MAR SABA

SHEPHERD'S
FIELD

DAHISHA

ARTAS

SOLOMON'S POOLS

HERODION

DARGA R.

Historic site

0   1   2
Kilometres

HEBRON 26

TEKOA R.

CONSTANTINIAN CHURCH

The site of the cave was selected by the Empress Helena in 325 for the building of the church. Constantine was particularly interested in the Bethlehem church as the memorial of his mother's piety. The Bordeaux and other fourth-century pilgrims describe the felling of the trees surrounding the cave and the levelling of rock to provide space for worship round the cave. Over this was built an octagonal shrine with a conical roof. In the centre of the shrine a circular opening was cut in the roof of the cave. Worshippers went up the octagonal steps to kneel at a rail looking down on to the sacred cave beneath, to see both the place of birth and place of the manger. The congregational part of the church, roughly square in shape, adjoined the octagon on the west and was divided by rows of columns into a central nave with two aisles on each side. A wide opening with three steps led from the basilica up to the octagon. The entrance down into the cave was probably from the east end of the nave and excavations in 1934 revealed a narrow flight of steps leading to a blocked doorway into the west end of the cave.

The three large doors to the basilica led out on to a square colonnaded forecourt, the size of the whole church – and this, in turn, led out on to the road. It is not difficult to picture this Constantinian basilica, standing at the back of the present church, if we imagine it carpeted with brilliantly coloured mosaics, some of which are still visible, decorated with rich furnishings, set against cream limestone walls, with a red-tiled roof.

JEROME

In the year 386, Jerome, a Dalmatian priest, travelled to Bethlehem with two ladies of a wealthy Roman family, Paula, a widow, and her daughter, Eustochia. Living in a neighbouring cave, Jerome translated the Vulgate – from the Hebrew and Greek of the Old and New Testaments into Latin. His tomb and those of the women are within a cave very near to that of the Nativity. Jerome describes innumerable pilgrims flocking to Bethlehem from Britain and India, Pontus and Ethiopia: 'The whole church in nocturnal vigils rang with the name of Christ the Lord. Tongues of diverse races but one Spirit sang in chorus the praises of God.'

JUSTINIAN

The Constantinian basilica, which had stood for 200 years, was demolished in the years 527–65 and replaced, at the plea of the Judaean Wilderness hermit, St Saba, by the Emperor Justinian. The first basilica, already liturgically too small, had been extensively damaged by the Samaritans with much looting and burning; its floors when excavated in 1934 revealed a thick layer of ashes and broken tiles.

Justinian's reconstruction to a large extent followed the lines of the first church. The nave was extended by one bay to the west and a porch added leading out into the courtyard. The octagon over the cave was replaced by the existing choir. Instead of an opening through which pilgrims could look down into the cave, two entrances were now provided, one on each side so that pilgrims could walk down into the cave. Arculf, a monk from Gaul, visited Bethlehem in 670 and describes a 'natural half cave', much the same as today, and even two separate places of 'the manger of the Lord' and the 'nativity'. The cave was lined with marble slabs and the church walls with mosaics and marbles. Outside, over the western triple doorways, was a great mosaic of the Wise Men in Persian costume.

PERSIAN INVASION

When in 614, the Persian invasion ravaged the Eastern Roman Empire and Syria, on their arrival at Bethlehem they were amazed at this mosaic of the Magi astrologers, depicted as their fellow countrymen. In respect and affection for their ancestors, they spared the church.

ISLAM AND OMAR

A few years later the Persians were expelled and soon afterwards the country was conquered by the Muslim invaders from Arabia. The first of their Caliphs, the tolerant and enlightened Omar, revered Jesus as a great prophet and, as a pious Muslim, believed in the Virgin Birth. He insisted on sparing both the Holy Sepulchre in Jerusalem and the Church of the Nativity. On arrival in

Bethlehem, he said his prayers in the south apse (not far from the Norman font today) which conveniently faced Mecca. Omar's agreement with the Patriarch Sophronius inhibited the Muslim call to prayer in Bethlehem, but allowed Muslims to pray singly in the south aisle. Although, after Omar, this agreement was spasmodically broken, yet in 951 a Muslim writer refers to the great reverence in which the church was held for its associations with both David and Jesus. Even the fanatical Caliph Hakim, who destroyed the tomb of Christ at Jerusalem, spared the basilica at Bethlehem.

CRUSADES

The early good relations between Christians and their Muslim rulers faded fast with the arrival of the Crusades! When in 1099 the Crusaders were approaching, the Christians in Bethlehem were in some danger, but Godfrey de Bouillon sent 150 knights under Tancred to defend them. A community of Augustinian monks was established there and lived in happy relations with the Greek clergy. In 1101 Baldwin I was crowned in the basilica at Bethlehem, as King of Jerusalem, refusing to be crowned with gold in the city where Christ was crowned with thorns.

MOSAICS

His successor, Baldwin II, was also crowned there in 1109. The church was completely restored in the reigns which followed. A seventeenth-century Franciscan, Custos of the Holy Land, described the Crusader mosaics. A vast Tree of Jesse covered the west wall. Out of the side of the sleeping Jesse came three stems, each leading through the prophets to Mary the Mother and Jesus. All has perished. On the south wall, seven half-life-size figures from the descent of Jesus from Abraham remain – also five of the seven motifs of the General Councils of the Church. The most beautiful surviving mosaic is perhaps the 'Doubting Thomas' in the north transept. Among the Crusader paintings is one of King Canute, on the fourth pillar on the right-hand side.

DISREPAIR

Saladin recaptured Bethlehem towards the end of the twelfth century and gave permission for the re-establishment of the Latin rite, but Beibars expelled all Christians from Bethlehem. The church survived, however, and a French pilgrim in 1325 described a pilgrimage of 5000. The Saracens permitted worship, but discouraged restoration; by the time of the occupation by Turks in 1516, the church was in poor repair. Following the Reformation, the rivalry between Christian denominations, and the Ottoman policy of status quo maintained by bribery, caused little to be done to repair the ravages of fire in 1809 and earthquake in 1834.

RESTORATION

Following the Crimean War, through the negotiation of Napoleon III of France, the Roman Catholic Church of St Catherine was reconstructed in 1888 from the older buildings of the Augustinians and Franciscans. From the end of the Ottoman Empire, British Mandate, Jordanian and Israeli regimes have been much more effective in preserving the oldest standing basilica in Christendom for contemporary pilgrims. The early Christian patriarch Sophronius wrote: 'There, upon the famous floor whereon the Christ God was placed, I would press my eyes, my mouth and my forehead, that I might bear away from thence a blessing.' And the Christian pilgrim still does today.

SHEPHERDS' FIELDS

In the year 384, the Spanish nun Egeria described her visit to the Church 'Of the Shepherds . . . a splendid cave with an altar'. The Orthodox Shepherds' fields just below the Village of the Watching, Beit Sahur, enclose a cave which from the fifth century formed the crypt of a church, whose pillar bases are still clearly visible. This served the local Orthodox community until 1955, and a new church now stands nearby. The cave was once near the centre of a basin of fields, which was the 'night-flocking-area' of the district, hence the 'Village of Watching'.

Here in these fields the shepherds pooled their flocks by night, discussing and allotting the morrow's pastures round their camp fires and taking their guard duties in turn. Others lay down to sleep in the neighbouring cave. In the morning each shepherd would call his own flock from a different point of the compass, on the higher ground surrounding the flocking place. Each shepherd has his own peculiar call – often a mixture between a gruff grunt and a whistle! And soon the flocks of sheep would be moving out in single file, like the spokes of a wheel to their own shepherds, the old ram leading. The Good Shepherd said: 'My sheep hear my voice. I know my sheep and am known of mine. A stranger they will not follow, for they know not the voice – or call – of strangers' and 'when he has put forth his own sheep he goes before them and the sheep follow him'.

1. Introductory prophecy: Mic. 5: 2–3.
2. Cave-stables or gleaning women, en route. Ruth 2: 19 ff, 3: 1–3, 4: 13–17.
3. Sheep by the way: 1 Sam. 16: 1–13, 17: 12–20.
4. Rachel's tomb: Gen. 35: 19–20.
5. Shepherds' Fields: John 10: 1–5, 7–15, Ps. 23.
6. Shepherds' Fields, Shepherds' cave: Luke 2: 8–16.

A Franciscan chapel, built by the road on the north of the Shepherds' Fields in 1954, may be on the site of an early Byzantine monastery, but does not accord with Egeria's description.

> GLORIA IN EXCELSIS DEO
> Eternal God,
> who made this most holy night
> to shine with the brightness of your one true light
> bring us, who have known the revelation
>   of that light on earth,
> to see the radiance of your heavenly glory;
> through Jesus Christ our Lord.

HEROD'S PALACE TOMB – HERODION

Two miles south-east of Bethlehem is a conical hill reminiscent of a volcano. Here in about 20 B.C., Herod the Great had built into the top of the hill a fortified palace, protected by one circular and three half-towers, approached across a causeway and draw-bridge. This was one of several of Herod's summer palaces. It may well have been intended as his mausoleum and Josephus describes his death at Jericho, the torch-light funeral procession and burial here. If he was buried here, it would most probably have been in the one circular tower, but excavations in 1962 revealed nothing. The towers, however, had been destroyed by the Romans in A.D. 70 and the fortress was occupied by the rebel forces of Bar Cochbar in 132.

The marble staircase has long since disappeared, though fragments remain. The visitor arrives at the top on the north-east perimeter, circles the northern half tower and descends a stairway on the west side. There is a Roman bath on his left and – across a courtyard – the dining hall on his right with the living quarters built into the northern perimeter wall. Ahead is an apsed peristyle, around a rectangular colonnaded courtyard, under the circular tower. It was essentially the palatial keep of a whole complex of buildings at the foot of the hill, including a hippodrome, a large rectangular building, a pool and system of cisterns fed by aqueduct from Solomons' Pools.

Piles of Roman catapult-missiles, in the central courtyard, reveal the vulnerability of even this seemingly impregnable fortress!

7. Matt. 2: 1–11.

> Heavenly Father,
> whose children suffered at the hands of Herod,
> though they had done no wrong:
> give us grace neither to act cruelly
> nor to stand indifferently by,
> but to defend the weak from the tyranny of the strong;
> in the name of Jesus Christ who suffered for us,
> but is alive and reigns with you and the Holy Spirit,
> one God, now and for ever.

BETHLEHEM CHURCH

The Church of the Nativity at Bethlehem, like that of the Holy Sepulchre at Jerusalem, can shock the unprepared pilgrim. It is wise to form a mental picture from scripture and scenery on the way to Bethlehem and to carry this with you to the cave-stable.

Therefore, do not arrive in Bethlehem by the main road and go straight to the church and down into the grotto. Rather, visit the Shepherds' Fields and Herodion, looking out for cave-dwellings between the limestone strata of the hillsides – caves for refugees, cattle, donkeys and even camels. If you have managed to visit the oldest inn (ninth-century) still in use at Jerusalem, with its donkey stables below the 'guest-chambers', its courtyard, cistern and drinking trough – the Sultan's Inn in Chain Street – you can take this illustration with you. There are cave-stables for cattle on the Ras-Al Amoud road to Bethlehem, complete with mangers, stores, drains and smells that all help to form the impression when you reach the 'actual' cave stable. Did St Francis of Assisi bring back from here the idea of the Christmas Crib? He certainly worshipped in the church which had already been standing 600 years.

The Oriental Churches have survived Muslim occupation and preserved Christian sites partly by concealment and decoration with marbles and tapestries. Their idea of beauty is often in quantity as much as quality; and a single shrine may be lit by a selection of lamps each 'representative' of each of the different Churches who share that shrine.

Forewarned is forearmed. You will be able by imagination to strip off successive layers of occupation, in reverse order: Franciscan, Saracen, Crusader, Byzantine and Constantinian, and to penetrate the protective layers of marble, mosaic and tapestry hangings – to find the limestone walls and ceiling of the original cave. As you step from the road on to the courtyard, remember you are now inside the limits of the colonnaded atrium of the Constantinian church. Look at the triple doorways, with their moulded lintels, of the Justinian church. Bend low through the little wicket gate, built to keep camels out in Turkish times, and notice the Crusader archway above.

You will then pass through the Justinian porch, through the huge central wooden door into the back of the church. Stay at the west end to absorb the atmosphere, layout and mosaics of the first church. Picture the steps up to the octagon shrine, the circular rail at which pilgrims could kneel looking down into the cave below. Walk up to the present choir, descend the step down into the cave from the right side, then kneel at the very back facing the shrine. When your eyes are accustomed to the darkness, come and kneel at the manger 'in spirit' with the babe wrapped in swaddling clothes so tightly, like a Bedouin child on his mother's back, that he could bounce without harm. Reflect on the depth of limitation and self-emptying which that babyhood cost God Almighty! Look through the grille and the candles at the painting of the cave-stable, shepherds kneeling, many pointing and the 'babe, lying in a manger' at floor level. The traditional veneration is to 'press eyes, lips and forehead and to carry away from thence a blessing'. Finally as you stand up, touch the limestone ceiling of his manger and make an act of love for 'Word made flesh' in the babe of Bethlehem. Turn and reverence the place of the birth marked by the Silver Star, and make your way out up the left-hand stairway.

8. Courtyard: 2 Sam. 23: 17–27.
9. Doorway: Turkish, Crusader, Justinian, Persian Magi motif above.
10. Through porch into nave, up into choir.
11. Within Cave: Luke 2: 1–7.
12. Jerome Cave.
13. Cave of the innocents: Matt. 2: 1–18.

> Almighty God,
> who wonderfully created us in your own image
> and yet more wonderfully restored us
> through your Son Jesus Christ:
> grant that, as he came to share in our humanity,
> so we may share the life of his divinity;
> who is alive and reigns with you and the Holy Spirit
> one God, now and for ever.

HEBRON AND MAMRE
FIRST PATRIARCHAL
SETTLEMENT

PATRIARCHAL BURIAL PLACE

It was at Hebron that God made with Abraham a covenant that he would be the father of a chosen people. According to tradition, Abraham lived at the Oak of Mamre, about a mile from the town centre, at a site now in the possession of the Russian Orthodox Church. It was at Beersheba that Abraham made a treaty with Abimelech, purchasing the right to dig a well, the traditional site of which is still pointed out.

On the death of Sarah his wife, Abraham purchased the Cave of Machpelah from Ephron the Hittite as a burial place, which became the patriarchal vault. This cave has for centuries been preserved beneath a vast shrine, the Haram El-Khalil, in Arabic the Shrine of the Friend of God. Surrounded by an enormous Herodian wall enclosing a mosque of Byzantine, Crusader and more recent masonry, this cave is the focus of both Jewish and Muslim devotion. The impressive catafalques of Abraham and Sarah, Isaac and Rebecca, Jacob and Leah, remind us of their burials below.

Herodian Enclosure
At the same time as Herod the Great enclosed the Temple area at Jerusalem and built the Third Temple, so he enclosed a sacred area over the Cave of Machpelah. In the year 1115 a Crusader church was built on the site, within the Herodian enclosure.

Crusader Excavation
During Crusader times, the Augustinian Canons explored the cave below and built a stairway down into a narrow corridor which led into a circular chamber, opening into a large rock-hewn cave. It is this cave which lies below the present opening to be seen in the church. The Crusaders noted a similarity between the subterranean corridor and the Herodian perimeter wall, and reported finding a quantity of bones within the cave.

Temple Masonry Pattern
Whatever other shrines, Jewish, Christian or Muslim, may have briefly adorned this sanctuary, the present Haram el-Khalil, Shrine of the Friend, is a conversion of the Crusader church into a large Muslim mosque. The outer enclosure is of fine Herodian masonry. From these walls with their alternation of pilaster and recess, one gains a good notion of how the outer walls of the Third Temple must have appeared, with their enormous blocks of stone and the delicate inward sloping of their corner stones. The upper courses of the wall are of Arab construction.

Mosque Today
The cenotaphs of Abraham and Sarah occupy two octagonal chapels to the north and south. Those of Isaac and Rebecca are within the mosque itself, those of Jacob and Leah in chambers to the north. In a separate enclosure is a cenotaph of Joseph. In a

corner beside the cenotaph of Abraham is a small window. Inside it is a stone with a depression in it which is said to be the footstep of Adam. All the catafalques are covered with richly embroidered palls. The pulpit is of splendid Muslim carving, having been presented by Saladin. Yet to the Jews Hebron, apart from its connection with Abraham, was also the capital of David before his capture of Jerusalem. After their capture of Hebron in the recent fighting, the Israelis have turned the greater part of it into a museum. Only a small part of it near the entrance is still carpeted, reserved for the Muslims, labelled 'Holy Place'. The Muslims are admitted there for prayers four times a day and on their holy day, Friday, when Jews are not allowed in.

The ancient town is famous for its *suqs*, potteries and glass blowers, all within easy reach of the mosque.

HISTORY AND REFERENCES

1 Abraham at Mamre, marked by another Herodian enclosure and well, two miles north of Hebron and east of the main road, 'entertained angels unaware'. Here Abraham pitched his tent and built an altar on his arrival in the land of Canaan – Gen. 13:18.

Here God gave him the covenant of circumcision – Gen. 17: 10.

Here the three angels were entertained, on their journey to destroy Sodom and Gomorrah, and rewarded Abraham and Sarah with the promise of a son – Gen. 18:10.

2 Abraham bought the Cave of Machpelah from Ephron the Hittite, for the burial of Sarah his wife – Gen. 23.

3 Hebron, the ancient stronghold of the Anakim, Giants of Canaan – Num. 13: 22.

4 Captured by the Calebites, during the invasion of Canaan – Josh. 14: 12, 15: 14.

5 A City of Refuge – Josh. 20: 7.

6 David's temporary capital for seven years – 2 Sam. 5: 5.

7 The rebellious Absalom's headquarters – 2 Sam. 15: 7.

8 Fortified by Rehoboam – 2 Chr. 11: 10.

9 Colonised after the return from exile – Neh. 11: 25.

10 Captured by Judas Maccabaeus – 1 Macc. 5: 65.

RIFT VALLEY – FROM JERUSALEM ANCIENT & HERODIAN JERICHO – QUMRAN – MASADA – EIN GEDI

NOMAD TO CITIZEN

Nowhere else in the Holy Land is the primitive settlement of mankind better illustrated than at Jericho, the earliest known fortified and organised township (at least 8000 B.C.) and the lowest on earth (838 feet below sea level).

Long before then, the nomadic hunters must have enjoyed the strong spring, yielding still today a thousand gallons every minute, creating a magnificent oasis for the present 'City of palm trees'. As with the process of evolution, there must have been a 'first', a hunter or a nomad who chose to settle and produce, rather than to gather, food – as the Bedouin of today plant and reap in circuit. It is not difficult to picture the process and expansion that followed from the occupation of a single cave beside the spring, to a tent circle protected by a thorn hedge, to the clearly visible walled and towered city of 8000 B.C. accommodating thousands of citizens.

EXCAVATION

Excavated for several successive years in the fifties, by the British and American Schools of Archaeology, under Dame Kathleen Kenyon, the site has not been as well preserved as more recent Israeli excavations. It is well worth while finding the basic items of interest, while traces still remain, visiting trenches in a circuit clockwise.

In the western trench, is a sequence of perimeter defences expanding outwards, beginning with a neolithic tower set in a stone wall. The tower can still easily be climbed by an internal staircase.

The defences include a glacis, a polished white plaster slide at an angle of about 40°, enough to turn over a wheeled chariot let alone the horses. This was the most effective defence against the Hyksos warriors from 1800 B.C. From this point the walls include brick, which was introduced by the Hyksos themselves.

One of the most remarkable finds in this trench was of seven or more skulls, shell-eyed and mud-sculptured to the features of their owners. These were not standard, but individual representations of city sages or respected ancestors.

In a nearby, north-westerly shaft, the various levels of occupation were analysed into twenty-three successive cities.

In the northern trench, the glacis defence is very clear. By the arrival of the Hyksos, successive occupations and destructions had raised the city level to nearly fifty feet above the present road level. One can therefore imagine the formidable sight presented by a glacis of that height from road level: a sheet of white glistening in the sun, whose polished slide gave no grip to hoof or wheel, hand or foot.

In the northern refugee camp, among the bare patches in the centre were discovered the Hyksos tombs, equipped with inlaid wooden beds and tables, while bowls of meat and cereal, together with their personal weapons, were to meet the needs of the warriors on their journey into the next world. A reconstruction of such tombs is to be found in the Rockefeller Museum, Jerusalem, and illustrates the aristocratic physiognomy of the Hyksos.

The north-eastern shaft was the 'temple area' of the city, reminiscent of the Canaanite altar and temple area at Megiddo.

The eastern shaft overlooking the oasis is the only one to include any Joshua-period evidence upon the whole tell. Only a 'postage-stamp in an acre' is late enough to include the thirteenth century B.C.! Except perhaps that depressing verse, 1 Kings 16: 34, the rebuilding of Jericho in the time of Ahab.

Nevertheless, the story of Rahab and the spies is magic in this setting, looking down towards the camp fires at Gilgal in the Ghor! – Josh. 2: 1–16 and 26.

HERODIAN JERICHO

In addition to Tel Es-Sultan, Ancient Jericho, there are three other Tels at Jericho. All these three are linked with Herod the Great, two on either side of the outflow of the Wadi Qelt and one half a kilometre south of Tel Es-Sultan. The first two were specifically to protect Herod's Winter Palace and Water Garden, on either side of them. The third, Tel Es-Samrat, was a hippodrome/theatre built by Herod.

The Winter Palace, built in the diamond pattern red brick which Herod brought back from Rome, stood on the north side of and facing across the Wadi towards the Water Garden, built on the south side in the same brick pattern. The garden was typically Italianate with rows of statues in niches from which water spouted, rather as one gigantic nymphaeum.

The Winter Palace and Water Garden may be reached, by turning west off the main road at the old police station, before the crossing of the Qelt. They can also be reached down the Wadi Qelt road, with its superb views of the Qelt Ravine, St George's monastery and many hermit caves, or *'skiti'*.

Almighty God,
whose Son Jesus Christ fasted forty days in the wilderness,
and was tempted as we are, yet without sin:
give us grace to discipline ourselves
    in obedience to your Spirit;
and, as you know our weakness,
so may we know your power to save;
through Jesus Christ our Lord.

Lord God Almighty,
grant your people grace
to withstand the temptations
    of the world, the flesh, and the devil,
and with pure hearts and minds
to follow you, the only God;
through Jesus Christ our Lord.

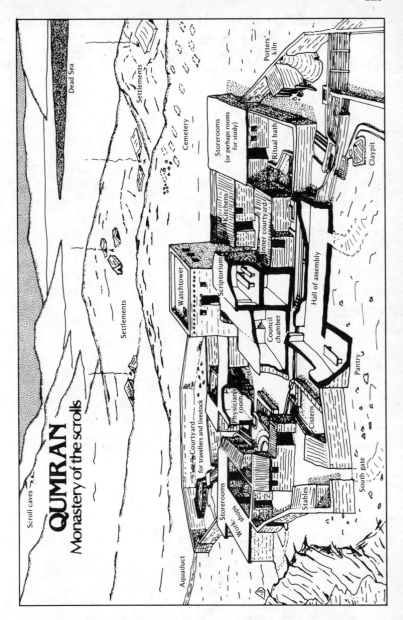

QUMRAN
Monastery of the scrolls

Scroll caves

Dead Sea

Settlements

Cemetery

Settlements

Settlements

Aquaduct

Watchtower

Scriptorium

Courtyard
for travellers and livestock

Physician's
room

Work
shops

Storerooms

Council
chamber

Kitchens

Inner courtyard

Storerooms
(or perhaps rooms
for study)

Ritual bath

Potters'
kiln

Claypit

Hall of assembly

Cistern

Pantry

Stables

South gate

QUMRAN – MONASTERY OF THE DEAD SEA SCROLLS

APPROACH TO SITE

Travelling south from Jericho to the Dead Sea, the limestone cliffs which form the western edge of the Rift Valley stretch away into the distance. A kilometre or so down the Dead Sea coast, the traveller can discern through the heat haze a low white marly plateau at the foot of the cliffs. As the road approaches nearer the cliffs, the cleft of the Wadi Qumran is now clearly visible, its deep ravine running white down the cliff face. This water supply is the key to the occupation of the plateau below it, which is just high enough above the floor of the valley to give a commanding view for miles to north and south.

OBSERVATION POINT

From the watch tower of the monastic settlement on that plateau, in the year 63 B.C., the watchman saw a shining snake creeping down the valley several miles to the north. As it moved inexorably closer, he realised it was the advance guard of a Roman legion. The Roman commander, Pompey, had decided that so tactical an observation point must be in Roman hands. From the moment the watchman sounded the alarm, the scriptorium was emptied and all the current scrolls deposited in a concealed cave (now known as number four) within a hundred metres of the settlement. When this 'waste paper basket' cave was discovered, the very mixed contents presented a puzzle, until its purpose was realised.

DISCOVERY OF SCROLLS

In the summer of 1947 a little Arab shepherd boy, Muhammad, the Wolf, was grazing his goats below the cliffs. His semi-nomadic Ta'amireh tribe ranged south-east of Bethlehem. Casually, throwing a stone into a cave on the cliff face, he heard it

QUMRAN

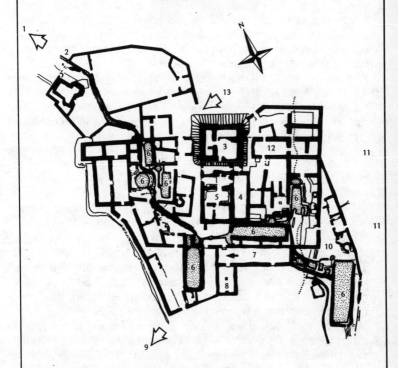

ORDER OF VIEWING QUMRAN

1 Aqueduct from cliff-cleft wadi.
2 Aqueduct enters settlement and runs through to SE corner.
3 Watchtower and storerooms.
4 Scriptorium, once in 2 storeys with desks and inkwells.
5 Council room, with running water and hand basin.
6 Numerous cisterns within water system, some damaged by earthquake 31BC, some with steps down for ritual bath.
7 Assembly hall and refectory, oriented to face Jerusalem.
   The community sat as follows:
   The Teacher of Righteousness on a raised plinth within doorway.
   His Council of three (equivalent: Peter, James and John) under west wall.
   His Twelve Elders (equivalent to the 12 Apostles) east of plinth in 3 rows.
   His 'Many' followers (equivalent to the 70 disciples) in rows behind the 12.
   Novices at the back of the hall.
   Here the community met for worship, twice a day, for teaching and meals.

8 Pantry for refectory, where much pottery was found in pieces.
9 Cave Four, the waste-paper basket, for security, a nearby hidden cache.
10 Pottery, workshops, wheels and round kiln.
11 Cemetery, in which both male and female were found, indicating that although the community was celibate, it had 'camp followers'.
   No accommodation was within the settlement perimeter, but in tents and caves.
   A freshwater farm at Ein Feshka supplied the settlement.
12 A communal kitchen.
13 Main entrance to settlement.

land in a pile of crockery. Intrigued, he climbed up through the opening into a long cave lined with tall jars with bowl-like lids. Some time later, he and a friend dug their hands into the jars and brought out tattered parchment and linen cloths, without any clue as to the value of these musty bundles. In the years that followed, some thirty caves proved a remunerative and happy hunting ground for Muhammad's Bedouins!

A fragmentary scroll manuscript of the Rule of the Community at Qumran, thought to have been an Essene monastery, reads: 'God considered their works, how they sought him with a perfect heart, and he raised up for them a Teacher of Righteousness to direct them in the way of his heart.'

ESSENES

The Essenes were a schismatic movement of Jewish priests, who broke off from the Temple and theocratic rule of the Maccabean high priesthood in about the year 150 B.C., for the following reasons:

1 They considered that the Maccabees were not entitled to be high priests – not being of the correct tribe of Levi – but as conquerors in war had claimed the high priesthood. If, therefore, the priesthood was invalid, so were its sacrifices.

2 During the Greek domination, there had been many cultic innovations and the calendar had been remodelled to the more exact lunar (cf. solar) calendar. The conservative Essenes considered the new calendar invalid and consequently the sacrifices. There was feasting on fast days and fasting on feast days, and God was displeased.

3 The Essenes were highly apocalyptic, and, following the Book of Daniel, expected the end of the world. Remembering the experience of Moses in the wilderness as necessary to purification, they retired to Qumran to prepare for the final battle between good and evil.

So, led to Qumran by a teacher of Righteousness, a community of guaranteed purity, of priesthood and calendar, they set up a framework of monasticism as early as 150 B.C.

Teacher of Righteousness

This Teacher of Righteousness, in spite of cruel persecution by the high priest(s) of his day, continued to teach his disciples how they could play their part in God's plan of salvation. He gathered round him a 'Council of Twelve' from whom he chose an inner circle of three or so closer companions. The wider community attracted by his teaching and leadership were called the Many, who gathered morning and evening for prayer in their Assembly Hall facing Jerusalem. Each Sabbath they shared a ritual meal of bread and wine. On festivals, they held a 'love banquet' in preparation for the Last Day, when the Messiah would come to conquer the world and invite the faithful to his triumphal feast.

Pattern Repeated

The familiar pattern of the teacher and his school of disciples was to reappear a century later, heralded by a desert prophet whose name 'the Baptiser' reflected the initiation rituals of the water channel at Qumran. For Jesus of Nazareth, as for the teacher at Qumran, the group of twelve personal disciples and founder-members was essential to his purpose.

MASADA ROCK FORTRESS SCENE OF HEROIC ZEALOT RESISTANCE

TACTICAL POSITION

Masada has been aptly described by several (including Murphy O'Connor) as 'curiously like an aircraft carrier moored to the western cliffs of the Dead Sea'. Its history is matched by its setting. It is well worth seeing an aerial photograph of Masada, before viewing it from either the Dead Sea or western approach. Most visitors will reach it from the Dead Sea side, by cable-car or climbing the Snake Path. It stands a good 1,000 feet above the floor of the Rift Valley, rising almost sheer – to a flat diamond-shaped top, oriented north to south. The 'prow of the ship' facing north consists of a three-terraced royal palace-villa, descending in three levels down the cliff face. Also in the 'bows of the ship' are the vast area of storerooms, administrative buildings and a magnificently complete bath house.

GATES

There are four known gates in the perimeter wall: a North Water-gate just port-side, or west, of the administration complex, an East Gate at the top of the Snake Path, a South Water-gate through a fortified section of the casement wall, and the West Gate – below Herod's Western Palace.

FORTIFICATION

The perimeter fortification consisted of a thick casement wall, four-fifths of a mile long, of packed earth sandwiched between stone walling, with thirty-eight towers each ten metres in height. These are best seen at the Southern Citadel, at the stern of the ship, and at the South Water-gate. The defenders – in addition to short-range personal arms, such as bows, arrows and javelins – would have rolled sizable stones and had some medium-range catapults.

ACCOMMODATION

It is probable that Herod and his family would have occupied the northern palace-villa, that visiting VIPs would be accommodated in the Western Palace (in which there was a throne room and reception patio), that the fortress officers and staff would have lived in the variety of apartment buildings scattered over the central area. Under siege, the defenders built living quarters along the casement walls.

FOOD AND WATER

Water was conserved in huge cisterns and countless smaller ones over the total area of thirty acres. Given some former (autumn) and latter (spring) rains, together with donkey transport from springs and wadis up through the water-gates, the fortress water supply was sufficient, except in drought. Foraging raids on Ein Gedi and other oases' date and grain stores would replenish the vast storage accommodation. Some cereals were grown actually on the top of the fortress. Even after several years' siege, when the fortress finally fell in April A.D. 73, there was no shortage of food or water.

THE SIEGE

Herod's Hide-out
Josephus is the sole historical source but it is unlikely that he was present at Masada, as he undoubtedly was at the siege of Jerusalem, which he describes with all the vivid detail of an eye witness. Masada was first fortified by Alexander Jannaeus, 103–76 B.C., but it was Herod who transformed the rock into a palace-stronghold cum desert foxhole, between the years 37 and 31 B.C. He did so partly from fear of Cleopatra, partly from fear of Jewish revolt, and actually evacuated his family there when threatened by the Hasmonean Antigonus in 40 B.C. and again in 31 B.C. In the years which followed, Masada was controlled by the procurators and occupied by a Roman garrison.

Zealot Occupation
In A.D. 66 a group of Zealots killed the Roman detachment and occupied the stronghold, where they adapted the sophisticated Herodian palaces to their more primitive needs. On the fall of Jerusalem in A.D. 70 they were joined by a few survivors, bent on continuing their struggle for freedom. From Masada, they harried the Roman troop movements and surrounding townships for two years, before Flavius Silva the Roman governor decided to eliminate this last outpost of Zealot resistance, towards the end of the year 72.

Roman Encirclement
Silva marched down the spine of Judaea with the 10th Legion and the type of siege machines developed by Vespasian and Titus at Jerusalem, together with several thousand Jewish prisoners of war carrying provisions, timbers and water. He approached from the west and arrived underneath the fortress walls, where their height above the surrounding ground was at its lowest – only 500

feet – half that of their height from the Dead Sea valley. Silva set up his own command camp on a slope facing the fortress on the north-west, establishing his own headquarters in the farthest corner from the Rock. From here he was within shouting range of the top!

Both the Zealots up on the Rock, under Eleazar Ben Yair, and the Romans below prepared for a long siege. Silva established eight fortified camps round the base of the Rock, linked by a ditch and wall formed from the excavated vallum, to prevent any possibility of escape or reinforcement.

Ramp and Siege Tower

Josephus described a small 'white' mound, under the West Gate; the mound still has traces of white quartz today. Silva decided to build a ramp of stones and packed earth from the white mound up to the West Gate, some 500 feet above. At immense cost in life and effort to his massive force of Jewish prisoners of war, the ramp was raised, packed hard and tight and broad enough to take a stone road for its last 100 feet. On this 'track' he ran up an iron-plated siege tower, the top of which was lined with rapid-firing catapults, which – when the tower appeared over the casement wall – were able to force the defenders to remain under cover. At a longer range, the roman ballistae cast half-hundredweight stones a quarter of a mile. These were visible in the air, until painted black, and killed not only those they hit, but all behind them for some distance.

Battering Ram

Silva had a huge battering ram ready made separately and specifically to operate through the structure of the siege tower against the fortress wall. On a day in the spring of A.D. 73, after constant battering, a breach was made in the casement wall which was rapidly replaced by the Zealots with a timber wall. The Romans on the tower threw torches to burn the new wall, but the wind blew back the fire and ignited the siege tower. Not long afterwards, the wind changed – as it usually does in the evening – to a west wind, quickly transferring the flames from the Roman tower to the Zealot timber wall. When night fell, the defensive wall was again breached and the Zealot position hopeless. The 960 men, women and children were faced with surrender or suicide.

THE END OF MASADA FROM JOSEPHUS

Eleazar's Plan

'Since we, long ago, my generous friends, resolved never to be servants to the Romans, nor to any other than to God himself, who alone is the true and just Lord of mankind, the time is now come that obliges us to make that resolution true in practice. And let us not at this time bring a reproach upon ourselves for self-contradiction, while we formerly would not undergo slavery, though it were then without danger, but must now, together with slavery, choose such punishments also as are intolerable; I mean this, upon the supposition that the Romans once reduce us under their power while we are alive. We were the very first that revolted from them, and we are the last that fight against them; and I cannot but esteem it as a favour that God hath granted us, that it is still in our power to die bravely, and in a state of freedom, which hath not been the case with others who were conquered unexpectedly. It is very plain that we shall be taken within a day's time; but it is still an eligible thing to die after a glorious manner, together with our dearest friends. This is what our enemies themselves cannot by any means hinder, although they be very desirous to take us alive. Nor can we propose to ourselves any more to fight them and beat them. It had been proper indeed for us to have conjectured at the purpose of God much sooner, and at the very first, when we were so desirous of defending our liberty, and when we received such sore treatment from one another, and worse treatment from our enemies, and to have been sensible that the same God, who had of old taken the Jewish nation into his favour, had now condemned them to destruction; for had he either continued favourable, or been but in a lesser degree displeased with us, he had not overlooked the destruction of so many men, or delivered his most holy city to be burnt and demolished by our enemies. To be sure, we weakly hoped to have preserved ourselves, and ourselves alone, still in a state of freedom, as we had been guilty of no sins ourselves against God, nor been partners with those of others; we also taught other men to preserve their liberty. Wherefore, consider how God hath convinced us that our hopes were in vain, by bringing such distress upon us in the desperate state we are now in, and which is beyond all our expectations; for the nature of this fortress, which was in itself unconquerable, hath not proved a means of our deliverance; and even while we have still great abundance of food, and a great quantity of arms and other necessaries more than we want, we are openly deprived by God himself of all hope of deliverance; for that fire which was driven upon our enemies did not, of its own accord, turn back upon the wall which we had built: this was the effect of God's anger against us for our manifold sins, which we have been guilty of in a most insolent and extravagant manner with regard to our own countrymen; the punishments of which let us not receive from the Romans, but from God himself as executed by our own hands, for these will be more moderate than the other. Let our wives die before they are abused, and our children before they have tasted of slavery; and after we have slain them, let us bestow that glorious benefit upon one another mutually, and preserve ourselves in freedom, as an excellent funeral monument for us. But first let us destroy our money and the fortress by fire; for I am well assured that this will be a great grief to the Romans, that they shall not be able to seize upon our bodies, and shall fail of our wealth also: and let us spare nothing but our provisions; for they will be a testimonial when we are dead that we were not subdued for want of necessaries but that, according to our original resolution, we have preferred death before slavery.'

The Final Destruction

'Now as Eleazar was proceeding on in this exhortation, they all cut him off short, and made haste to do the work, as full of an unconquerable ardour of mind, and moved with a demoniacal fury. So they went their ways, as one still endeavouring to be before another, and as thinking that this eagerness would be a demonstration of their courage and good conduct, if they could avoid appearing in the last class: so great was the zeal they were in to slay their wives and children, and themselves also! Nor indeed, when they came to the work itself, did their courage fail them as one might imagine it would have done; but they then held fast the same resolution, without wavering, which they had upon the hearing of Eleazar's speech, while yet every one of them still retained the natural passion of love to themselves and their families, because the reasoning they went upon, appeared to them to be very just, even with regard to those that were dearest to them; for the husbands tenderly embraced their wives and took their children into their arms, and gave the longest parting kisses to them, with tears in their eyes. Yet at the same time did they complete what they had resolved on, as if they had been executed by the hands of strangers, and they had nothing else for their comfort but the necessity they were in of doing this execution, to avoid that prospect they had of the miseries they were to suffer from their enemies. Nor was there at length any one of these men found that scrupled to act their part in this terrible execution, but every one of them despatched his dearest relations. Miserable men indeed were they! whose distress forced them to slay their own wives and children with their own hands, as the lightest of those evils that were before them. So they not being able to bear the grief they were under for what they had done, any longer, and esteeming it an injury to those they had slain, to live even the shortest space of time after them – they presently laid all they had in a heap, and set fire to it. They then chose ten men by lot out of them, to slay all the rest; every one of whom laid himself down by his wife and children on the ground, and threw his arms about them, and they offered their necks to the stroke of those who by lot executed that melancholy office, and when these ten had, without fear, slain them all, they made the same rule for casting lots for themselves, that he whose lot it was should first kill the other nine, and after all, should kill himself. Accordingly, all those had courage sufficient to be no way behind one another, in doing or suffering; so, for a conclusion, the nine offered their necks to the executioner, and he who was the last of all, took a view of all the other bodies, lest perchance some or other among so many that were slain should want his assistance to be quite despatched; and when he perceived that they were all slain, he set fire to the palace, and with the great force of his hand ran his sword entirely through himself, and fell down dead near to his own relations. So these people died with this intention, that they would not have so much as one soul among them all alive to be subject to the Romans. Yet was there an ancient woman, and another who was of kin to Eleazar, and superior to most women in prudence and learning, with five children, who had concealed themselves in caverns underground, and had carried water thither for their drink, and were hidden there when the rest were intent upon the slaughter of one another. These others were 960 in number, the women and children being withal included in that computation. This calamitous slaughter was made on the fifteenth day of the month (Xanthicus) Nisan.'

SUGGESTED ORDER OF VISIT TO MASADA

1. Snake Path Gate.
2. Zealot quarters, south wall.
3. Mikve and Southern Water-gate.
4. Underground cistern.
5. Southern Citadel.
6. 'Columbarium', dovecote or funerary urns.
7. Palace swimming pool.
8. Western Palace:
   - Entrance, guardroom.
   - Muralled patio and throne room.
   - VIP apartments including:
     - Zealot fireplace on Roman pavement.
     - Bath and toilet rooms.
     - Staircase down to servants' quarters.
9. Western Gate and Ramp.
10. Byzantine church.
11. Synagogue – perhaps the oldest in Israel.
12. Roof of Bath-house to view storerooms.
13. Bath-house.
14. Parade ground.
15. Palace-villa including:
   - lower terrace, with murals.
   - middle terrace, with circular pavilion.
   - upper terrace, with semi-circular porch.
16. North Water-gate.

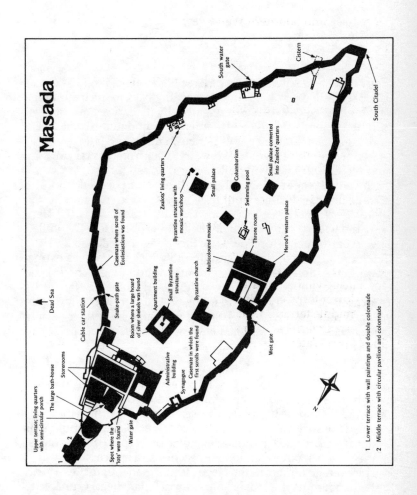

Masada

Dead Sea

Upper terrace; living quarters with semi-circular porch

The large bath-house

Storerooms

Spot where the 'lots' were found

Water gate

Cable car station

Snake-path gate

Casemate where scroll of Ecclesiasticus was found

Room where a large hoard of silver shekels was found

Apartment building

Small Byzantine structure

Administrative building

Synagogue

Casemate in which the first scrolls were found

Byzantine church

Multicoloured mosaic

West gate

Zealots' living quarters

Byzantine structure with mosaic workshop

Small palace

Columbarium

Swimming pool

Throne room

Herod's western palace

Small palace converted into Zealots' quarters

South water gate

Cistern

South Citadel

N

1 Lower terrace with wall paintings and double colonnade
2 Middle terrace with circular pavilion and colonnade

CITIES OF THE NEGEV
BEERSHEBA, AVDAT,
MAMSHIT & SHIVTA

THE NEGEV

'Four thousand square miles of Israel's south – a limitless sea of sand, stone and scrub, grandeur reaching back to the beginnings of time. A golden ocean navigated by Bedouin and camels, islanded by emerald green settlements, bounded by barrier reefs of rising peaks. Lunarscape of rainbow craters and craggy gorges seared by fiery heat; yet today, with water from the far north, a land reclaimed, a land of challenge and hope.'

The name Negev means literally the dry, or parched land, the land of the Amalekites, until they gravitated to the more fertile soil of Gaza and Philistia (Exod. 17: 8 ff.; 1 Sam. 30: 1 ff.) Here were the wicked cities of Sodom and Gomorrah. Here David fled like a partridge before Saul to the caves of Ein Gedi. Here Solomon mined copper, in addition to which the Israelis extract phosphates, potash, bromine and magnesium. Here the Essene communities sought the purity of the desert. Here the Nabateans from their capital city at Petra in the first century B.C. alternately pillaged and protected the passing caravans, built their supply cities and farmed the parched land with remarkable expertise to supply their sizable city populations.

Desert Farms
Modern Israeli agriculturists have established, over the last twenty-five years, experimental farms to rediscover the Nabatean and Byzantine methods of desert agriculture. Such methods enabled the survival in the desert of considerable city populations and today produce handsome crops of carobs, figs, grapes, pomegranates, olives, almonds, peaches and apricots.

The average rainfall in the Negev is less than four inches a year, but when it rains the crusty soil, compacted by heat, is unable to absorb the water, which tends to cascade down the wadis – unless carefully controlled by irrigation channels. The Nabateans in the first centuries B.C. and A.D., and the Byzantines of the fourth to seventh centuries A.D. blocked shallow wadis with a sequence of locks, from which low walls (serving as conduits) directed the overflow water along the terraces on either side. A proportion of the overflow continued down the wadi from lock to lock, and at successive levels was diverted to water each terrace. Such catchment areas included also a farmhouse, whose cistern was fed by pipes from its own roof and courtyard.

BIBLICAL BEERSHEBA

One tradition ascribes its origin to Abraham, another to Isaac, but in either case the story is similar: the Patriarch purchased the ground from Abimelech for the price of seven ewe lambs and dug a well which was named 'The Well of the Seven' or 'The Well of the Covenant'. There are in fact seven wells in Beersheba today – ancient and modern: Gen. 21: 22–31; 26: 26–32.

Jacob visited and sacrificed at the ancient sanctuary here, on his way north to Haran and on his way south to Egypt: Gen. 28: 10; 46: 1 ff.

The prophet Samuel sent his sons to judge, in the circuit of Beersheba: 1 Sam. 8:2.

The prophet Elijah fled to Beersheba for sanctuary from Jezebel: 1 Kgs 19: 3.

The prophet Amos linked Beersheba with the sanctuaries of Bethel and Dan: Amos 5: 5; 8: 14.

It is regarded as the southern boundary of Southern Kingdom: 2 Kgs 23: 8; 2 Chr. 19: 4.

A Roman garrison was established here in the time of Eusebius (fourth century) and also a Christian bishopric.

Beersheba is now an expanding frontier town of over 100,000 population, scientists, builders, teachers and traders – though it is still a Bedouin centre. Every Thursday is market day.

HISTORICAL AND GEOGRAPHICAL

Within the vast triangle of the Negev, the area south of Beersheba as far as the Ramon Crater straddled the desert trade routes. These ran between Arabia Felix and the borders of Egypt from Kantara to El Arish, between Elath on the Red Sea and Gaza on the Mediterranean.

The Nabateans settled in Petra about 800 B.C.; by 400 B.C. they dominated the caravan routes with a policy of 'piracy' or 'protection'. By 200 B.C. they had established settlements of desert farm units at tactical points. The one-time desert raiders settled skilfully and successfully in the most inhospitable climate and became themselves vulnerable to nomads who envied their comfort and security!

When nomadic incursions into cultivated valleys again threatened the trade routes, the Romans – particularly under Trajan in A.D. 105 – intervened. Roman camps were established from which the roads were patrolled. Roman engineers cut a stepped road in the cliff of the 'Ascent of Scorpions', from the Arava gorge from the east, up on to the Negev. Water holes were dug every twenty miles or so along the routes, which were now usable by pack-mules as well as camel-trains.

In the fourth century, the Byzantines occupied most of the Nabatean settlements and expanded them, carefully preserving the existing water channels, and conserving water from wide streets and open spaces to fill reservoirs. Some of these townships may have had populations of 2000, judging by the numbers of housing units among the ruins.

DESERT CITIES

The following share this same pattern of history and are well worth visiting. The National Parks Ticket Office at each site will supply a groundplan of the main features.

Avdat (forty miles south of Beersheba)
Burial place of the Nabatean king Obodas II, 9 B.C., and renamed Oboda – in Hebrew Avdat. His son, Aretas IV, ruled as far north as Damascus in the time of St Paul. The Byzantine ruins include a castle, Church of St Theodore and monastery. There is a Roman camp and a Nabatean altar, gateway and terrace.

Shivta/Subeita (thirty-five miles south-west of Beersheba)
Unwalled city, whose street-ends were gated, whose layout is still clear and whose water-system is channelled from cistern to cistern. There are three churches, the central of which has three apses. The north church has a cruciform baptismal font and

monastic quarters. The entrance bears carvings of the Chi-Rho monogram, Alpha & Omega.

Mamshit/Mampsis (twenty-six miles south-east of Beersheba)

The northernmost Nabatean settlement in the Negev, a walled city set on a hill and on the north bank of the Wadi Kurnub, with a number of dams. Of the two churches, the western one – next to the town hall – has a floor-mosaic inscription: 'Lord, help your servant Nilus who built this church. Amen.' There are two large blocks of administrative buildings.

PROVINCIAL SHRINES OF ISLAM

HEBRON AND BETHLEHEM

Among the remaining Muslim Holy Places are Hebron, El Khalil, or the 'Friend of God' (meaning Abraham), and the Tomb of Rachel, Qubbat Rahil. These indeed they were, long before the time of Muhammad, and were accepted as such by the Christians, St Jerome and Eusebius the historian. Long before Jerome and Eusebius, Herod built his sanctuary over the Cave of Machpelah and Josephus knew Rachel's Tomb near Bethlehem. Muslim veneration of these two and other early Hebrew shrines is, in a sense, retrospective and under Muslim rule was apt to be protectively exclusive. Consequently the Muslim annexation of sites sacred to the Jews has not been popular; nor perhaps nowadays is the virtual control at the Haram El Khalil and the Qubbat Rahil by the Orthodox Jews very popular with Muslims. Whereas in Ottoman times Jews were excluded from the Harams in Jerusalem and Hebron, now there is limited freedom of access to both for all faiths.

LYDDA

Of Lydda, Muqaddasi writes: 'Lydda lies about a mile from Ar-Ramlah. There is here a great mosque, in which are wont to assemble large numbers of the people from the capital [Ar-Ramlah], and from the villages round. In Lydda, too, is that wonderful church [of St George] at the gate of which Christ will slay the Antichrist.' The Church of St George mentioned by Muqaddasi must have been the original church which the Crusaders restored, for the present ruins are those of a building of the Crusading epoch. According to local tradition, St George the Cappadocian martyr came from Lydda, and over his remains was built a church mentioned in the fifth century. On the approach of the Crusaders, the church was burnt, but was rebuilt and again destroyed in 1291. Today the white minaret, rebuilt after the 1927 earthquake, and the mosque occupy the site of the Byzantine church. The remainder of the Crusader church was acquired by the Greek Orthodox, who built the present church over a crypt in which is shown the Tomb of St George. St George is revered by the Muslims as Al-Khadr (the green and living one).

RAMLAH

Ramlah was the provincial capital from its foundation by Suleiman, son of Abdel Melik, until the coming of the Crusaders. Then, the famous White Mosque stood in the centre of the city, but its shrine was that of Nebi Salih, a Muslim prophet mentioned in the Quran who was sent to the tribe of Tamud. The Tower of Ramlah is an interesting and outstanding monument of the fourteenth century, originally erected as the minaret of the mosque, and now six storeys and thirty metres high. In its basic features it is an imitation of a gothic belfry, perhaps that of the Holy Sepulchre, but the decorations are Moorish. It stands within the White Mosque enclosure which was itself built six centuries earlier. It is called by Christians the Tower of the Forty Martyrs and by Muslims that of the Forty Companions of the Prophet. The Tomb of Nebi Salih lies to the west of the tower. Ramlah is also the traditional site of Arimathea, the home of Joseph in whose tomb Jesus was buried.

NABLUS

Nablus was built in A.D. 72 by Titus and named Neapolis. It was the see of a Christian bishopric and also a Samaritan stronghold. It was occupied by the Muslims in 636, until it fell to the Crusaders in 1100. Today Nablus is a centre of cultural and political thought as well as a centre of light industry. The two fine mosques were in origin Byzantine churches. Ali of Herat, in 1173, wrote:

> Outside the town is a mosque where they say Adam made his prostration in prayer . . . the Samaritans are very numerous in this town. Nearby is the spring of Al-Khadr [Elijah] . . . further, Joseph is buried at the foot of a tree at this place.

Of Nablus, the geographer Idris wrote:

> There is here the well that Jacob dug – peace be on him! – where also the Lord Messiah sat, asking of water to drink from a Samaritan woman. There is at the present day a fine church built over it. The people of Jerusalem say that no Samaritans are found elsewhere but here.

ACRE

Among the provincial cities of Muslim interest is Acre, ancient Ptolemais, a naval base under the Omayyads second only to Alexandria, and a key port throughout the Crusader occupation. On the fall of Jerusalem, Acre became the capital of the Ottoman province of Sidon, under the Albanian soldier of fortune Ahmed al-Jazzar, justly nicknamed 'The Butcher' for his indiscriminate cruelty towards all classes of his subjects. He has left behind a magnificent mosque, square in plan and roofed with a great dome. With its slender minaret it stands in the middle of a large rectangular court, which is surrounded on three sides by arcades resting on ancient columns with modern capitals. The columns, which are partly of granite and partly of marble, were brought from the ruins of Tyre and Caesarea. Along these arcaded walks or cloisters are domed cells for the servants of the mosque and the pilgrims who come to visit it. In the courtyard, near the northwest corner of the mosque, stands a small domed chamber containing the white marble tombs of Jazzar Pasha, the founder of the mosque, and of Suleiman Pasha his successor.

TOMB OF MOSES

Although the Book of Numbers denies that anyone knows the Tomb of Moses, in 1269 the Mamluk Sultan Beybars built a mosque at a point on the old pilgrim road, from which pilgrims could view Mount Nebo, to enclose a representative Tomb of Moses. What began perhaps as a pilgrimage provision soon developed into political expedient, to ensure that there was a large Muslim contingent in Jerusalem over the Christian Easter festival. Since the Middle Ages it has been the custom to make an annual pilgrimage to Moses' tomb and shrine. The villagers used to come from all over Palestine; after services in the Haram es-Sharif, they would proceed in a picturesque procession to the shrine of Nebi Musa. After festivities lasting about a week, there was a return procession to Jerusalem, the whole festival coinciding exactly with the Holy Week services of the Eastern Churches!

BROTHERHOOD OF ISLAM

It is a solemn thought that if Jews and Christians had set out more purposefully to share their faith with the Arabic tribes in the early centuries of the Christian era, they might not now be confronted with the vast brotherhood of Islam throughout the world. This brotherhood is drilled to a pattern of prayer, from preliminaries to prostrations, which binds together its members of all colours and countries. Hardened by the burning fast of Ramadhan, united in its single focus of pilgrimage, this brotherhood has developed its own exclusiveness, without reference to the universal fatherhood of God. 'Only believers are brothers,' says the Quran, in which the mercy and compassion of God are outweighed by his justice and judgment. Islam still remains in character a brotherhood, whose words of witness, 'There is no God but God: Muhammad is the Apostle of God' are of great power, both to the simple and the wise.

Part Four:

TRANSFER TO GALILEE

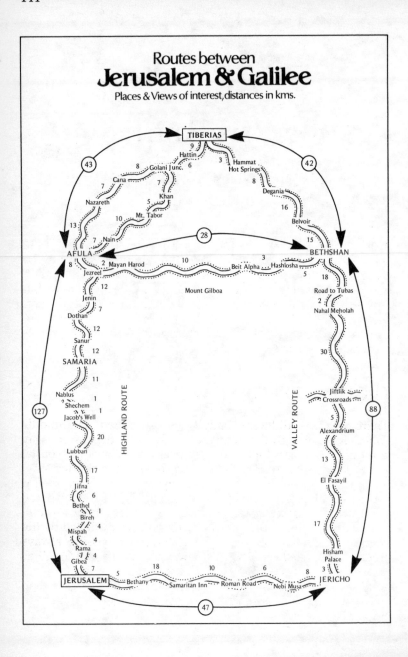

Routes between
Jerusalem & Galilee
Places & Views of interest, distances in kms.

TIBERIAS

43   42

9

Hattin

Hammat
Golani Junc.   Hot Springs
8   6   3

Cana   8   Degania
7   7   8

Nazareth   Khan   16

13   5   Belvoir

7   Nain   Mt. Tabor   15

28

AFULA   BETHSHAN

8   2   Mayan Harod   10   3   18

Jezreel   Beit Alpha   Hashlosha   5

12   Mount Gilboa   Road to Tubas

Jenin   2

7   Nahal Meholah

Dothan   30

12

Sanur   HIGHLAND ROUTE   VALLEY ROUTE

12   Jiflik

SAMARIA   Crossroads

11   5

Nablus   Alexandrium

1

Shechem   13

1

Jacob's Well   El Fasayil

20

Lubban   17

17

Jifna   Hisham

6   Palace

Bethel   Jericho

1   3

Bireh   JERICHO

4

Mispah   127   88

4

Rama

4

Gibea

7   5   18   10   6   8

JERUSALEM   Bethany   Samaritan Inn   Roman Road   Nebi Musa

47

JOURNEY TO OR FROM JERUSALEM CHOICE OF PILGRIM ROUTES

The principal Christian Holy Places are naturally to be found in those districts where Jesus was born and brought up, where he lived and taught, where he suffered, died and lived again. Broadly speaking, this means Nazareth and the lakeside within Galilee, also Jerusalem and Bethlehem within Judea. There are, however, a number of places sacred to Christians for their association with the visits of Jesus or his mother, on their travels between Galilee and Judea.

HIGHLAND ROUTE

There are three different roads to be considered. The middle route leads through the highlands of Samaria, the eastern way through the Jordan Valley and the western follows the coastal plain. Josephus describes the middle route as the shortest one, able to be covered on foot in three days, and the usual one for Jewish pilgrims from Galilee to Jerusalem. The main disadvantage of this was the possible trouble when travelling through Samaritan territory. On the whole, this was outweighed by the greater safety and speed of a shorter route passing always through inhabited localities, in which provisions and lodgings were plentiful. It is very probable that there were sizable caravanserais at staging posts near El-Lubban and Sanur. On more than one occasion, Jesus is described as needing to spend a night in Samaria (Luke 9: 51–5).

VALLEY ROUTE

The eastern route, via the Jordan Valley, might have taken nearly
twice as long, though St John indicates that Jesus and his disciples
went from Jericho to Cana in three days (John 2: 1). This road may
have served Jesus' purpose better than the shorter route on those
occasions when he wished to avoid the pilgrim traffic, or when he
wished to stay outside Judean territory as long as possible, or
simply when he wished to travel alone with his disciples.

COASTAL ROUTE

The western route passing through either Emmaus (Amwas) or
Antipatris seems to have been little used by Jesus, though Joseph
and Mary with the child Jesus would have returned from Egypt to
Nazareth by the Via Maris.

TRAVEL TO 'TERMINAL'

If we think of the 'Highland' and 'Valley' routes as the two main
arteries, we must expect that – in the districts both of Galilee and
of Jerusalem – smaller capillary roads would lead to the terminal
of the main route. So, Jesus must have visited many villages
among the glens of Galilee and in the environs of the city, on link
roads to the pilgrim terminals.

A number of events within the gospel story took place at
specific points on his journeys. One would expect Galilean
pilgrims to gather in the plain of Jezreel, near the modern town of
Afula at the foot of the hill of Moreh. Indeed, Afula has always
been at a crossroads and the obvious communication centre for
southern Galilee. This would explain the visit to Nain and the
raising of the widow's son (Luke 7: 11–15).

DAILY DISTANCES

The 'Highland' route can be divided into three days' travel,
between Jezreel and Jerusalem. The total distance is some one
hundred and twenty-two kilometres, just over seventy-five

miles, with each day's travel forty kilometres or twenty-five miles. Each day in turn was divided by a noonday halt. This accords exactly with known sites and scriptural references:

DAY 1: Afula to Jenin – first noonday halt.
   – Healing of the Ten Lepers – the 'Grateful Samaritan' – Luke 17: 11–19.
   Jenin to the Plain of Sanur, near Akaba – first night stop.
   – Caravanserai.

DAY 2: Sanur to Sychar – second noonday halt.
   – Samaritan woman at Jacob's well – John 4: 1–43.
   Sychar to Lubban, an ancient inn site – second night stop.

DAY 3: Lubban to Bireh – third noonday halt.
   – Mary and Joseph lost the boy Jesus – Luke 2: 41–51.
   Bireh to Jerusalem – pilgrims' terminal and dispersal.

CHOICE OF ROUTES THEN

This route would have been followed by Mary on her way to visit her cousin Elizabeth for the Visitation. Most pilgrims would weigh up the advantages between one route and the other. The 'Valley' route would have been insufferably hot in mid-summer, 120°F in the shade, but safer – if slower. The 'Highland' route in large caravans or convoys was fairly secure – if very cold in winter. For individual travellers or small groups, the Samaritan territory was a perpetual hazard. The irony of the story of the 'Good' Samaritan is just in the fact that he was on the *wrong* road! The 'certain man who went down from Jerusalem to Jericho' may well have selected his route to *avoid* Samaritans!

Jesus may well have chosen the solitude of the 'Valley' route, as providing a quiet opportunity to teach his disciples. Perhaps, however, for him the most important advantage of this route was its proximity to the River Jordan and the baptism centres of his cousin, John.

CHOICE OF ROUTES NOW

The choice of routes for the traveller today will depend firstly upon the security situation in the area of Jacob's Well, Nablus and Sebaste – and secondly upon his personal purpose. The tourist primarily concerned with agricultural and industrial settlements in the modern State of Israel may do well to choose the 'Coastal' route. The Christian pilgrim will probably prefer the 'Highland' route with its superb sequence of Old and New Testament associations: northwards: Bireh, Jacob's Well, Shechem, Samaria, Dothan, Jenin and Jezreel. Should this route, however, be 'closed' there is much of interest on the 'Valley' route, despite the present inaccessibility of the places of baptism linked with John the Baptist.

On leaving Jericho, the road passes successively a fine Ummayyad palace at Khirbet Mafjir and the Herodian town-site of Phasael (Herod's brother's name) now El Fasayil. Only seven kilometres later, the road passes below the Herodian palace stronghold of Alexandrium on the conical hill of Sartaba, before the crossroads at Jiftlik – leading up the fertile vale of Faria to Nablus and down to the Damiya bridge across Jordan. Here Jacob crossed from Haran into Canaan and Joshua crossed with the Children of Israel. Nearly fifty kilometres north, the route passes through the well-populated township of Bethshan, whose remarkable tell is clearly visible from the road and whose theatre is the largest in modern Israel.

Whichever route is accessible, as far as Jenin or Bethshan, there is a sequence of sites along the south of the Plain of Esdraelon which are always open. These include, from east to west, Bethshan, Beit Alpha, Mount Gilboa and Mayan Harod. The superb Crusader castle of Belvoir and the synagogue at Hammat can also be visited on the final approach to Tiberias.

SAMARITAN TERRITORY
JACOB'S WELL, SHECHEM, SAMARIA

THE SAMARITANS

Then

In 722 B.C. the Assyrians invaded and captured Samaria, deported a proportion of the population and imported several alien tribes to take their place. It is commonly said that the intermingling of the aliens and Israelites who remained formed the Samaritan race of later days who were not recognised by the Jews as Jews. The Samaritans repudiated completely any obligation to go up to Jerusalem to worship. They built their own temple on Mount Gerizim above Shechem. This was destroyed by the Hasmonaean prince, John Hyrcanus, in 129 B.C.

And Now

The Samaritans in our time have been reduced to a small community of under two hundred, who live mainly in Nablus. Even this diminished survival they owe in part to the Jews. In 1841, for example, when the Muslims of Nablus threatened to exterminate them, the chief rabbi of Jerusalem saved them by giving a certificate that 'the Samaritan people are a branch of the children of Israel who acknowledge the truth of the Torah'.

Samaritan Torah

The Samaritans continue to observe their ancient separatist rites which they claim to be purer than those of the regular Jews. They admit the canonical authority only of the Books of the Pentateuch. They wear long hair and beards and in their synagogue is a volume of the Torah written in the Samaritan script, which is similar to ancient Hebrew.

Passover Today

They celebrate the Passover on the summit of Mount Gerizim. On the Passover eve, the entire community ascends the mountain.

Surrounding their altar, they slaughter seven sheep for an offering, while the high priest stands on a rock and reads aloud the twelfth chapter of Exodus. When he comes to the sentence 'the congregation of Israel shall kill it', the people kill the sheep. They then pour water over the carcasses and, stripping off the fleece, extract the fat and burn both fat and fleece. The forefoot of each sheep is cut off and given to the priest in accordance with the biblical command. After being cleaned, the sacrifices are thoroughly salted and each sheep is then spitted on a rod and roasted.

Roasted Whole

Close to the altar is a pit, or *tannur*, heated by the burning of brushwood. In this primitive and vast oven, the carcasses are roasted. After prayers and at about midnight they take the roasted sheep out of the pit and put them into huge casseroles. They then all sit round, fully clothed and shod, to eat their sacrificial portions. No bone must be broken nor anything edible left unconsumed. When all is finished they gather up the bones, hooves, horns and also anything, such as the spits, which has come in contact with the sacrifice, and solemnly burn everything.

JACOB'S WELL

Then

Just south of the Ebal–Gerizim Pass, as St John the Evangelist describes, Jesus rested at Jacob's Well and sent his disciples on to the next village to buy lunch. It was over his midday rest that he had that wonderful conversation with the much-married woman of Samaria, who teased him for his thirsty request for a drink: 'You Jews have no dealings with us Samaritans, besides the well is deep and you have no bucket and rope!'

Now

Today the well is still thirty-two metres deep and its identification is unquestioned. A Byzantine cruciform church, with the well beneath the centre of the crossing, was described by Arculf in 679. Antoninus records that the well entrance was in front of the altar rail. Jerome describes the building of a church in the fourth century and the Bordeaux Pilgrim as early as 333 identified the well by its proximity to Joseph's Tomb. Since then the site has had an unbroken tradition. In Crusader times the well was within a crypt below the high altar of a three-aisled church. Today it still forms the crypt of an unfinished Orthodox church, in exactly the same position and plan. Here, without doubt, was the scene of Jesus' refusal to participate in the Jewish-Samaritan controversy and also of his dictum, 'Neither in this mountain, nor yet at Jerusalem . . . God is a Spirit and they that worship him must worship him in spirit and in truth.'

Scriptural References
1 Jacob's purchase of property near Shechem: Gen. 33: 18–20.
2 Joseph visits his brothers at Shechem: Gen. 37: 12–14.
3 Joshua built an altar on Mt Ebal and read the Law: Josh. 8: 30–4.
4 The bones of Joseph buried on Jacob's property: Josh. 24: 32.
5 Jesus and the woman of Samaria, at Sychar: John 4: 1–26.

SHECHEM

The ancient patriarchal city, at the mouth of the only east–west pass through the spine of Samaria. Tel Balata was first settled in the fourth millennium B.C. and must have been an important town at the crossroads of trade routes, at the time of Abraham (Gen. 12: 6–7). An obvious feature of the city was the monolithic south gate, still to be seen today.

SAMARIA – A TALE OF FOUR CITIES

Omri, 880–721 B.C.
Royal capital of the Northern Kingdom (2000 chariots and 10,000 men): 1 Kgs 16: 24. Ahab's death at Ramoth Gilead: 1 Kgs 22: 31–9. Lepers and the Syrian siege: 2 Kgs 7: 3–11.

Illustrated by the Israelite walls – two headers to each stretcher – short, short, long – best seen south of the Roman forum.

Sargon, 721–331 B.C.
The administrative headquarters of a backward province in the vast oriental empire of Assyria: 2 Kgs 17: 6. Deported Israelites replaced by colonists: 2 Kgs 17: 29.

Illustrated by crude stone walls in the Acropolis area.

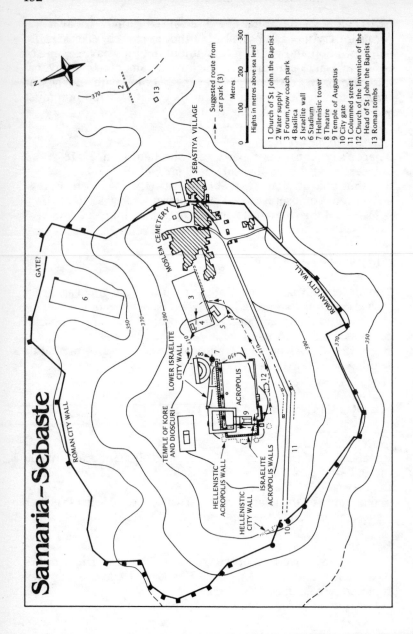

Samaria–Sebaste

1 Church of St John the Baptist
2 Water supply
3 Forum, now coach park
4 Basilica
5 Israelite wall
6 Stadium
7 Hellenistic tower
8 Theatre
9 Temple of Augustus
10 City gate
11 Columned street
12 Church of the Invention of the Head of St John the Baptist
13 Roman tombs

Hights in metres above sea level

--- Suggested route from car park (3)

Metres
0   100   200   300

Alexander 331–107 B.C.

Alexander's personal visit, followed by a colony of 6000 Macedonian veterans. The Greek colonial city captured and destroyed by Hyrcanus 108 B.C.

Illustrated by the fine Hellenistic tower.

Herod, 30 B.C.

Presented to Herod by the Roman Emperor Augustus. Herod imported 6000 mercenaries and renamed the city Sebaste, in honour of Augustus – a provincial city. New circuit of walls, two and a half miles long.

Illustrated by colonnaded street, temple of Augustus and forum. An early Christian tradition of the burial of the body of John the Baptist, at Sebaste, resulted in the building of a Byzantine basilica and later – in the twelfth century – a Crusader cathedral of St John. This is within the perimeter of the present Arab village.

Order of Visit

Begin in the Roman forum and circle the site anti-clockwise:

1 Enter site by South Gate.
2 Forum.
3 View of Roman hippodrome and Persian polo posts, to the north.
4 Graeco-Roman theatre.
5 Hellenistic tower.
6 Acropolis, possible site of the Ivory Palace.
7 Temple of Augustus.
8 Cycloptic Assyrian Wall.
9 Byzantine Church of John the Baptist.
10 View Imrin village, which retains name of Omri.
11 Return to Forum, noting Israelite Wall.
12 Crusader cathedral in village, if desired.

VALLEY OF JEZREEL
GILBOA, HAROD, BEIT
ALPHA, GAN HASHLOSHA,
BETHSHAN

The valley of Jezreel extends along the southern fringe of the Plain of Esdraelon, from the fortress/tells of Megiddo and Ta'Anach in the west to Bethshan in the east.

JEZREEL

The 'Highland' pilgrim route between Jerusalem and Galilee emerges north of Jenin at a junction, just north of the old West Bank boundary. Near the present crossroads was the ancient city of Jezreel, associated with the story of Naboth's vineyard (1 Kgs 21) 'hard by the palace of Ahab King of Samaria', also the execution of Jezebel by Jehu (2 Kings 9: 30–7). At this point the valley runs west and east. To reach the lakeside cities, the more direct route continued north round the Hill of Moreh, via Nain (Luke 7: 11–15) and perhaps Endor (1 Sam. 28: 7–25) and the foot of Mount Tabor (Luke 9: 28–36).

GILBOA

Another road turned East along the Valley of Jezreel to link up with the Jordan Valley pilgrim route at Bethshan. This road passes under the mountains of Gilboa, with all their vivid associations with the killing of Saul and Jonathan by the Philistines, on the heights above (1 Samuel 31 and 2 Samuel 1):

> 'Thy glory, O Israel, is slain upon thy high places! . . .
> How are the mighty fallen,
> and the weapons of war perished!'

HAROD

Some five kilometres from the crossroads a road turns right under the Gilboa range, towards Mayan Harod, near Kibbutz Gideona. Such names conjure up memories of Gideon selecting his 300 commandos, at the Well of Harod, to fight the Midianites as thick as 'locusts for number' in the Vale of Jezreel (Judg. 6 and 7). Once again, the setting is so vivid that the story only needs reading against the background of the scenery: 'At the beginning of the middle watch, when they had just set the watch; and . . . they blew the trumpets and smashed the jars . . . holding in their left hands the torches, and in their right hands the trumpets to blow; and they cried: "A sword for the Lord, and for Gideon!"'

BEIT ALPHA

Returning to the road along the valley, another five kilometres east takes us to the forbidding Shitta prison. Turning right towards the hills again another five kilometres brings us to Kibbutz Heftziba, in which is a quite remarkable sixth-century synagogue mosaic floor. This was discovered in 1928, in the course of irrigating land owned by the neighbouring kibbutz Beit Alpha.

Synagogue Plan
The basic ground plan is very clear and it is easy to imagine the elevation. The whole will help relate to synagogues at Capernaum, Hammat and elsewhere. An open courtyard facing south (towards Jerusalem) leads through two doorways, into a vestibule the width of the building. From this, three doorways lead into the prayer hall, the central one into the nave and the other two into side aisles, all with mosaic floors. Above the side aisles, galleries looked down into the nave, at the southern end of which was an apse housing a Torah cupboard. Off the right or west aisle is a courtyard, half the length of the building with its separate entrance to the front and from which a staircase led up into the gallery.

Nave Mosaics
Within the central doorway between a lion and a bull is an Aramaic and Greek inscription: Greek: 'In honoured memory of

the artists who made this work well, Marianos and his son Aninus.' Aramaic: 'This mosaic was laid down in the . . . year of the reign of the Emperor Justinus in honoured memory of all sons . . . Amen.'

This is the only dated inscription found in a Holy Land synagogue and refers to the time of Justinian, who ruled from 518 to 527 A.D.

The nave mosaics are divided into three panels: The first depicts the sacrifice of Isaac (Gen. 22: 1–14). In the top of the picture the hand of God reaches down out of the cloud and the words 'Lay not thine hand upon the lad' appear over the figure of Abraham with his knife ready, while the ram (hardly caught by its horns) is tethered behind the patriarch.

The middle panel has a central medallion of Apollo driving his sun-chariot over the heavens, within a Zodiac circle of the signs of the twelve months, inscribed in Hebrew and running anti-clockwise from three o'clock. These are Aries the ram, Taurus the bull, Gemini the twins, Cancer the crab, Leo the lion, Virgo the virgin, Libra the scales, Scorpio the scorpion, Sagittarius the archer, Capricorn the goat, Aquarius the water bearer, Pisces the fishes. In the corners are the four seasons: top left, Spring; bottom left, Summer; bottom right, Autumn; top right, Winter.

The southern and furthest panel depicts the Torah cupboard, which stood in the apse beyond and above the mosaic, framed within tasselled curtains and flanked by *menorah* (seven-branched candlesticks), incense shovels and *shofars* (rams' horns). The doors of the Ark, heavily inlaid and decorated, together with the rich symbolism of the whole design, do honour to this one-time shrine of the Law.

GAN HASHLOSHA

Two kilometres on the road to Bethshan is the most idyllic bathing and picnic place, a sequence of pools along the same Harod stream, on its way to the Jordan River. There are few enough such facilities on either the 'Highland' or 'Valley' route from Jerusalem, and Hashlosha is included in the National Parks card.

BETHSHAN

B.C.

The tell is the site of eighteen successive cities, since 3500 B.C., and was finally destroyed during its Crusader occupation by Saladin. It was on the walls of ancient Bethshan that the Philistines hung the bodies of Saul and his three sons, after their defeat on Mount Gilboa (1 Sam. 31: 8–10).

The Israelite tribe of Manasseh made little impression on this great fortress city, which was successively in the hands of Canaanites, Egyptians and Philistines, whose powerful chariot forces and bowmen were too strong for the Hebrews – except perhaps in the time of Solomon. In Hellenistic times, it reappeared under a new name, Scythopolis, and was captured in 107 B.C. by John Hyrcanus, who sought to force circumcision upon the inhabitants. They mostly went into exile, until the arrival of the Romans in 63 B.C.

A.D.

In the time of Christ, the city was one of the Graeco-Roman cities of the Decapolis. The magnificent Roman basalt theatre – one of the most complete and best preserved in Israel – dates from A.D. 200. At that time, Scythopolis was a well-known textile centre and famous for its fine linen. In 325, its first Christian bishop attended the Council of Nicea.

Part Five:

IN & FROM GALILEE

GALILEE: THE GREENHOUSE OF THE GOSPEL

'Yahweh created seven seas, but Gennesaret is his delight'
A rabbi
'O Sabbath rest by Galilee . . .'
A Quaker

DISTRICT

To the Christian the very word Galilee has an emotive impact. It conveys in a word the scene of Jesus' lakeside Ministry. It conjures up memories of his calling, of his disciples, his miracles and his teaching – as does no other word. To most of us, however, it is the *Sea* of Galilee rather than the district, which we hold in such affection.

The name Galilee – from the Hebrew *Galil*, meaning a circuit or circle – is applied to any well-defined region. 'Galil Ha Goyim' – 'Galilee of the Gentiles', literally 'encircled by Gentiles' – was the name given to the northern province. The region, or district, was actually surrounded by foreigners on at least three sides – on the west by the Phoenicians, on the north by the people of Tyre and Sidon, on the east and south-east by the Ten Towns, the Graeco-Roman colonials of the Decapolis. Following the return from Babylon, the district remained largely Gentile, but by the time of Jesus it was thoroughly Judaised. The words 'of the Gentiles' – 'Ha-Goyim' – were dropped from its title, which then became proudly known as '*The* Region or District'.

Rift
The main feature of the District is the 'Rift' or Jordan Valley,

whose waters are fed from the melting snows of Mount Hermon, sixty miles to the north-east. The name Jordan can mean 'descender', and its waters descend from 9000 feet above sea level to 682 feet below the level of the Mediterranean, to form the Lake or Sea of Galilee.

Rising out of the Rift Valley and running west to the coastal plain are three parallel and rising steps: the Plain of Esdraelon, much of which is below sea level; the Lower Galilee ranges of up to 1800 feet; and finally the plateaux of Upper Galilee of up to 4000 feet. It is as though the Lebanon has cast her mountainous roots southwards, channelling her snows and rains down the valleys of Galilee. Consequently, the District enjoys a great fertility and profusion of flowers, corn, oil and wood – also hot sulphur springs and a tendency to earthquakes.

Roads
The most striking feature in the time of Jesus was the system of roads crossing the District in all directions: from the Levant to Damascus and the east, from Jerusalem up to Antioch, from the Nile to the Euphrates. The fertility and good communications resulted in the growth of a considerable population – engaged in local industries and concentrated largely on the lakeside.

Climate
Unlike the District of Judea to the south, whose desert borders exerted an austere influence on that province, Galilee was surrounded by pagan and colonial townships, which poured in their full influence of Greek life and leisure. All these features: the wealth of water, the extreme fertility, the great highways, the considerable population, the Greek influences, were crowded into the Rift Valley, in tropical heat round a blue and lovely lake. These were the conditions in which Jesus taught and worked – and under which Christianity began to grow.

Galilee was indeed the 'Greenhouse' of the Gospel. If the seed was sown in Nazareth or Bethlehem the seedling was planted out in the greenhouse atmosphere of Galilee with its intense humidity and heat. Here in the hearts of its very Latin-temperament population the seed of the Word of God was quick to germinate.

LAKE

St Luke, the Traveller, like Josephus the historian, had weathered the Mediterranean, therefore he calls the Sea of Galilee a 'lake' – the Greek word 'limnē' – rather than 'thalassa' – a 'sea'. This lake is thirteen miles long north to south, and seven miles across at its widest, between Magdala and Kursi. In the clear eastern atmosphere it looks smaller than it really is. The scenery – ravines, hills and valleys – remains unchanged by the centuries. The maximum depth along the course of the River Jordan, north to south, is 150 feet. Deep water is reached very soon from the shore, except in the north-west on the plain of Gennesaret. The hot sulphurous springs flow into the lake on all sides – particularly at Tiberias, which was in Roman times a spa, famous for its medicinal waters. Folklore takes its origin back to Solomon! Tiberias was, in the time of Jesus, despised by the local Jewish population as the capital city of Herod Antipas, whose artificial oriental court was held in the castle on a crag, dominating the hot springs and harbour.

TIBERIAS

Tiberias, one of the four holy cities of the Jews (the others are Jerusalem, Hebron and Safed) was founded by Antipas in A.D. 17 and named after the Roman emperor. From the third century Tiberias was a Jewish religious centre, where the Mishmah and later the Talmud were completed. The second-century Rabbi Akiba and the twelfth-century Jewish-Spanish physician-theologian, Maimonides, were buried here. South of the town above the hot springs are the remains of the third- and sixth-century synagogues at Hammat. Above these is the tomb of Rabbi Meir, a second-century Jewish patriot.

Most visitors to Galilee are accommodated in Tiberias and tour the lakeside clockwise round to Ein Gev, on 'the other side'. The prevailing wind on the lake is the west wind, which rifles down a steep gorge, 'the Gulf of Pigeons', above the ancient site of Magdala, to churn up the surface of the lake in the early evening. In the caves of the overhanging cliff, Galilean partisans have hidden from Roman to British mandate times – only to be winkled out by force from Roman legionaries to Palestine police.

MAGDALA

Magdala had a sizable harbour and was known for its weaving industry. Here was the home of Mary Magdalene. Here were traditionally the looms of the robe worn by Jesus to his crucifixion and gambled for, by the execution squad. Here we turn north on to the fertile plain of Gennesaret – the market garden of the populous lakeside towns. Josephus described Gennesaret as 'the ambition of nature', supplying the principal fruits (grapes and figs) continually during ten months of the year and the rest of the fruits as they ripen together throughout the whole year.

BEATITUDES

The road rises from the plain, over a tell and round the lake to the Mount of Beatitudes, the traditional site of the Sermon on the Mount. From there we shall come down the Valley of Tabgha to the lakeside. The name 'Tabgha' or 'Tabigha' is an Arabic corruption of the Greek words 'Hepta pēga' meaning 'seven springs', whose warm waters still flow into the lake.

It is so easy to picture Jesus retreating up the hillsides to escape from the crowded lake shores – in order to pray or plan or select and teach his team of disciples. When he wished to speak to the crowds, he remained down at lake level, often speaking from a boat in one of those little bays on the north shore, with the people surrounding him on the rocks or grass. That is just how St Mark (or was it Peter?) describes it: 'There was gathered to him a great multitude, so that he entered into a boat and sat in the lake; while the whole multitude was by the sea – on the land.' With the lake as a sounding-board at his back his voice would carry far up the hillside.

Such was the scene below the Mount of Beatitudes when Jesus first taught and then fed the five thousand. Two successive Byzantine churches were built in the fourth century, both focused on the traditional altar stone on which Jesus took, blessed, broke and gave the bread and fish to be distributed. Set within that stone is a fifth-century mosaic of a basket of five little barley loaves flanked by two Galilean mullets – now called Peter's fish. The surrounding mosaics are a superb picture-guide to the flora and fauna of the lake with peacocks, flamingos and snakes, cormorants, herons and doves, ducks and geese among the lotus leaves and oleander bushes.

Only two hundred yards away, at the water's edge, is the traditional site of Jesus' post-resurrection commission to Peter – described in the last chapter of St John's Gospel. An enormous rock projects out over the water and back into the little basalt 'Chapel of The Primacy'. This rock, the traditional scene of Jesus cooking breakfast on the 'fire of coals', was known to medieval pilgrims as the 'Mensa Christi' – the Table of the Lord.

CAPERNAUM

Two kilometres further round the lake shore is the site of the frontier town of Capernaum, headquarters of Jesus' Galilean Ministry. Of all the towns of Israel none was more appropriate for Jesus to launch his message than the little metropolis of Capernaum. It was the commercial centre of a chain of fishing villages or *Beth-saidas* (from Magdala on the west to Gergesa on the east) whose inhabitants brought their daily catch to the wharves and salteries of their market town. Boats loaded and off-loaded not only fresh or dried fish, but all the local weaves and wares of Galilee, the fruit and produce of Gennesaret, and even silks and spices from Damascus.

Half a mile of lakeside ruins and a considerable depth of water witness to the harbour and warehouse installations of long ago. The town was in fact one vast sea-bound market place, a cosmopolis teeming with merchants from Phoenicia and Damascus, Greeks and Romans from the Ten Towns, and wholesale buyers from Jerusalem. Less conspicuous among the jostling crowds along the jetties were the stevedores and shipwrights and local fisher-folk – sorting fish, pickling, packing, mending nets, making sails, painting boats. Along the coastal highway, which crossed into Herod Philip's territory at the fords of Jordan less than a mile away, rolled the ox-carts heaped high with vegetables and fruit – to the sound of camel bells. Camel-trains, roped nose to tail, plodded through the dust or stood bored yet patient under vast loads in the thick of the traffic jam. Ubiquitous donkeys and mules pushed through, like mopeds at traffic lights. Every now and then amid the crush appeared the plumed helmet of the legionary, the black gown of the rabbi – Pharisee or Scribe – and the brass badge of the publican, each about his own particular business in the melee of men and animals.

SYNAGOGUE

You will see there nowadays a twentieth-century reconstruction of a third-century synagogue – which still includes stones from its first-century predecessor. The main prayer hall, overlooked from a women's gallery, the Gentiles' courtyard with gaming boards carved on the flagstones and an amazing medley of both Roman and Jewish symbols carved in stone. Surely this must go back to the centurion commander of troops in Capernaum, who sought Jesus' healing for his batman – and was commended by local elders: 'This man, Roman though he is, loves our nation and has built us our synagogue.'

Opposite the front of the synagogue was discovered only in 1921 a Byzantine mosaiced octagonal shrine, covering houses of the first century. On leaving the synagogue Jesus used immediately to enter the home of Simon Peter. Could this be the site of the cottage of the trawler skipper, Simon son of the Dove, who was called with these words: 'Simon, son of the fluttering dove, I will call you the Rock and upon this Rock I will build my Church'?

LAKESIDE TOWNSHIPS

Now let us look at the soil of the greenhouse chosen to take the seedling of the Christian movement. There were at least nine townships round the shores of the lake, each of which had a population of 10–15,000. Within this huge population Jesus chose the fishermen. He went to a trade with no private wrongs, whose members were content to escape from the crowds, to the peace of their fishing grounds, out on the lake. Thus it was not the jargon of hot-headed Zealot guerillas – the brigand highlanders – of Galilee; it was the speech of the fishermen and their patient craft which became the language and symbolism of Christianity; their tools and techniques, their catches, boats and nets.

The seed could not have been planted in more fertile soil than in the climatic conditions of the Rift, where the Latin temperament and frustrated hopes of the Galilean nationalists had something in common with the Palestinians of today. Within this explosive situation Jesus selected a team of twelve, half of whom were professional fishermen, whose lives were governed by very simple and basic facts and experiences.

FISH

First of all: the fish which were dependent for their feed, mainly the rotting vegetable matter swept down by the fast-flowing Jordan, whose currents (and you will see them) sweep out into and round the north of the lake. These currents are followed by shoals of feeding fish, followed in turn by the fishermen – whose *Beth-saidas* tended to be mostly round the north shore.

The fishing industry then was far more extensive than it is today and concentrated round the lake, rather than in modern fish farms. It involved not only the netting and landing of the catch, but the whole process of sorting, pickling, transporting and marketing – down to Jerusalem, up to Damascus and all round the country – especially the Ten Towns. 'Zebedee & Sons' and their partners 'Jonah & Sons' were likely to be involved in all strata of the fishing industry. There is a little Crusader church in the Old City *suq* at Jerusalem, dedicated to Zebedee's fish shop!

There were and are (broadly speaking) three kinds of fish in the lake:

The sardine or sprat – still fished and trawled at night, nowadays drawn to the surface by floodlights, canned on the other side of the Lake at Ein Gev and sold in Marks & Spencer.

The 'musht' or Peter's fish – so-called as it was the fish which Peter caught on a hook, at Jesus' command, to find the silver piece in its mouth, with which to pay tax. The young of the *musht* tend to swim back into the buccal cavity, or gills, of their parents when frightened. Consequently the parents, at spawning, tend to carry a flat stone, or any other flat round object, to block their mouths. A bright silver half-shekel would be an obvious choice (Matt. 17: 27).

The barbut or cat-fish – a formidable carnivore of smaller fish, was by Levitical Law reckoned 'unclean', being without scales or fins. It has some qualities of the snake and can live on land for up to four days. This is the fish referred to in the question: 'If he asks him for a fish, will he give him a serpent?' The *barbut*, like a barbel, is bearded – but his name comes from the 'squeak' he emits when out of water.

BOATS

The 'tools of the trade' included two kinds of boat mentioned in the New Testament story:

The fishing smack (Greek: 'Ploios') with both sails and oars, probably square-rigged sail and half a dozen thwarts for rowers – not unlike a dhow. When the wind was contrary the crew had to row into the wind. One such first century boat is to be seen today at Ginnosar.

The dinghy (Greek: 'ploiarion) with paddles, and usually towed behind the larger fishing smack, from which the dinghy could land crew in shallow water.

There are nineteen references to boats in Mark's Gospel, thirteen in Matthew, eight in Luke and thirteen in John, Chapters 6 and 21. On all occasions the functions of the kind of boat fit the context. So in John 21 Peter jumps off the bows of the fishing smack and swims ashore, while the others follow in the dinghy. James and John mend their nets in the bigger boat. Jesus gives the Parable of the Sower from the dinghy.

A first century fishing smack found in 1986
It was only on 4th February that the boat was discovered on a part of the sea-bed which had turned into dry land, due to the recession of water from a severe lack of rain. Nautical archaeologists were shown the curving profile of one side of a sunken boat, buried beneath the mud, east of the ancient port of Magdala.

They exposed a section of planks and examined the joinery of the timber, the planks being jointed with mortice and tenon, hole and dowl. This method was a hallmark of boat-building in the Mediterranean world during the Roman period. A cooking pot was found outside and an oil-lamp inside the boat; the pot dated to the first century B.C., the lamp as late as first century A.D.

The excavation of the boat presented enormous problems of security, preservation and transport. Rumours of the discovery spread fast. The timber needed to be kept wet. The boat had to be moved whole to some conservation tank. It was decided to site this near the museum in Kibbutz Nof Ginnosar and to move the boat by sea rather than helicopter. It was given a strait-jacket of polyurethane foam inside and out. Thus packaged the whole was floated round to Nof Ginnosar and lifted by crane into the tank, where for the next seven years it will soak in a wax solution of preservative – while being visible to pilgrims. When stripped of its foam covering, the boat's ribs have become clearly visible across its width of seven feet and along its length of twenty-seven feet.

NETS

And the methods of fishing and type of nets – mainly three.

The deep – for use mainly at night, trawling – the skill at which Peter was the master-craftsman. The *Mubattan* is a long trawl net about eight feet deep and kept on the surface by corks.

The drag – called by the Arabs the *jurf* or broom because it sweeps the bottom, usually used with two boats moving in an arc to enclose and then drag an area of water. The ends of the net are hauled up the beach until all kinds of fish are landed in the loop of the net. As good and bad on the day of Judgment they need sorting and weighing on the scales (Matt. 13: 47–50).

The drop – a parachute-shaped casting net, with lead weights on the fringe and a hole in the top – such as is common in many primitive fishing communities throughout the world. When Jesus called them Andrew and Peter were casting this net *'amphiblēstron'* into the shallows. They would first see and then enclose the fish, the net lightly dropping in a circle over them.

CREW

Simon Peter was the skipper of his own fishing smack. The gospels term him 'No.1' 'Ho prōtos' – the boss. His house is central in Capernaum, the market centre of the fishing industry. The earliest mosaics show him as a sturdy, craggy, trawler man with a fringe of grey hair.

What better means of training a group could Jesus have chosen, than to select and then work with a boat crew? Take the story of the 'stilling of the storm' on the lake, and it is easy to reconstruct the function and places of the crew. It was too rough and the wind was contrary. The crew sat in pairs on the thwarts, rowing into the wind with little progress.

Jesus, as the steersman, slumbers on a cushion in the stern, his arm over the tiller. Before him, in pairs, the brothers are ranged on the benches of the boat.

Peter and Andrew are on the stroke's thwart to give the rhythm and call the course. Andrew is the dinghy-man, within reach of the tow rope – and, as you may remember, always bringing people to Jesus. In the earliest Ravenna mosaics Peter pulls the net while Andrew, the larger, younger and more bovine brother, uses the paddle.

The method by which Matthew lists the apostles in pairs indicates their places in the boat. Behind Andrew and Peter are successively: The Zebedee boys – Boanerges – *James* and *John*; the Sons of Alphaeus – *Matthew* and *James* the youngest, the publicans. *Philip*, the pessimistic provisioner and *Nathaniel*, his friend from Cana; *Judas Thomas* (the twin) next to *Judas Thaddaeus* (Busty Judas); *Simon*, the Zealot and *Judas of Kerioth*.

All the last three in the bows are probably Zealots, dagger-men who became pacifists (My peace I give unto you) for Christ's sake.

What a motley crew to become the intrepid Apostles of the Early Church!

How true that Galilee – the District, the lake, the crew-training and team work, the patience and the peace of the fisherman's trade – was the greenhouse of the early Christian movement. The seed sown, the seedling planted out, nourished through the itinerant Ministry, pruned by the Passion, flowering in the forty days of Resurrection teaching, to burst like a pod at Pentecost!

THE LAKE OF GALILEE: PRESENTED CLOCKWISE

1. *Tiberias: West Coast*
   Hot sulphur spring spa.
   On site of two fenced cities of Naphthali – Hammat and Raqqat – Josh. 19: 35.
   Hammat: third- and sixth-century synagogue ruins, Tomb of Rabbi Meir. Tomb of Rabbi Akiba – martyr of Bar Cochbar revolt – west of the town.
   Tomb of Maimonides – Saladin's personal physician – town centre.
2. *Gulf of Pigeons*
   Cleft in cliff above the ancient strand of Magdala.

The prevailing west wind descends suddenly through the cleft to disturb the lake.

Possibly a breeding place for sacrificial doves.

3. *Magdala*

Lakeside township, with long strand harbour, famous for its weaving industry.

Associated with Mary Magdalene, 'last at the Cross and first at the Tomb' of Jesus.

Linked by the Catholic Church with the notorious prostitute who became the 'passionate penitent' of Luke 7: 36 and John 20: 1–18.

Tim Rice's *Jesus Christ Superstar* lyric of Mary Magdalene's song:

> I don't know how to take this.
> I don't see why he moves me.
> He's just a man; he's just a man.
> I've had so many men before.
> In very many ways, he's just one more!
> I never thought I'd come to this,
> Yet, if he said he loved me,
> I'd be lost and frightened.
> I just couldn't cope – just couldn't cope.
> I'd turn my head and back away.
> I wouldn't want to know.
> He scares me so
> I want him so
> I love him so!

> Almighty God,
> whose Son restored Mary Magdalen
>   to health of mind and body
> and called her to be a witness to his resurrection:
> forgive us and heal us by your grace,
> that we may serve you in the power of his risen life;
> who is alive and reigns with you and the Holy Spirit,
> one God, now and for ever.

4. *Plain of Gennesaret*

Market-garden of the Lakeside Townships, 680 feet below Mediterranean Level.

Banana plantations and date palms.

Overlooked by Tell Kinneret on the north side, one of many *Beth-saida*'s (the tell above the pumping station).

Good bathing at Kibbutz Nof Ginnosar, first century boat.

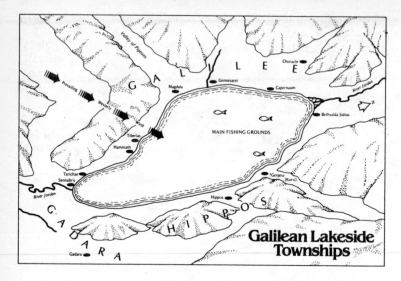

Galilean Lakeside Townships

5. *Mount of Beatitudes*
   Italian Hospice, Basilica and viewpoint – Matt. 5: 3–12.

> O blessed Lord, who on the mountain didst teach thy disciples
> the laws of thy kingdom of love: Implant this love within us, that,
> loving thee with all our heart, we may love all men for thy sake,
> to the glory of thy Name.

6. *Tabgha*
   Easy walk down to Lakeside at fresh-water springs.
   a) Church of Multiplication over two successive Byzantine
      church sites. Mosaics of flora and fauna – John 6: 1–14.
   b) Church of Peter's Primacy – Mensa Christi rock – the
      post-resurrection breakfast over a 'fire of coals' and com-
      mission of the Rock Man – John 1: 40–42 and 21: 5–24.
7. *Sower's Bay*
   Natural theatre, enclosed by a small bay and lake sounding-
   board. Reader at water's edge can be heard high up the
   hillside, and by all 'beside the sea on the land . . . "He who
   has ears to hear . . ."' Mark 4: 1–9.
8. *Capernaum*
   Frontier town headquarters of the Galilean Ministry, commer-

cial centre of the fishing towns. In the centre of the bustling waterside township:

a) The twentieth-century reconstruction of a third-century synagogue – with water canal entrance and stairway, prayer hall, gallery, Gentiles' courtyard; mixed Roman and Jewish carving motifs: Tenth Legion crest, Roman equivalent of V.C., of Ark and Manna pot – Luke 7: 1–10.

b) 'Peter house', cottage of the trawler skipper discovered 1921 outside the synagogue, mentioned by Christian pilgrims of fourth century and recently excavated to reveal first-century houses – Mark 1: 16–21, 27–32.

c) Gentiles' courtyard, with knucklebone gaming board, probably used by soldiers and with locking doorway to main prayer hall – Isa. 42: 1–7, Acts 26: 22–3, Rom. 3: 29–31.

d) Stairway of interlocking steps down to canal entrance.

e) Ruins, olive presses and basalt corn-mills – Luke 10: 15–16, John 1: 11–12.

f) Harbour jetties – scene of the call of Matthew – Matt. 9: 9, Luke 5: 27–32.

In this small area, 100 metres square, the core of the Christian Gospel was preached in parable, miracle of healing and argument. Healings include: the paralytic, Mk. 2: 1–13; the centurion's batman, Luke 7: 2; the nobleman's son, John 4: 46–54; Jairus' daughter, Mark 5: 21–43.

> Heavenly Father,
> giver of life and health:
> comfort and restore those who are sick,
> that they may be strengthened in their weakness
> and have confidence in your unfailing love;
> through Jesus Christ our Lord.

> Almighty God,
> who through your Son Jesus Christ
> called Matthew from the selfish pursuit of gain
> to become an apostle and evangelist:
> free us from all possessiveness and love of riches
> that we may follow in the steps of Jesus Christ our Lord
> who is alive and reigns with you and the Holy Spirit,
> one God, now and for ever.

9. *Jordan Delta*

Frontier between territories of Herod Antipas and Herod

Philip. A superb sanctuary for waterbirds – herons and kingfishers of many species.

The unexcavated ruins between the Delta and Kursi may be those of Beth-saida Julius.

10. *Kursi*

Scene of the dramatic exorcism of 'Legion', in the 'Land of the Gadarenes' – a place of pilgrimage since fifth century. Remains of a sizable Byzantine monastery and – nearer the Lake – traces of a first-century town and harbour – Mark 5: 1, Luke 8: 26–39.

11. *Ein Gev*

Modern Jewish kibbutz, the successful defence of which in 1947 ensured the retention of a strip of lake shore the length of the east coast for Israel. The Israeli equivalent of East Anglian Aldeburgh – with a vast concert-hall and musical tradition. This settlement has a flourishing dairy farm and forest of date palms – not to mention the fishing and canning industry. The huge Mount Susita, once the site of Hippos, a city of the Decapolis, overlooks the settlement and still boasts a Graeco-Roman forum on its summit.

NAZARETH: BOYHOOD AND FAMILY HOME

TODAY

The large, predominantly Arab town covers a hillside which commands the plains of Jezreel and Esdraelon. The Arab town since 1948 has been enfiladed by an Upper and Jewish town on the hill above. The Arab town was largely Christian until the influx of Muslim refugees during the War of Independence 1947–8. Today, Nazareth is still a centre of Christian activities with a wide range of institutions: Orthodox, Roman Catholic,

Melkite, Anglican, Baptist, Lutheran and other Protestant groups.

HISTORY

Signs of occupation on the hillside date back to patriarchal times, but by the first century Nazareth seems to have been little more than a small Orthodox township within a mile or so of the large provincial centre of Sepphoris to the north. During the youth of Jesus, the Carpenter's son, following a revolt against the Roman occupation forces, a punitive expedition crucified a large part of the population of Sepphoris. No doubt the Carpenter's son was well aware of, if not actually involved in, the process of making crosses for crucifixion.

Unlike Jerusalem and its neighbour Bethlehem, which early became Christian, Nazareth, not being linked with the Passion and Resurrection, remained Jewish. It is not mentioned by Josephus, Origen or Jerome; it seems to have been neglected by friend and foe alike. Perhaps the Lucan narratives – of the Annunciation, residence of Joseph the Carpenter and Jesus' return to the synagogue as a mature rabbi – resulted from Paul's imprisonment at Caesarea and Luke's freedom to research among the Lord's friends and relations at Nazareth.

The only member of the third-century Nazareth Christian community whose name we know was Conon, martyred during the persecution of Decius. In his defence he declared: 'I am of Nazareth, a relative of the Lord, whom I serve, as did my ancestors here.' Persecution seems to have been concentrated upon the family of Jesus, including even the first two Christian bishops of Jerusalem, James his brother and Simeon his cousin.

RECENT DISCOVERIES

Recent Franciscan excavations have resulted in exciting discoveries: in 1955, an Iron Age village and a Herodian-period network of grottos, cisterns and silos – besides glass and pottery. Not only did the excavations localise the Gospel Nazareth, but confirm the existence of successive Byzantine and Crusader complexes.

Byzantine

The Byzantine basilica was built at the expense of a converted Jew, Count Joseph of Tiberias, by a deacon from Jerusalem, called Conon. A sixth-century historian attributed the original initiative to the Empress Helena who 'turned to Nazareth and having sought the house where the Mother of God, all worthy of praise, received the Hail of the Archangel Gabriel, thereat she raised the temple of the Mother of God'.

The Byzantine church was destroyed during the Persian invasion of 614. A Jewish contingent, alongside the Persians, sacked the town which was recaptured by the Byzantines in 629.

Crusader

The Crusader church is attributed by William of Tyre (1095–1184) to Tancred, who 'founded with infinite care and endowed with vast patrimonies the churches of . . . Nazareth, Tiberias and also Mt Tabor'.

Second Century

The most sensational discovery, in 1960, was of a pre-Byzantine shrine dating back almost to Apostolic times. Some twenty squared stones, faced with plaster, bore recognisable charcoal incisions of graffiti. These included the Greek for 'Hail Mary', 'Lord', 'Christ' and many cross motifs. The outline of this primitive 'synagogue-church' is to be seen in the lower church of the modern basilica, but the main cave is the 'Mary's kitchen', which has been the central focus of all successive churches. The Upper church walls are covered with representations of Madonna and Child from all over the world.

CARPENTER'S SHOP

The exit from the Upper church faces across the courtyard and up the steps to the Church of the Carpenter's Shop, dedicated to the Holy Family. The value of this site is that of a visual aid and vivid illustration, rather than of any exact association with the Family home. Here stood a simple, single-roomed cottage, used as a workshop by day and a bedroom by night. While above, on the flat roof, a booth of green branches gave shade or shelter to those who sat or slept out on summer evenings. Below the church is a Byzantine baptistry. Below this again is a cave basement, formed by the limestone strata of the hillside, which was the kitchen and living room. In the centre was the low table round which a family reclined to eat their simple meals. Set in the floor are the openings to grain stores, carved out of the rock below. Above each store and carved in the cave wall is the staple, through which on a rope a basket could be lowered into the store below.

CHURCH OF THE WELL

Pilgrims are sometimes worried by the existence of another – the Greek Orthodox – Church of the Annunciation, over an ancient well and spring.

Their doubts may be resolved by the early Apocryphal Gospel of St James, which relates how the Archangel first tried to meet the little peasant girl – probably in her teens – as she went to draw water at the village well. Where else could a man expect to meet the much-protected, eligible daughter of an Orthodox Jewish household? The Gospel tells how she was so embarrassed at his approach that she hurried back home to her kitchen and began to spin. There again, the Archangel attempted to discharge his commission and successfully delivered his invitation.

HILLTOP

The hilltop behind the present Arab town is the natural viewpoint and picnic place of the people of the town. From here Jesus, boy and man, could read the history of his people in the surrounding scenery, seeing anew the victories of Deborah, Barak and Gideon in the plain below, the defeat of Saul and Jonathan on the mountains of Gilboa beyond. Further south is the hill country of Samaria, the capital of the Northern Kingdom, Mt Ebal and Mt Gerizim. From here he could see the long range of Carmel, where Elijah competed with the prophets of Baal, and north of which Asher kept the coastline. Down in the plain of Esdraelon is the long, low 'lion couchant' – 'Little Hill of Hermon' – of the Psalms. On its slopes are the villages of Endor and Shunem, also of Nain, the scene of Jesus' raising of the widow's only son.

SALESIAN ORPHANAGE

The hilltop is crowned appropriately with the Salesian Orphanage Chapel, above the altar of which is a statue of the boy Jesus. It is a lovely figure of a lad of about sixteen years, with sensitive features and the eyes of a poet. At first glance he seems to be walking the hilltop, dreaming of the Kingdom of God, but at second glance he seems a very shrewd young Hebrew whose lessons have been learnt in the market place of this commercial and cosmopolitan market town overlooking the highway of the ancient world.

Is it far fetched to think of the Nazareth upbringing and experience as providing a useful preparation for his open-air itinerant Ministry and even for those last few fateful days avoiding arrest in Jerusalem?

SYNAGOGUE DRAMA

Within the hilltop view, looking towards Jezreel, a precipitous hill on the near skyline has been associated with the story of Jesus' near execution – following the riot on his return to speak in the synagogue. Within the town *suq* is a Melkite church, reputedly on the site of an early synagogue. It was Jesus' striking choice and application to himself of the Messianic passage, Isaiah Chapter 61: 'The spirit of the Lord is upon me!' that evoked the scandalised protest: 'Is not this the Carpenter's Son?' The 'eyes of all were fastened upon him' as he went on to castigate them for their lack of faith in him: 'No prophet is accepted in his own country.' Rising up in fury, they expelled him from the town, leading him to the 'brow of the hill whereon their city was built' that they might cast him down. The 'Hill of Precipitation' may appear too far out to be appropriate, but its crag could well have been the local 'Execution Hill'. On either side of it are two chapels 'of the Fright' – one Orthodox, one Catholic – commemorating a legendary fainting of Mary, the Mother of Jesus, as the crowd returned without her son, who had 'passed through the midst of them'.

The Highland Route north, via Samaria, to Galilee – along the spine of Judaea. pp144 ff.

A Samaritan High Priest reading a scroll of the Torah in the Samaritan script. p149.

Jacob's Well near Samaria, an undisputed site nearly 4,000 years old. p150.

The 'Parable of the Sower', given from a boat at the water's edge of a bay with the Lake as a natural sounding board. p168.

The Parable is illustrated by the soil, the rock, the thistles and crops on the hillsides above and around the bay.

The modern Italianate basilica on the traditional site of the Sermon on the Mount. p164.

The blind man at Bethsaida saw 'men like trees walking'. So the trees march across the Bethsaida skyline today. p165.

Lake-view from the Mount of Beatitudes.

Left: Part of triple doorway into the synagogue at Capernaum, a 3rd century reconstruction, with 1st century materials. p165.

Below: Early basalt olive press, among the ruins of Capernaum, whose destruction Jesus predicted. p165.

The possible regimental crest of X Legion, the eagles suspend a victor's laurel wreath. p173.

The synagogue at Capernaum with steps leading up from a lake inlet and a women's gallery above. p166.

Ark of the Covenant on wheels motif. Mobility on the Exodus! p173.

Manna-pot stone motif: 'Your fathers did eat manna in the wilderness'. p173.

Above: Upper Church of the Annunciation, over 'Mary's Kitchen', with murals of the Universal Church. p176.

Left: View from The Hill of Precipitation, where Jesus escaped execution. p178.

Below: Summer flowers: marguerite, poppy, flax.

Roman aqueduct at Caesarea Maritima, carrying water from Mount Carmel to the Roman base port and barracks. p187.

St George's Desert monastery within the Wadi Qelt, once Brook Cherith. p122.

Excavations of Herod the Great's Winter Palace at Jericho, with protecting fort in the background. p122.

The ancient and Crusader harbour at Acre once held eighty sizeable ships at a time. p192.

The Crusader sea walls withstood many attackers from Saladin to Napoleon. p192.

The underground refectory of the Knights Hospitaller. p194.

NAZARETH

1. *Orthodox Church of the Annunciation and St Mary's Well*
Original village water supply in Crusader crypt. Note steep steps from road level down to water are carved in rock. Down here came the women of days gone by. Among them, perhaps, a young toddler clinging tightly to the flowing dress of his teenager mother.
– Apocryphal Gospel of St James.
2. *Village fountain today*
The same spring water piped under the street to the crossroads.
3. *Franciscan Church of the Annunciation*
   a) Synagogue Church in lower church.
   b) Graffiti board showing second-century 'Hail Mary' etc.
   c) Cave crypt of St Mary's Kitchen.
   d) Upper church, mural and East End mosaics
   e) Museum and excavations
   – Luke 1: 26–38
4. *Church of the Carpenter's Shop*
Baptistry and Grottos.
   – Luke 2: 39–40
5. *Melkite Church of the Synagogue*
   – Luke 4: 16–30
6. *Christchurch (Anglican) within* suq
7. *Salesian Orphanage Chapel on hilltop*

> We beseech you, O Lord,
> to pour your grace into our hearts;
> that as we have known the incarnation
>   of your Son Jesus Christ
> by the message of an angel,
> so by his cross and passion
> we may be brought to the glory of his resurrection;
> through Jesus Christ our Lord.

> Almighty God,
> who called Joseph to be the husband of the Virgin Mary,
> and the guardian of your only Son:
> open our eyes and our ears
> to the messages of your holy will,
> and give us the courage to act upon them;
> through Jesus Christ our Lord.

CANA OF GALILEE SCENE OF THE MARRIAGE FEAST

HOLY PLACES

Six kilometres along the road from Nazareth to Tiberias is the Arab village of Kefar-Kanna, the disputed site of Jesus' first miracle at the Wedding Feast of Cana, when he turned the water into wine. A medieval tradition favoured Khirbet Kanna for the site of Cana, but a Byzantine tradition is evident at Kefar-Kanna.

Latin Church

In the Latin church there is an old Hebrew mosaic inscription, probably of the third or fourth century, which says: 'Honoured be the memory of Yosef, son of Tanhum, son of Buta and his sons who made this mosaic, may it be a blessing for them. Amen.' This Yosef was probably the converted Jew, Joseph of Tiberias, of Constantine's period, on whom Constantine conferred the title of count and who founded many churches in Galilee. The church possibly stands, therefore, on the site of the old synagogue. In its early days it still held what were believed to be the relics of the marriage feast. In 570, Antonius of Piacenza visited Cana where, as he records, 'Our Lord was at the wedding, and we reclined upon his very couch upon which I, unworthy that I am, wrote the names of my parents!' It is customary to condemn the vulgarity of modern tourists who cover walls with their graffiti, and perhaps in these days of easy travel it should be condemned, but at Cana, as indeed at Bethlehem and at Jerusalem, early pilgrims thought it no vulgarity to write up their names on holy walls, and the inscriptions and crosses of crusading soldiers on the stairs up from the Chapel of St Helena at the Holy Sepulchre are a moving memorial.

Orthodox Church

From the level of the mosaic within the Latin church, steps lead down into a crypt containing a cistern. Perhaps the synagogue enclosed ritual washing facilities. There is an old pitcher, with no claim to authenticity but which serves to illustrate the story. On the opposite side of the village street is the Orthodox Church of the Marriage Feast in which stands a large and ancient water jar, again with no pretensions to direct association with the story. Further east along the same street is the Franciscan Chapel of St Nathaniel Bar-Tolmai, an apostle of Jesus and a native of Cana.

ORDER OF VISIT

As follows, if approaching from Tiberias. Reverse, if approaching from Nazareth.

House of Nathaniel Bartholomew
The Orthodox Jew, meditating under his fig tree or reading Jacob's dream of the ladder between earth and heaven, wrestled with rumours of an upstart Messiah from Nazareth, over the hill.

Philip introduced him to Jesus, who reached into his very prayers and evoked his confession: 'You really are the Messiah.' He was flayed alive at Albanopolis in Armenia and commemorated as the figure, with his own pelt, in the foreground of the Sistine Chapel mural. John 1:43–51 and hymn 'Nearer my God to Thee'.

Franciscan Church of the Marriage Feast
Synagogue inscription 'Joseph, Tanhum's Son'. Third- or fourth-century Byzantine mosaics and cistern top. John 2: 1–11 or John 4: 46–54.

Greek Orthodox Church of the Marriage Feast
John 2: 1–11 or John 4: 46–54.

MEDITATION ON MARY

Mary is the person whose holiness is expressed in simple faith and obedience. Millions of Christians the world over and down the centuries, Roman Catholic, Orthodox, Monophisite, Anglican, Protestant have been attracted in a very special way to her son Jesus by the holiness of this little Jewess.

Her patience and simplicity, humility and obedience, faith and love still inspire both Christians and Muslims, who share the shrine of her tomb in the Kedron Valley.

She was betrothed, when still in her teens, to the local carpenter. She was chosen by God to be the means of his arrival into his world, to be his channel, as the Mother of Jesus. She was invited and she obediently accepted to share God's will and purpose for mankind – even at the cost of becoming an unmarried mother in an Orthodox Jewish community.

Mary is to the Christian Church what Abraham is to both Jews and Muslims – the person whose obedience to God's call enabled his coming to his people. As Abraham was the first of a team of twelve patriarchs, so Mary was the first of a team of twelve apostles, with whom she received the Spirit at Pentecost.

In the Old Testament, the presence of God was thought to be conveyed within the Ark of the Lord; so in the New Testament Mary is the Ark by whom God is present with us – Emmanuel.

In the lovely story of the Annunciation, notice what happened: the awe and reverence of the Archangel before the little peasant girl, the moment of silence when he puts his proposal and awaits her consent and finally the stupendous humility and simplicity of her 'fiat': 'I am the Lord's servant – let it happen to me!' In that moment the Spirit descended and God's plan had already been transformed into action.

Mary generated Jesus in her midst and brought him forth into his world. 'The Word became flesh'. She made a home for him first within her own body, then in the cottage at Nazareth. She carried him, fed him, cleaned and clothed him – and he was God. She cared for him and cultivated his character – and he was God. Under her influence, 'he grew in wisdom and stature, in favour with God and men'. Through it all, her life was a perpetual losing and finding. Puzzled and perplexed, crowded out of her own Son's presence, at Capernaum, on the Via Dolorosa, at the foot of the Cross, in the Upper Room, even at Easter and Pentecost, the sword turned in her soul.

Consider that, if Jesus' sense and experience of the loving Fatherhood of God was the basis of all his personal prayer and teaching – just what must have been his respect and reverence for his mother? Should we not share his feelings for her, to whom the Archangel said – 'Hail Mary, full of grace, the Lord is with thee. Blessed art thou among women'? Should we not recognise her as the Mother of both the Man and the Church – and like John bar Zebedee beneath the cross – take her into our own home and affections. Do not let Jesus have to introduce us with: 'Oh, I don't think you know my Mother!'

MOUNT TABOR
SCENE OF THE
TRANSFIGURATION

TABOR OR HERMON

Some nine kilometres east of Nazareth the Hill of Tabor rises 588 metres above the Plain of Jezreel. This remarkable hump-backed feature is one of the possible sites of the transfiguration of Jesus, the spiritual experience which strengthened him for his final journey to Jerusalem. The other possible site is Mount Hermon, on the Anti-Lebanon range. If this latter site conforms more to the description of a high snow-clad mountain near Caesarea Philippi (Banias), it is Tabor which can claim the Byzantine tradition. There are reasons, however, for believing that this tradition may have been mistaken. From the times of Barak and Deborah, whose name is recorded still in that of the village of Daburiyah at the foot of Tabor, Tabor has been of tactical, if not strategic, importance. In the first book of Chronicles, it is referred to as a Levite settlement and must have been a fortified stronghold. In the year 218 B.C. Antiochus the Greek captured it, and as late as 100 B.C. Alexander Jannaeus conquered it. In A.D. 66, only some thirty-six years after the transfiguration, the whole stretch of hillside, 1300 metres by 300 metres, was enclosed by Josephus with a still recognisable encircling wall. It would seem unlikely that the transfiguration, as described in the Gospels on a silent, snow-clad mountain, could have taken place on this fortified stronghold, overlooking the great high road through the Plain of Esdraelon.

BYZANTINE TRADITION

An early Palestinian tradition linking this remarkable hill with the story of Jesus' transfiguration was universally accepted in the fourth century. On the summit, three churches were built in the sixth century, in memory of the three booths which Peter wished to set up for Jesus, Moses and Elijah. They were visited by the pilgrims Antoninus and Arculf. In the twelfth century, the Cru-

saders built a church incorporating a deep-lying apse of Byzantine origin, perhaps as their crypt. On each side of this there was a
chapel and one of these is still clearly visible. On the top of the hill
there is a long thin plateau; on the eastern end of this are the
churches overlooking the Plain of Ahmra and the Lake of Galilee.
The modern Franciscan basilica, erected in 1921–3, incorporated
portions of the Crusader and Byzantine churches. Nearby is the
Greek Church of the Holy Elijah, built in 1911, next to a traditional
cave of the mysterious Melchizedek. This last church covers the
site of a fourth-century basilica, some of whose mosaics are still
preserved. Mark 9: 2–9. Luke 9: 28–36.

> Almighty Father,
> whose Son was revealed in majesty
>   before he suffered death upon the cross:
> give us faith to perceive his glory,
> that we may be strengthened to suffer with him
> and be changed into his likeness, from glory to glory;
> who is alive and reigns with you and the Holy Spirit,
> one God, now and for ever.

MEGIDDO – HILL OF BATTLES
ESDRAELON THE
BATTLEFIELD

The Prophet Ezekiel wrote: 'Thus saith the Lord God: This is
Jerusalem. I have set it in the midst of the nations and countries
that are round about here.'

Strategically, Palestine was the centre of the ancient world,
lying on the routes between Egypt, Babylon, Persia, Greece and
finally Rome. In fact it was virtually the crossroads between the
early civilisations. The geography of the country is remarkably
simple. Running from west to east, the pattern is coastal plain,
foothills, spine and mountainous desert descending to the Rift
Valley far below sea level, through which runs the River Jordan.

Megiddo

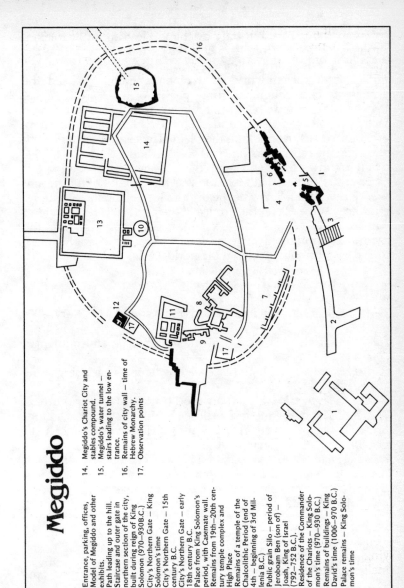

1. Entrance, parking, offices, Model of Megiddo and other exhibits.
2. Path leading up to the hill.
3. Staircase and outer gate in northern section of the city, built during reign of King Solomon (970–930 B.C.).
4. City's Northern Gate — King Solomon's time
5. City's Northern Gate — 15th century B.C.
6. City's Northern Gate — early 18th century B.C.
7. Palace from King Solomon's period, with Casemate wall.
8. Remains from 19th–20th century temple complex and High Place
9. Remains of a temple of the Chalcolithic Period (end of 4th — beginning of 3rd Millenia B.C.)
10. Public grain Silo — period of Jeroboam Ben (son of) — Joash, King of Israel (792–752 B.C.).
11. Residence of the Commander of the Chariots — King Solomon's time (970–930 B.C.)
12. Remains of buildings — King David's time (1006–970 B.C.)
13. Palace remains — King Solomon's time
14. Megiddo's Chariot City and stables compound.
15. Megiddo's water tunnel — stairs leading to the low entrance.
16. Remains of city wall — time of Hebrew Monarchy.
17. Observation points

This pattern is broken only by the fertile plain of Esdraelon, running south-east from Carmel to the Jordan. Below Carmel the coastal plain is reduced to a narrow bottleneck avoided by the armies of the ancient world, as an obvious ambush. Instead, the armies struck through the three passes of the Carmel range, between the coastal plain and the plain of Esdraelon. These tactical passes were commanded on the Esdraelon approach by great fortresses overlooking the plain. The central fortress commanding the central passage was Har Medeiddo, the hill of battles – better known to us as Megiddo, the scene of Armageddon. It can be thus argued that Megiddo was the cock-pit of the ancient world, that Esdraelon is the theatre and Jezreel the stage, with set entrances and exits for the armies of the great empires. Megiddo was for much of the Old Testament period controlled from the mountain stronghold of Jerusalem. Solomon's chariot system included enormous stables at Megiddo, Gezer and Hazor.

HISTORY OF SITE

Earliest settlement, Neolithic period, flints and early pottery, 4000 B.C.

Later settlement, pavement drawings of animals and hunters *c.* 3000 B.C.

Early Canaanite cities, high places, stone temples enclosing stone altars, *c.* 2000 B.C.

Hyksos 'Shepherd Kings', import mud-brick and own culture, *c.* 1700 B.C. The entire mound enclosed within an enormous mud-brick city wall, thirteen feet thick and still in places ten feet high. Cobbled streets, burials under houses, children in jar burials.

New Egyptian imperial occupation, 1479 B.C. Pharaoh Thutmosis III defeats the king of Kadesh, after forced march across the Sinai Desert. A rich and flourishing period, ornaments of ivory and gold and well-built palaces.

Hebrew invasion. 'Habiru' marauders mentioned in Tel el Amarna Cuneiform Tablets, written by the Governor of Megiddo requesting help from the Pharaoh of Egypt and quoting the fall of the neighbouring fortress of Ta'anach. Deborah defeats the army of Jabin, king of Hazor under Sisera at the waters of Megiddo, 1100 B.C.

Philistine occupation, household utensils and furnishings reflect culture, 1000 B.C.

City fortified by Solomon, huge stone city wall, iron gates, well-

paved streets, stabling for 500 horses in this 'Chariot city', 950 B.C.
I Kgs 9: 15–19.
Division of the Kingdoms, Shishak of Egypt invades Judea and
Samaria, 925 B.C. I Kgs 14: 25.
Ahaziah, king of Juda, killed at Megiddo by Jehu, 843 B.C. 2 Kgs 9: 27.
Conquest by Tiglath-Pilezer III of Assyria, 732 B.C.
Josiah, King of Juda, killed at Megiddo by Pharaoh Necho, 610 B.C. 2
Kgs 23: 29–30; 2 Chr. 35: 30–34.
The Traditional Hill of Battles, 'Har-Mageddon' or 'Armageddon',
from its strategic position commanding the 'Way of the Sea'. Rev.
16: 16.

SUGGESTED ORDER OF VIEWING (AS CLEARLY MARKED ON SITE)

Model Room in Curator's building – to the east of the tell.
Iron Age gateway – on the north side.
Canaanite temple area – with circular stone altar, to the south.
Grain silos of eighth century – in the centre of the tell.
Chariot stables, a garrison headquarters under Solomon, Omri and
Ahab, on the west.
The water shaft, underground conduit and cave well – emerging on to
the plain outside the north-west of the city perimeter. This is the
most impressive feature of the whole magnificent site and must
not be missed. Vehicles can await visitors at the cave-well exit.

CAESAREA MARITIMA

IN SCRIPTURE

St Peter Baptised Cornelius
A Roman centurion of the Italian band, stationed at Caesarea in
the great Roman harbour fortress, was the first Gentile to be

baptised a Christian. Prompted by a vision, he sent messengers to Simon Peter, at the house of Simon the Tanner in Joppa (Jaffa) thirty-two miles to the south. Peter, also prompted by a vision ('What God has cleansed, that call not thou unclean'), at first hesitating to visit a Gentile, yet was reassured and accompanied the messengers back to Caesarea. There, he baptised Cornelius together with a number of his Gentile companions, who spoke with tongues and received the Holy Spirit to the astonishment of the Jewish Christians (Acts 10).

St Philip 'the Evangelist's' mission

In the year 58, St Paul and St Luke were entertained by Philip and his four daughters, on Paul's final and fateful journey to Jerusalem. Philip was the first missionary to the maritime plain and had settled in Caesarea, the administrative capital of the districts of Judea and Samaria, some twenty years before. Philip and Paul were both apostles to Gentiles (Acts 21: 8–10).

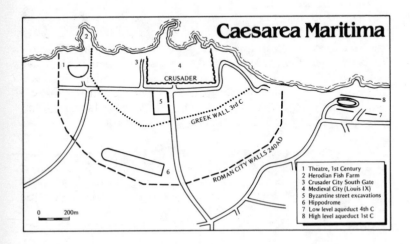

Caesarea Maritima

CRUSADER

GREEK WALL 3rd C

ROMAN CITY WALLS 240AD

1 Theatre, 1st Century
2 Herodian Fish Farm
3 Crusader City South Gate
4 Medieval City (Louis IX)
5 Byzantine street excavations
6 Hippodrome
7 Low level aqueduct 4th C
8 High level aqueduct 1st C

0   200m

St Paul and St Luke imprisoned

Paul was sent down under escort by Claudius Lysias to Caesarea to await trial before the procurator Felix. Eventually brought to trial, Paul, detained for two whole years, was left in chains by Felix to his successor Festus. Knowing that he was unlikely to obtain justice from the new procurator under Jewish diplomatic pressure, Paul appealed – as was his right as a Roman citizen – to be tried in Rome by the Emperor himself. He again defended himself before Herod Agrippa and his Queen Bernice, who declared his innocence. Having appealed to Caesar, Paul was despatched by sea to Rome under the escort of another centurion, Julius (Acts 23: 23–6 ff.).

St Luke gathers his Gospel

During the two years of Paul's imprisonment under Felix, Luke, under Paul's direction, would be free to travel inland to meet Mary the Mother of Jesus and other apostles, to gain first hand information for his Gospel.

HISTORY

Early Occupations of this Site

These began with the building of a fortress by one of the kings of Sidon, during the Persian period of the sixth century B.C. 'Strato's Tower', as it was called, formed an intermediate port of call between Dor and Joppa and was regarded by Egyptian merchants as one of the most important on the coastline. In the second century B.C. the port was captured by Alexander Jannaeus and incorporated into the Hasmonaean kingdom.

The Roman Occupation

This began with the capture of the port by Pompey, who severed the coastal cities from Judea and gave them some measure of independence under the Roman governor of Syria. Augustus later gave the coastal region to Herod.

In 22 B.C. Herod began to build a magnificent city and deep-water harbour. Twelve years later he named the new city Caesarea and its port Sebastos (the Greek form of Augustus). An excellent road linked the port with Jerusalem, through Antipatris (now near Ras-El-Ain). The city covered an area of three square kilometres and included some magnificent public buildings: a temple of Augustus, theatre, amphitheatre and hippodrome, with a fortified harbour and aqueducts. At this time, Caesarea was a Gentile city with an influential Jewish minority.

When Herod's son Archilaus was exiled, Judea became a Roman province ruled by procurators, whose official residence was at Caesarea. Pontius Pilate and his successors came up from Caesarea to 'stand to' with their troops in Jerusalem at times of national emergency and festivals. So it was that he was present in Jerusalem over Passover for the trial of Christ. Here in Caesarea, Paul appeared before the procurators Festus and Felix. In the year A.D. 66, according to Josephus, 20,000 Jews were massacred – from a total population of 50,000 – in disturbances which culminated in the destruction of Jerusalem in A.D. 70. After the war, Vespasian granted the city the status of a colony. In fact, he was in Caesarea when he was proclaimed emperor.

Following the Bar Cochbar rebellion, Rabbi Akiba was imprisoned and executed here. In the third century Origen taught and studied here, and Eusebius the historian was bishop of Caesarea in the following century.

The Crusader Occupation
This began with the conquest of the city by Baldwin I in 1101. Louis IX of France fortified the very much smaller Crusader city with the walls and moat still to be seen today. In 1265 the Sultan Beybars captured and destroyed the city, which was not repaired until the nineteenth century under the Turks.

SUGGESTED ORDER OF VISIT

Roman perimeter wall and hippodrome
South Theatre
Crusader town and harbour
Byzantine excavations
Amphitheatre and aqueducts.

These have all been magnificently excavated by the Israeli Government Department of Antiquities.

Recent underwater excavations have revealed the long stone jetties of Herod's vast harbour – now sunk a quarter of a mile off shore.

Almighty God,
who caused the light of the gospel
    to shine throughout the world
through the preaching of your servant Saint Paul:
grant that we who celebrate his wonderful conversion
may follow him in bearing witness to your truth;
through Jesus Christ our Lord.

MOUNT CARMEL

The long and undulating range of Carmel (the name means
'garden') was once covered by prehistoric forest and still boasts
today an incredible variety of flora and fauna – including wolves!
If any part of Palestine has rain, Carmel does (1 Kgs 18: 41).

The Carmel skeletons to be seen in the Rockefeller Museum in
Jerusalem were found in the caves of the Wadi Maghara, near
Athlit. Here primitive man lived, wore beads and killed his
enemies some 300,000 years ago.

Today, there are a number of Druze villages on Carmel and the
Druze town of Daliyat-El-Carmel up on the ridge some twenty
kilometres south of Haifa. The Druzes began as a heretical sect
from Islam, defying the mad Fatimite Khalifa at the close of the
tenth century A.D., under the teaching of a Muslim missionary
called Darazi – hence the name 'Druze'.

Near the Druze town of Daliyat is the traditional Place of
Sacrifice, now marked by a Franciscan convent with a superb
view of the plain of Esdraelon and southern Galilee. It is a
magnificently appropriate and graphic site for Elijah's important
and significant victory for Yahweh over the Canaanite Baalim. (1
Kgs 18: 19 ff. and 40 ff.)

The slaughter of the prophets of the Tyrian Baal took place by
the Brook Kishon in the plain below. The pilgrim planning to visit
the Place of Sacrifice will need to allow plenty of time on the steep

and winding roads. Distances are deceptive, on Carmel! (Amos 9: 3, Isa. 35: 2; S. of S. 7: 5.)

The Carmelite Order, founded in the twelfth century, has its headquarters at Stella Carmel, the centre of devotion to Our Lady of Mount Carmel.

ACRE – ONE-TIME CAPITAL OF THE CRUSADER KINGDOM

Until the nineteenth century Acre was the most important sea port on this coastline and it is still a medieval city, in total contrast to the modern port of Haifa.

EARLY HISTORY

Originally, a Canaanite town on Tel El Fukhar, a mile inland on a strategic mound, Akko, was captured by the Egyptian pharaohs Thutmosis III and Rameses II, and also mentioned in the nineteenth century Egyptian 'Curses'. The harbour and town were successively occupied by Phoenicians, Persians, Greeks and again by Egypt, at which time Ptolemy renamed the city 'Ptolemais'. This is the name mentioned by St Luke, in Acts, as the port at which St Paul and St Luke called on their way to Rome. The emperors Augustus and Vespasian visited the city in 30 B.C. and A.D. 67 respectively. The city flourished in the Byzantine and Omayyad periods.

FIRST CRUSADE

The First Crusade landed on the beaches south of the port, but never took the city until 1104. From then on, it became the main port of the Latin Kingdom of Jerusalem and harboured ships from

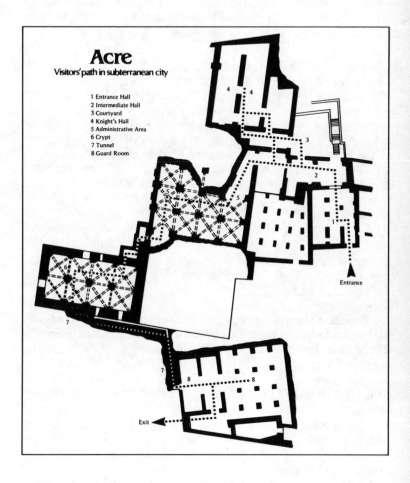

Acre
Visitors' path in subterranean city

1 Entrance Hall
2 Intermediate Hall
3 Courtyard
4 Knight's Hall
5 Administrative Area
6 Crypt
7 Tunnel
8 Guard Room

Entrance

Exit

Venice and Genoa, Pisa and Amalfi – bringing stores, pilgrims and soldiers from Europe.

HOSPITALLERS' HEADQUARTERS

The Orders of Chivalry established their headquarters: the Hospitallers in an underground fortress at Acre, still to be seen, and the Templars in the Aqsa Mosque at Jerusalem. The former, the Knights of St John, gave the name 'St Jean d'Acre' to the city and were primarily responsible for the health and accommodation of pilgrims. The latter were primarily responsible for the security, defence and travel arrangements of pilgrims. Each maritime nation and each order established trading depots and hospices within their own jealously guarded quarters of the city.

CAPITAL OF THE KINGDOM

With the fall of Jerusalem and Crusader defeat at the Horns of Hattin, Acre surrendered to Saladin in the same year, 1187, but was recaptured by Richard Coeur de Lion four years later after a vicious siege. Acre replaced Jerusalem as capital of the Kingdom for the next century, the saintly King Louis IX of France; Francis of Assisi; and Marco Polo all landed here before the fall of the city to the Mamelukes in 1291.

RECENT HISTORY

For more detail of the Crusader siege and occupation, see the chapter on the Crusades, p. 197 and of the subsequent Muslim occupation, see Provincial Shrines of Islam, p. 139. In 1799, following his defeat at the Battle of the Nile, Napoleon Bonaparte failed to capture Acre, when his artillery was sunk by the British Admiral Sir Sidney Smith off the Cape of Carmel. The British finally took the city from the Turks in 1918. During the Mandate and particularly during the last World War, members of the Irgun and other underground movements were imprisoned and executed in the citadel-fortress, which still has eighteenth-century cannonballs buried in its walls. Today, the Arab township is almost surrounded by Jewish suburbs and the citadel cells have become a museum of Israeli heroism.

ACRE TODAY

The pilgrim can easily grasp the strategic importance of the town as both port and fortress through the centuries. Although there is little trace above ground of Crusader fortifications – except for the lower courses of masonry in sea and land walls, and corner towers – yet the pilgrim can easily visualise the Crusader fosses and ramparts from the remaining but more recent fortifications.

Among many items of interest and best seen in this order are:

The River Belus – Wadi Naamin, two kilometres south of town – whose sand was used in Phoenician glass factories and which was famous for the shells of murex, used for making the famous Tyrian purple dye.

The White Bazaar – the Suq el Abyad – eighteenth-century, near the Land Gate.

Jazzar's Mosque – largest in Israel – eighteenth-century, at the end of bazaar.

The underground fortress headquarters of the Knights of St John including entrance hall, inner hall, courtyard, knights' quarter, administrative offices, refectory (crypt), escape tunnel and guardroom.

Ancient Inns: Khan El 'Umdan, El Faranj and Esh-Shawarda.

Sea and land walls and fortifications, Tower of Flies prison. The sea gate and southerly harbour, used by St Paul and St Luke, when Acre was called Ptolemais (Acts 21: 7).

The citadel – Burj el Khazna, many times destroyed and rebuilt, includes the old Turkish arsenal and barracks – in Mandate times a prison and asylum, and Crusader vaults still below the prison.

Aqueduct from the north; Jazzar and Suleiman Pasha, eighteenth century.

Tel El Fukhar: east of town, the strategic headquarters of all besieging forces, including those of kings Guy, Louis and Richard Coeur de Lion, Mamelukes and Napoleon.

CRUSADER CASTLES ACCESSIBLE FROM ACRE

Early in the thirteenth century a great part of the Acre district of Galilee passed into the hands of the Teutonic Order, the German order of chivalry which was founded on the model of the Templars and Hospitallers soon after the recapture of Acre. With the support of the German Emperor Frederick II, the Teutonic Knights purchased the rights of the feudal lords and acquired:

Three Castles
1 The King's castle – the village of Mi'ilya near Tarshiha.
2 Montfort – the present Qual'at El Qurein on the Wadi Qarn.
3 Judin – now the well-excavated castle of Jiddin.

These three form a triangle dominating the coastal plain. The site of Judin is now marked by a later adaptation of the original Crusader castle. Montfort, the northernmost of the three, was the depot and treasury of the Teutonic Order, and has the most Crusader remains. It was heavily damaged, when besieged and captured by the Mameluke Sultan Beybars in 1271. It was not afterwards occupied. Of the castle at Mi'ilya, little remains but a single Crusader hall on the side of the village facing Tarshiha.

Montfort
The Teutonic Castle of Montfort can be reached from Mi'ilya, along an ancient road or track to the north-west for about three kilometres. The pilgrim should keep to the right-hand descent into the Wadi Qarn. The castle occupies the shoulder of a spur jutting out into the wadi. A rock-cut ditch or fosse cuts it off from the higher ground on the east. West of this, the main buildings stand along the ridge in a line end to end. Highest of all is the keep – a massive square tower built of large well-dressed blocks. Below this are the knights' lodgings, then the chapel and the hall – once vaulted on a huge octagonal pier – and finally the commander's residence, flanked by one tall and well-preserved tower.

On the slope of the hill below this there remain parts of the outer ring wall, which surrounded the castle at that level. At the bottom of the valley below the castle, there is a large gothic grange. Opposite this are remains of a dam and aqueduct which probably brought water to a well in the ground floor of the grange.

A contemporary Arabic account of the siege of 1271 describes the undermining of the defences, stone by stone!

Jiddin

The Teutonic castle of Judin was already in ruins by 1284, but in the late eighteenth century was largely reconstructed on the old foundations by Daher el 'Omar. As it stands today, the castle consists of an upper and lower court. The upper court contains the principal buildings – the lower the farm accommodation. Only one remains of the two Crusader towers, but much of the basement vaulting is of Crusader workmanship.

The domed reception hall and fireplace, the surrounding quarters, the round towers and enclosing walls belong to a feudal residence of the Turkish period.

THE CRUSADES – A BRIEF HISTORY

GODFREY DE BOUILLON

In response to the call to reopen and secure the pilgrimage routes, the First Crusade set out in 1097. After marching down from Syria, they by-passed Acre and captured Jerusalem in 1099. They breached the wall to the north-east of the city – the only place where the ground level was higher outside than inside the wall. They cut their way through to the site of Calvary and, sheathing their dripping swords, fell upon their knees. Their cruel massacre of the city's inhabitants appalled the Muslims, whose preachers proclaimed revenge and the recovery from the Infidel of the site of the Prophet's heavenly flight. The leader of the First Crusade was Godfrey de Bouillon, who was elected ruler of the city, with the title of 'Defender of the Holy Sepulchre'. There is an impress-

The Crusading Period
Map & Town plans

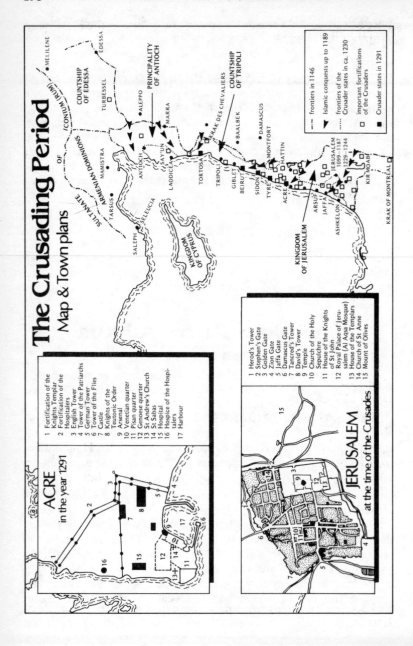

MELITENE

COUNTSHIP
OF EDESSA

EDESSA

TURBESSEL

PRINCIPALITY
OF ANTIOCH

COUNTY OF (CONIUM (RUM))

ALEPPO

KRAK DES CHEVALIERS

COUNTSHIP
OF TRIPOLI

MARRA

SULTANATE

ARMENIAN DOMINIONS

MAMISTRA

TARSUS

ANTIOCH

SAVÜN

LAODICEA

BAALBEK

DAMASCUS

MONTFORT

SELEUCIA

SALEPH

TORTOSA

TRIPOLI

GIBLET

BEIRUT

SIDON

TYRE

HATTIN

ACRE

JERUSALEM
1099–1187
1229–1244

KINGDOM
OF CYPRUS

KINGDOM
OF JERUSALEM

ARSUF

JAFFA

ASHKELON

KIR MOAB

KRAK OF MONTREAL

— · — frontiers in 1146

◣ Islamic conquests up to 1189

······ frontiers of the
Crusader states in ca. 1230

▢ important fortifications
of the Crusaders

■ Crusader states in 1291

ACRE
in the year 1291

1 Fortification of the
  Knights Templar
2 Fortification of the
  Hospitalers
3 English Tower
4 Tower of the Patriarchs
5 German Tower
6 Tower of the Flies
7 Castle
8 Knights of the
  Teutonic Order
9 Arsenal
10 Venetian quarter
11 Pisan quarter
12 Genoese quarter
13 St Andrew's Church
14 St Sabas
15 Hospital
16 Hospice of the Hospi-
   talers
17 Harbour

JERUSALEM
at the time of the Crusades

1 Herod's Tower
2 Stephen's Gate
3 Golden Gate
4 Zion Gate
5 Jaffa Gate
6 Damascus Gate
7 Tancred's Tower
8 David's Tower
9 Temple
10 Church of the Holy
   Sepulchre
11 House of the Knights
   of St John
12 Royal Palace of Jeru-
   salem (Al Aqsa Mosque)
13 House of the Templars
14 Church of St Anne
15 Mount of Olives

ive portrait, together with his sword and spurs, in the Franciscan vestry of the Holy Sepulchre.

KINGDOM OF JERUSALEM

Godfrey's successors, Baldwin I and II, established a kingdom of Jerusalem, defended by a series of forts and castles, ultimately extended to join up with the Christian states of Edessa, Tripoli and Antioch. Apart from the period of the Crusader Kingdom of Jerusalem, Palestine ceased to have an identity of its own from the Arab conquest in the seventh century to the Mandate in the twentieth century! As in Roman times, Palestine was regarded as South Syria. During the Crusader Kingdom, two Orders of Knights were created. The Templars – originally guardians of the temple – had their headquarters at the erstwhile Church of St Mary in the temple area, which the Muslim had changed into the present Mosque el Aqsa – the mosque more remote from Mecca and Medina. Here the Templars kept their stables and armoury, establishing the Dome of the Rock as their chapel, whose altar surmounted the rock itself. The Templars also policed the pilgrim routes and provided escorts for pilgrims. The Order of Hospitallers, as their name suggests, were responsible for the care of pilgrim routes. Their headquarters was a large hospice and hospital in Jerusalem. Today, their successors are the Order of St John of Jerusalem, who have a large new ophthalmic hospital, in the Sheikh Jarrah quarter – to the north of the Old City.

The main port of the Latin kingdom of the Crusaders was Acre, the lesser ports Jaffa and Caesarea. Tyre and Ascalon were still held strongly by the Fatimite rulers of Egypt. Both Hospitallers and Templars had establishments at Acre and an eye witness in 1172 describes the port with eighty ships at anchor. Another Muslim traveller tells of the Christian customs clerks writing and speaking in Arabic. He comments too on their courtesy and upon the grandeur and traffic of the town: 'It resembles Constantinople!'

DEFEAT AT HATTIN

In 1144, the Turkish prince Zanki captured the Christian state of Edessa. A Second Crusade failed to recover it. Christian influence began to wane in Syria. The Sultan Saladin annexed Damascus and became the greatest enemy of the Crusaders. In the mid-summer of 1187, during a *khamsin* (a hot desert wind) the Crusaders in full armour suffered a crippling defeat from the lightly horsed and mailed Saracens at the Horns of Hattin in Galilee. The Crusaders rallied to the Frankish Knights on the crest of the hill, but the Saracens set light to the surrounding camel-thorn and scrub. The Crusaders left the field of battle and were allowed to embark from their ports with military honours. This disastrous engagement marked the end of the Latin kingdom and Jerusalem returned once more to Muslim control.

FALL OF ACRE

After the defeat of the entire Crusader army at Hattin in July, Acre surrendered to Saladin without resistance. Of all the seaports south of Beirut, Tyre alone remained in Crusader hands. Aware of the importance to the Crusaders of Acre as a port, Saladin personally supervised the strengthening of its fortifications that winter. Sure enough, less than two years later, Guy de Lusignan, king of Jerusalem, advanced down the coast from Tyre to besiege Acre. The Crusaders, like Napoleon in future years, took up position on the large tel (El Fukhar) east of the town. Saladin collected his forces on the plain north of Nazareth and hastened to relieve his garrison at Acre, advancing along the line of prominent tels, or mounds of ancient settlements. Gradually Saladin encircled and surrounded the Crusader force itself, block-ading and besieging the town.

THIRD CRUSADE

In the spring of 1191, the bulk of the Third Crusade arrived, consisting of large contingents under King Philip of France and King Richard Coeur de Lion of England. Now the siege operations began in earnest, directed against the strongest towers and walling. These were undermined by sappers and battered by artillery, whose stone missiles are still to be seen in the citadel at Acre. Repeated assaults from movable towers of scaffolding approaching right up to the walls were repulsed. The garrison set light to the wooden towers with a naphthalene preparation, known as 'Greek fire'. All Saladin's efforts to interrupt the siege, however, failed and in July 1191, the weary and starving garrison surrendered.

Acre Made Capital

The port then became the base of Richard's attempted reconquest of the coast and capture of Jerusalem. When this failed, Acre became the capital of the revived Latin kingdom, both king and patriarch taking up residence there, together with the Templars and Hospitallers. During the years which followed, the Teutonic Knights built their castles of Montfort and Judin, still to be seen in the foothills of North Galilee, facing down upon the coastal plain. Subsequent pilgrimages during the thirteenth century converged upon Acre, as their base-port and bridgehead. The religious enthusiasm and single-hearted purposefulness of the earlier Crusades were diluted by political intrigue, commercial competition and ambition. A Fourth Crusade in 1203 only got as far as Constantinople, and a Fifth Crusade as far as Egypt. The Sixth and Seventh Crusades of 1227 and 1243 exercised greater diplomacy and negotiated with the Muslims the restoration of the Kingdom of Jerusalem only to suffer a crippling defeat from a new opponent – the nomad Turks. The Eighth Crusade and Ninth Crusade of 1250 and 1270, both led by St Louis IX of France, failed to defeat either the Kharezmian Turks or the Mameluke (Egyptian) Sultan Beybars. In fact, the Ninth Crusade only reached Tunis. The Mameluke Sultan Beybars and later Kala'un proceeded to conquer the Crusader territories step by step. A ten-year truce was signed with Beybars, but only after he had already won back most of the remaining Crusader strongholds. (Beybars has left his sign of the two lions over St Stephen's Gate at Jerusalem.)

Destruction of Acre

In 1290 Beybars' successor Kala'un determined to wipe out the fortress-port of Acre and the final Crusader footholds on the coast. It was, however, his successor Malik El Ashraf who ultimately besieged, burnt and devastated Acre and occupied Athlit, the last of the Templar castles, in 1291.

LEGACY OF CRUSADES

Thus ended the Crusades, originally inspired by an earnest spiritual longing to open up the pilgrim routes to the sites of the Incarnation and Redemption. The pilgrim today, faced with the amazing evidence left behind during their brief century and a half of spasmodic occupation, will find it hard to assess the value of the Crusades. The sheer industry of their occupation, recorded in enduring buildings, commands respect. There is little reason to expect the rank and file of the crusading armies to have been more pious and devoted or better informed and cultured than those of other medieval forces at arms. There were, of necessity, the camp following of traders, merchants and adventurers who exploited their opportunities in competitive commerce. It is not surprising, however, that the reputation of the Crusaders in both the Jewish and the Muslim world is one of imperialism, avarice and cruelty, senseless slaughter and intolerance. Sometimes the Arab opinion of the West today reflects their opinion of the Crusaders! Certainly the Crusaders returned to Europe with a sense of Arab chivalry, courtesy and hospitality, besides a hearty respect for the fanatical religious zeal of the Muslim. The Crusaders brought back too a vision of the pointed arch, reflected in the later architecture of many medieval European cathedrals. The spirit of the Knights Hospitallers and Knights of St John lives on in the Red Cross and St John's Ambulance brigades of today.

GOLAN HEIGHTS DAY FROM TIBERIAS
SAFED – ANCIENT CITY OF REFUGE, CENTRE OF JEWISH MYSTICISM

Safed was the great intellectual centre of the Jewish revival. Today the town circles a hilltop eight hundred and fifty metres above the Mediterranean and well north of the Sea of Galilee. Both these seas can be seen simultaneously from the top of the town.

HISTORY

In A.D. 66 the priest Flavius Josephus, who led the Jewish rebels of Galilee against the Romans, fortified the town of Zef (or Seph). The surrounding hills acted as beacons, to signal to the Jewish people. During the Crusader occupation, Fulke, King of Anjou, built a citadel here in 1140, which was destroyed by Saladin, rebuilt by the Knights Templars and again destroyed by the Sultan Beybars in 1266. The Muslims made the town the capital of the northern district of Palestine. Here a Jewish community gathered and reached the height of its fame in the sixteenth century. Together with Tiberias, Safed became the centre of Jewish study of the Scriptures, mysticism and symbolism, based upon the Mishnah and Talmud.

RABBI ISAAC LURIA

'In Safed,' it was said, 'is the purest air of the Holy Land and there is not a place where they understand better the profundities and the secrets of the Holy Torah.' In the sixteenth century the first printing press in Asia was established in Safed. The great exponent of its Cabbalist learning was Rabbi Isaac Luria, nicknamed Ha'ari, the lion, in whose name there are two synagogues in Safed today. When it was destroyed by earthquake in 1738, it was said that 'since the destruction of the Temple we have not known such disaster in Israel'. Safed was said to contain in the cave of Shem va'Ever the place where Shem. the son of Noah, expounded the secrets of the Torah to his grandson.

RABBIS SIMEON BAR JOCHAI AND ELEAZAR

Seven kilometres to the west at Meron are the tombs of Rabbi Simeon Bar Jochai and his son Rabbi Eleazar. The Rabbi Simeon lived in the second century A.D. He was one of the leading exponents of the Talmudic literature. Simeon had to take refuge from the Romans in a cave at Pekin, where he composed his Cabbalistic treatise on The Brightness, or the Zohar. In the great pilgrimage to Meron, the people sing:

> In a cave he lay hidden
> By Roman law forbidden
> Our Rabbi bar Yohai
> In the Torah he found his guide
> With spring and carob at his side

Part of Simeon's tomb projects into the adjoining prayer room and the wooden shelf above it is always covered with a large number of notes of supplication, praying that he will intercede with God to obtain the supplicant's desire. On the holiday of Lag Beomer, about a month after the Passover, a pilgrimage is held to the rabbi's tomb, a pilgrimage which has taken place since the sixteenth century. The pilgrims assemble in Safed bearing the flag-bedecked Scroll of the Law and, singing and dancing, process round the city. Then, towards evening, they ride from Safed to Meron where they dance again in the courtyard of Simeon's Tomb. The two tombs are covered with lighted candles and when darkness falls two bonfires are lighted and kept up all through the night, the pilgrims throwing on them clothes soaked in oil to keep them alight. By a Cabbalistic rule, young children have their hair cut for the first time and the cut hair is cast into the bonfires.

SAFED BEACON

Mount Safed was, in ancient times, the site of one of the bonfires by which the news of the new month was passed from Jerusalem throughout the country. 'They used to take long cedar wood sticks and rushes and oleander wood and flax-tow. A man bound these up with rope, went up to the mountain and set light to them. He waved them to and fro and up and down, until he could see his fellow doing the like on the top of the next mountain.'

HILLEL AND SHAMMAI

There are also tombs in Meron which are said to be the tombs of Hillel, the famous rabbi of the years shortly before Jesus, by whose teaching Jesus is thought to have been influenced, also that of his rival, Shammai. At Shammai's Tomb is the traditional Tomb of the Messiah, a rock on which the Messiah will sit at the Last Judgment, after Elijah has blown his trumpet in order to summon all the people to judgment. The synagogue there dates from the second century. Its central doorway consists of huge stones and the upper lintel is also a monolith. It is the Jewish belief that if the lintel should fall of its own accord this would presage the coming of the Messiah. Once, when the lintel was moved by an earthquake, the people of Safed held a feast of celebration for the coming of the Messiah.

PLACES OF INTEREST

The Ari Synagogue of the Ashkenazim, the Jews who came from East Europe through the Balkans. A highly colourful building with medieval vaulting.

The Joseph Caro Synagogue of the Sephardic Jews, who fled from the Spanish Inquisition over the Straits of Gibraltar.

The castle site on the top of the hill, affording views of Mount Hermon, Galilee and the Mediterranean.

The synagogue of Meron, seven kilometres to the west of Safed – much frequented by Jewish pilgrims to the tombs of Rabbi Simeon Bar Jochai and his son Eleazar.

Many other synagogues in Safed town.

Mount Canaan, above Safed, affording magnificent views over Syria.

Relics of the 1948 action include the bullet-scarred police station and the 'Little David' bombard.

HAZOR – STRATEGIC OLD TESTAMENT CITY

EARLY HISTORY

As early as the nineteenth century B.C., Hazor is mentioned in the Egyptian Curses texts, listing enemies of the Egyptian Empire in distant provinces. Hazor is the only Palestinian city mentioned in the Archives of Mari, of the Middle Euphrates, in the same century. Hazor must have been a centre of commerce in the Fertile Crescent, on the caravan route between Egypt and Babylon. It is listed among the conquests of the Pharaohs Thutmosis III, Amenhotep II and Seti I. It occurs in no less than four Archives from El Amarna.

BIBLICAL REFERENCES

In the time of Joshua, Hazor was the chief of a league of northern Canaanite fortresses, gathered by Jabin King of Hazor at the Waters of Merom (once Lake Huleh) to fight against Israel. Joshua defeated them, captured all the cities of the north, but only burnt and destroyed the capital city Hazor. Of all the cities, however, he killed the menfolk, crippled the horses and burnt the chariots (Josh. 11: 1–15).

In the time of Deborah, the children of Israel were oppressed for twenty years by Hazor. Deborah and Barak with a force of infantry held Mount Tabor. Sisera, commander of the Canaanites had a force of some 900 iron chariots at Harosheth, a tell three kilometres north east of Yokneam. Harosheth was probably the iron-smelting furnace of such importance in a period of soft bronze weaponry. Deborah and Barak left their mountain stronghold and attacked the huge chariot force, which was hopelessly bogged down in the swamps of the Kishon, which runs along the base of the Carmel range. Sisera fled on foot and asked hospitality of a Kenite family (a gipsy-smithing tribe) possibly linked with Harosheth. While asleep, he was killed with a tent peg and handed over to Barak (Judges 4: 7–22).

In the time of Solomon, he rebuilt the strategic cities of Hazor, Megiddo and Gezer, dominating respectively the plains of Huleh, Jezreel and Ajalon. His plans of casement wall and city gate were identical in all three cities.

In the time of Pekah of Samaria, Tiglath-Pilezer III conquered Hazor and carried its population away captive to Assyria.

THE SITE AND EXCAVATION

The tell, 600 metres East to West, and 200 metres wide, is bounded by a large plateau on the north, some 1000 by 70 metres in size. The tell was protected by an earthwork, glacis and moat, the plateau by a perimeter earth wall. Solomon's city was on the tell. The gates and casement wall are to be seen in the centre of the excavations. Ahab extended the city and built a keep on the western end of the tell. Between the Solomon and Ahab areas is a vertical water shaft, some forty metres deep, approached by a staircase, as at Megiddo.

Occupation of the Upper City began well before 2000 B.C., but the occupation of the Lower City began in 1800 B.C. This second city was well fortified with a moat on the west side and earth ramparts on the east and north. This well-built Canaanite city was destroyed by fire in the thirteenth century B.C. and never rebuilt. This destruction was almost certainly the work of Joshua. Solomon's reconstruction was confined to the Upper City.

MUSEUM

The most exciting finds from the Lower City mostly came from a series of Canaanite temples and included stelae, statuettes, basins, bowls and a basalt altar. The centrepiece of the museum is an exhibit of two Canaanite temples. In one, the Holy of Holies is exactly as found – the stelae in a line, with one of raised hands towards a symbol of the moon. Beside the larger objects, including a whole sequence of pottery drainpipes, the smaller items – weapons, ritual objects, seals and jewellery – are very impressive.

ORDER OF VIEWING

Upper City from East to West:
Canaanite and Israelite fortifications.
Solomon's gate and casement wall.
Central storehouse.
Underground water system.
Citadel.

Lower City from East to West:
Town gates and Canaanite Temple area.

DAN THE NORTHERN LIMIT OF THE LAND

'From Dan to Beer Sheba.' On the deployment of the tribes, Joshua allocated Dan the coastal plain South of Joppa. When the Danites were unable to hold their territory against Philistine invaders, they moved to the extreme north and occupied the Canaanite city state of Laish (Josh. 19: 47). This city is mentioned in the same Egyptian and Babylonian texts as Hazor.

On the death of Solomon in 928 B.C., Jereboam created two rival shrines within his Northern Kingdom – Dan in the north and Bethel in the south – to establish the religious independence of the Northern Kingdom from the Temple in Jerusalem. At this time, he re-fortified and enlarged the city. Rebuilt in the times of Omri and Ahab, the city was finally destroyed and the population carried away to Assyria, by Tiglath-Pilezer III. Recent research into the practice of pilgrimage to Dan by the King and court of the Northern Kingdom has posed similarities in the 'ritual humiliation' of the king or his 'vicar' to the Passion of Jesus Christ. Among these is a sequence in which a priest, representative of the king, undergoes a process of imprisonment overnight in a bottleneck cell, followed by a ritual flogging and mocking.

ORDER OF VIEWING

The track leads to the *Southern* gate – in itself a sequence of four openings – leading into a courtyard. At the top of the slope is another gate leading through the line of the City Wall, visible on the right. On the *north side* of the tell is the High Place – a square platform on which may well have stood the Golden Calf – approached up a wide staircase from a courtyard. The whole shrine is formed from slabs of early Israelite masonry.

CAESAREA PHILIPPI, BANYAS – SHRINE OF PAN

SOURCE OF RIVER JORDAN

One of the three sources of the Jordan, called the River Hermon, forms the Banyas Waterfall, about two kilometres west of Banyas itself. Here the water gushes from the rock face into a deep cleft, with such strength and spray all the year round as to create a light mist. In the fast-flowing stream, fish over half a metre long are visible. Banyas is a corruption of Paneas, there being no 'P' in Arabic. In the red cliff face, a huge cave enshrining a spring was the outlet of the river. An earthquake has closed the outlet long since and the water now emerges below the cave. High above is a Druse Weli, or Tomb of El Khader. To the right of the cave opening are niches carved in the cliff face, with Greek inscriptions to the god Pan.

PETER'S CONFESSION

Here, Peter made his great confession of faith in Jesus, as the Christ of God, and received the keys of the Kingdom (Matthew 16:13–20).

HEROD PHILIP

The Emperor Augustus presented the District of Iturea in 20 B.C. to Herod the Great, who raised and dedicated a temple for the emperor near the spring. On his death, Herod left the district to his youngest son Philip, who established his capital at Banyas naming it Caesarea Philippi. Agrippa II was a great benefactor of the city. Titus celebrated his successful siege and capture of Jerusalem – according to Josephus spending the lives of many prisoners of war in the process, with mock battles and wild beasts.

CRUSADER CASTLE AND CAMP

The Crusaders used this idyllic setting as a rest camp and re-creational centre, building on the crag above a magnificent castle, Nimrud, which commanded both the approaches to Banyas and the road to Tyre. The castle fell to the Saracens in 1164.

> Almighty God,
> who inspired your apostle Saint Peter
> to confess Jesus as Christ and Son of the living God:
> build up your Church upon this rock,
> that in unity and peace
> it may proclaim one truth and follow one Lord,
> your Son our Saviour Jesus Christ,
> who is alive and reigns with you and the Holy Spirit,
> one God, now and for ever.

THE GOLAN HEIGHTS

NIMRUD

Leaving Banyas, the road climbs steadily, circling the fine Crusader Castle of Nimrud, much of which is still intact. (Nimrud was a 'mighty hunter before the Lord', listed among the descendants of Noah – Gen. 10: 9.) A good view of the castle can be obtained from the road above it.

BIRKET RAM

Eleven kilometres' continuous climb beyond Banyas, the road reaches the southern ridge of the Anti-Lebanon range at the Druse village of Mas'ada. Away to the left is the large Druse town of Majdal-Shams (Tower of the Sun) on the slopes of Mount Hermon. Just beyond Mas'ada is the mountain lake of Birket Ram (the High Pool) seemingly in a vast volcanic crater. Josephus described how Herod Philip had chaff thrown into the lake in hopes that it would reappear down at Banyas and confirm his theory that the lake was the highest source of the River Jordan. Only the prompt action of one of his court by throwing chaff into the river at Banyas ensured that Philip was not disappointed!

MOUNT HERMON

Mount Hermon, the southern high point on the Anti-Lebanon range, is some 2224 metres or 7228 feet high. It overlooks the city of Damascus, forty kilometres to the north-east, and Beirut, sixty kilometres to the north-west. It usually retains some snow for a good six months of the year and is noted for its plentiful dew (Ps 133: 3). Its height and remoteness accord with the description of the mountain of Transfiguration far better than Mount Tabor – quite apart from its proximity to Caesarea Philippi (Mark 8: 27–30, 9: 2–8 and Matt. 16: 13–20, 17: 1–8).

THE GOLAN

Returning south, along the Golan and occasionally within a kilometre or two of the Syrian frontier, Quneitra is reached within fifteen kilometres. Skirting the town, passing United Nations villages and heavily fortified volcanic hills, the route descends either over Jordan at Jacob's Daughters' Bridge, or more spectacularly to the Jordan Delta. The Delta is famous for its marvellous range of bird life with every species of heron and kingfisher. Thence, round either side of the lake, we return to Tiberias.

Part Six:

GENERAL INFORMATION

(inevitably subject to change)

THE CHRISTIAN CHURCH – EASTERN AND WESTERN – IN JERUSALEM TODAY

LANGUAGE

The notice of accusation of Jesus, on his cross, was in three different languages: Greek, Latin and Hebrew. Alexander's empire gave the Greek language to the Middle East, where it spread down the coast of Syria and Palestine to Egypt. St Paul preached and taught in Hebrew and Greek; he wrote his letters in Greek. The Gospels were mostly written in Greek. Even in Rome, the Christian services were Greek until the mid-second century. Certain local languages survived and developed, however: in Egypt the Coptic language, in the Caucasus the Armenian language, in the towns and villages of Palestine and Syria – Aramaic. This last is a Semitic language related to Hebrew and Arabic; it originated among the trading communities of Mesopotamia, from where the Jews of the exile brought it to Palestine. Jesus probably spoke in Aramaic. Latin was the language of the Roman Empire, which succeeded the Greek. Latin was the language of Roman law and order, and it spread throughout Europe. It was the language in which the Gospel was preached throughout the West.

ORGANISATION

From the Pentecost, there was a primitive unity within the Christian Church: common faith, sacraments, apostolic authority and later the threefold ministry of bishops, priests and deacons.

The inner organisation of the Church took form along the lines of civil divisions within the Roman Empire and beyond. The bishops of Antioch, Alexandria and Ephesus were the leading prelates in the East, in the West the bishop of Rome. When Constantine established his capital at Byzantium, the bishop there claimed an equality with the bishop of Rome. Jerusalem too grew in importance at this time, as a centre of Christian pilgrimage.

So, the organisation crystallised into four patriarchates in the East – Constantinople, Alexandria, Antioch and Jerusalem – and one in the West, Rome, which, as the old imperial capital linked with St Peter and St Paul, was regarded as the foremost patriarchate.

SCHISM

Doctrinal disputes were likely to develop on racial, linguistic, political and geographical lines. These broke out in the fifth century and largely concerned the nature of Christ. The patriarch of Constantinople, Nestorius, 426–431, proclaimed that in Christ were not only two natures, divine and human, but also two distinct persons, that of the Son of God and that of the man Jesus. This theory was condemned, as destroying the personal unity of Our Lord, at the Council of Ephesus in 431. Nestorius was exiled and his followers fled beyond the Roman Empire to find refuge among the Syriac Christians in Persia. Until the Mongol and Muslim invasions, this branch of Christ's Church flourished, reaching across Asia into Turkistan, India and China. Today, the Nestorians are still to be found in Iran, Iraq and Eastern Syria.

In Jerusalem, at the Church of John Mark, on a traditional site of the Upper Room, the house of John Mark, there is a Syrian Orthodox community which worships in their chapel in the Holy Sepulchre (west of the tomb) in Syriac, a language almost identical to Aramaic, the language of the Lord. Pilgrims to the House of John Mark may ask the Syrian priest to read the words of the institution of Communion, and then hear the sounds heard by the Twelve: 'This is my body . . . This is my blood. . . .'

After the vindication at Ephesus of the united personality of Christ, a priest at Constantinople declared that, following from the union of the two natures of Christ, he had only one single nature (a monophusis). The theory was condemned at a second council at Constantinople in 448 and, following a fourth Council of Chalcedon in 451, Christ was declared to be of two natures, human and divine united in one person. Disputes, however, persisted and led to permanent schism between Orthodox and Monophysite branches of the Christian Church in the East, though now the Monophysitism is more verbal than real and very little doctrinal divergence separates them. From then until the eleventh century the Orthodox Church held the patriarchates of Constantinople, Alexandria, Antioch and Jerusalem and was in full communion with the Latin West. The Nestorians were in Mesopotamia, the Monophysites in Antioch, Alexandria, Ethiopia and Armenia.

The two sides of the ancient Byzantine empire, the Latin West and Greek East, had grown apart. The barbarians had overrun the West, in which the power of the bishop or pope of Rome had greatly increased. Charlemagne received the imperial crown of the new Holy Roman Empire at the hands of the pope in 800. The popes of Rome claimed as St Peter's successors to rule both West and East. The disagreement fastened on a clause in the Nicene Creed, altered by the Western Church to assert that the Holy Spirit proceeds from the Father 'and the Son'. The East held that this introduced confusion into the Doctrine of the Trinity. So the drift apart became a break in the Great Schism between East and West in 1054. Since then, although present decrees in the Latin West – of the infallibility of the pope, the immaculate conception of the Virgin Mary – have widened the breach, they still have much in common. This includes the same sacraments and threefold Ministry, similar liturgies and moral law, a great respect for the Blessed Virgin and the saints. The last twenty years have gone far to bring closer together the patriarchs and peoples of East and West with the meetings of His All Holiness Athenagoras and His Holiness Paul in Jerusalem, Rome and Istanbul, also of the present patriarch Demetrius with the present Pope John Paul in Istanbul.

IN JERUSALEM TODAY

The Eastern Orthodox Church is the largest numerically in the Holy Land. The patriarch and the monastic community of the Holy Sepulchre, which has a peculiar part in the government of the patriarchate, are Greek-speaking, while the lay-people and their parish clergy are Arabic-speaking. Strangely enough, in Arabic the Orthodox Church is called the 'Roman' Church, because the Arab conquerors considered that the proper name for the Church of the eastern Roman Empire.

Among the other independent Eastern Churches, who went out of communion with the Orthodox Church in the fifth century, are the following:

The Armenian Church, sometimes called Gregorian, is the national Church of the Armenian people. They have a patriarch and monastic community of St James.

The Coptic Church is that of the majority of the native Christians of Egypt. They have an archbishop and monks.

The Old Syrian, or Jacobite, Church has a bishop and monastic community.

The Abyssinian Church is represented by an abbot and monastic community, and has been under the protection of the Egyptian, Coptic Church since the fourth century.

The Roman Catholic Church – commonly called the 'Latin' Church – has had a patriarch in Jerusalem since Crusader times. There are many religious orders in Jerusalem, of which the Franciscans since the thirteenth century have been entrusted with the protection of the Latin rights in the holy places and with the care of pilgrims. Others are the Dominicans, White Fathers, Benedictines, etc., and numerous religious orders of nuns and sisters. The Dominicans have the Ecole Biblique, the French biblical and archaeological centre, linked with the 'Jerusalem Bible'.

The Uniat Churches. Since the Great Schism, the Roman Catholic Church has offered the Eastern Churches the continuance of their national customs and rites provided they recognise the papal supremacy. Small groups have consequently transferred their allegiance to that of the pope to become the Greek Catholics, Armenian Catholics and Syrian Catholics. Their rites and ceremonies are practically the same as those of the independent Eastern Churches, but they follow the Western calendar. The national Syriac-speaking Maronite Church of the Lebanon, which at the time of the Crusades went over in its entirety to the Roman obedience, has a small chapel in Jerusalem. The Greek Catholic or Melkite Church has a seminary at St Anne's Church, under the care of the White Fathers. The Benedictines (a community from the Abbey of Bec-Hellouin in Normandy) have the care of the Crusader Church at Abu Gosh.

The Western pilgrim today can – within a short Sunday morning –

experience a cross-section of oriental liturgies within the Church of the Holy Sepulchre, as nowhere else in the world! What appears at first to be a strange cacophony of languages and cultures proclaims a common gospel of the Risen Lord.

A possible order and timetable might be:

The Syrian chapel, behind the Sepulchre (Syriac/Aramaic) – 08.00
The Coptic Shrine, behind the sepulchre   – 08.15
The Greek Orthodox, central space   – 08.30
The Armenian Chapels, on first floor   – 08.45
Arabic Orthodox Liturgy, Mar Yacoub (from courtyard)   – 09.00
Abyssinian/Ethiopian monastery chapel (from *suq*)   – 09.30

The 'Status Quo' principle of regulating ownership of space and facilities for worship in the Holy Sepulchre goes back centuries. Therefore, more recently arrived Protestant groups may feel excluded. Some of these groups have found hospitality within the Garden Tomb. Anglicans are welcome to celebrate the Eucharist in the Chapel of Abraham, within the Greek Orthodox convent, by arrangement with the Dean of St George's Cathedral.

RELIGIOUS COMMUNITIES IN JERUSALEM – AS IN 1987

ORTHODOX:

Armenian
Armenian Orthodox Patriarchate Road, P.O. Box 14001 – Tel: 282331

Coptic
9th Station, Christian Quarter, P.O. Box 14006 – Tel: 282343

Ethiopian
8th Station, Christian Quarter, P.O. Box 19025 – Tel: 282848

Greek
Greek Orthodox Patriarchate Road, P.O. Box 19633 – Tel: 284917

Roumanian
46 Shivtei Israel – Tel: 287355
Russian
25 Dabagha Street, P.O. Box 991 – Tel: 284580
Russian Orthodox Mission of Moscow
Russian Compound, P.O. Box 1042 – Tel: 222565
Syrian
St Mark's Road, P.O. Box 14069 – Tel: 283304

ROMAN CATHOLIC

Armenian
41 Via Dolorosa, 3rd Station, P.O. Box 19546 – Tel: 284262
Chaldean
Chaldean Street, opposite 'Ecole Biblique', Nablus Road – Tel: 284519
Coptic
St Francis Street, Old City, P.O. Box 186 – Tel: 282868
Greek-Catholic (Melkite)
Greek-Catholic Patriarchate Road, P.O. Box 14130 – Tel: 282023
Latin
Latin Patriarchate Road, P.O. Box 14152 – Tel: 282323
Maronite
25 Maronite Street, P.O. Box 14219 – Tel: 282158
Syrian
Chaldean Street, P.O. Box 19787 – Tel: 282657
Nativity Street, Bethlehem, P.O. Box 199 – Tel: 742497

OTHER:

Episcopal Church of Jerusalem and the Middle East (Anglican)
20 Nablus Road, P.O. Box 1248 – Tel: 287708
Christ Church (Anglican)
Jaffa Gate, P.O. Box 14037 – Tel: 282082
Southern Baptist Convention in Israel (Baptist House)
4 Narkis Street, P.O. Box 154 – Tel: 225942

Jerusalem House – Baptist Centre
35 Nablus Road, P.O. Box 20423 – Tel: 283258
First Baptist Bible Church
Ashafani Street, P.O. Box 19349 – Tel: 282118
Church of Christ
Museum Street (Alhalabi Bldg), P.O. Box 19529 – Tel: 282723
Church of God
Mount of Olives, Near Commodore Hotel, P.O. Box 19287
Church of God of Prophecy
Christian Quarter, 14 Jabsheh Street, P.O. Box 10184
Church of the Nazarene
33 Nablus Road, P.O. Box 19426
Christian and Missionary Alliance
International Evangelical Church, Native Alliance Church
55 Prophets Street, P.O. Box 50 – Tel: 234804
In the Old City: Christian Quarter, El Rasul Street – Tel: 854587
Danish Israel Mission (Lutheran)
48 HaPalmach Street, P.O. Box 20030 – Tel: 663251
Finnish Mission (Lutheran)
Christian Centre, 25 Shivtei Israel Street, P.O. Box 584 – Tel: 233701
Lutheran Church: Church of the Redeemer
Evangelical Lutheran Church in Jordan (E.L.C.J.)
Muristan Road, Old City, P.O. Box 14076 – Tel: 282543 – 285564
   German-speaking Congregation
   Evangelisch-Lutherische Propstei In Jerusalem
   Address: see above – Tel: 282543 – 285564
   English-speaking Congregation
   Address: see above – Tel: 282543 – 285564
Garden Tomb
Nablus Road, P.O. Box 19462 – Tel: 283402
Bible Evangelistic Church (Pentecostal)
32 Shivtei Israel Street, St Paul's Church, P.O. Box 216 – Tel: 717988
Presbyterian St Andrew's Scots Memorial Church
Near Railway Station, P.O. Box 14216 – Tel: 717701
Norwegian Home (Lutheran)
26, Hatzfira Street, Talpiot – Tel: 638923
Seventh Day Adventist Centre
4 Abraham Lincoln Street, P.O. Box 592 – Tel: 221547
Swedish Institute (Lutheran)
58 Prophets Street, P.O. Box 37 – Tel: 223822

Church of God 7th Day
8 Zorobabel Street, P.O. Box 10184 – Tel: 718814
Old Pentecosts (Fellowship of Sion)
Heleycon House, 13 Ragheb Nashashibi Street, Sheikh Jarrah –
Tel: 283964

PROTESTANT CHRISTIAN SERVICES IN JERUSALEM – AS IN 1987

Language Key: E English   G German S Swedish   D Danish
                FI Finnish   H Hebrew A Arabic   Ev Evening

Anglican Church

St George's Cathedral	Daily	7 a.m. (E) Eucharist
Nablus Road, P.O. Box 19018		6 p.m. (E) Ev. prayer
Tel: 282253/287708	Sunday	8 a.m. (E) Eucharist
		9.30 a.m. (A) Eucharist
		11 a.m. (E) Eucharist
		6 p.m. (E) Ev. prayer
Christ Church	Monday to	6 p.m. (E) Ev. prayer
Jaffa Gate, P.O. Box 191	Saturday	
Tel: 282082	Thursday	7.45 p.m. (E) Bible study
	Sunday	9.30 a.m. (E) Holy Communion
		11 a.m. (E) Family worship

Baptist Church

Baptist Congregation	Wednesday	10 a.m. (E) Bible study (women)
4 Narkis Street	Saturday	9 a.m. (E+H) Bible study
P.O. Box 154		10.30 a.m. (E) Worship service
	Sunday	7.30 p.m. (H) Prayer service
Indep. Baptist Bible Church	Wednesday	5.30 a.m. (A+E) Winter Bible study
Salah-ed Din Street	Sunday	10 a.m. (A+E) Sunday School
Tel: 282118		11 a.m. (A+E) Worship
		5.00 p.m. (A+E) Winter worship
		6 p.m. (A+E) Summer Bible study

Christian Brethren Assembly

9 M Smuts St., P.O. Box 1203	Sunday	9.30 a.m. (E)
Tel: 631178		
Church of Christ		
Ezzahara Street (Alhabibi)	Wednesday	6 p.m. (E+A)
P.O. Box 19529	Sunday	6.30 p.m. (E+A)
Tel: 282723		

Church of God of Prophecy		
14 Jabsheh Street	Thursday	8 p.m. (A+E)
Tel: 282205	Sunday	4 p.m. (A) Winter 3 p.m.
Church of God-7th Day		
Zerubbabel St, P.O. Box 10184	Saturday	10.30 a.m. (E) at Ein Rogel St
Tel: 718814		
Church of the Nazarene	Sunday	9.30 a.m. (E) Service
33 Nablus Road		11 a.m. (E)
Tel: 283828		5.30 p.m. (E)
Church of the Redeemer	Thursday	8.30 a.m. (G) Morning prayer
(Lutheran)	Sunday	9 a.m. (A+E) Worship
Muristan, P.O. Box 14076		10.15 a.m. (G)
Danish Israel Mission		
(Lutheran)	3rd Sun.	4 p.m. in Redeemer Church
42/98 14 Hapalmach St	in month	
P.O. Box 20030		
Tel: 357851		
Finnish Christian Mission		
(Lutheran)	Saturday	11 a.m. (H)
25 Shivtei Israel St	Saturday	
Tel: 233701 (Off.) 283300 (Pastor)	1st in month	4 p.m.
	Monday	6.30 p.m. (H) Bible study
	Wednesday	4 p.m. (FI) Bible study
Garden Tomb		
(Interdenominational)	Sunday	9 a.m. (E)
Nablus Road, P.O. Box 19462		
Tel: 283402		
Seventh Day Adventists		
Adventhouse	Saturday	9.30 a.m. (E+H) Bible study
4 Lincoln Street		10.30 a.m.
Tel: 221547		
11 Ali Ibn Taleb St	Saturday	9.30 a.m. (A+B) Bible study
Tel: 283271		10.30 a.m. (A+E) Divine Service
Pentecostals		
Church of God, P.O. Box 19287	Friday	6 p.m. (E) Bible study
Tel: 284436	Sunday	10 a.m. (E) Prayer
Mt of Olives nr Commodore Hotel		
Bible Evangelistical Mission		
32 Shivtei Israel	Saturday	7 p.m. (E) Communion
St Paul's Church	Sunday	6 p.m. (E) Worship
Church of Scotland Presbyterian		
St Andrews	Sunday	10 a.m. (E)
Harakevet St, P.O. Box 14216		

ROMAN CATHOLIC MASSES
IN JERUSALEM – AS IN 1987

| Language Key | (L) Latin | (E) English | (F) French | (S) Spanish | (Ar) Armenian |
| | (A) Arabic | (G) German | (I) Italian | (H) Hebrew | (Sy) Syrian |

CHURCH	SUNDAY		WEEKDAY
Latin Patriarchate Latin Patriarchate Road P.O. Box 14152 Tel: 282323	Summer: Winter:	7.00 a.m. (A) 8.30 a.m. (A) 9.30 a.m. (A) 7.00 a.m. (A) 8.30 a.m. (A) 9.30 a.m. (A)	7.00 a.m. (A)
Greek-Catholic Patr. Greek-Catholic Patr. R P.O. Box 14130 Tel: 282023	9.00 a.m.	(A)	7.00 a.m. (A) except Thurs. & Sat. 6.00 p.m. (A)
Maronite Vicariate 25 Maronite St, P.O. Box 14219 Tel: 282158	10.00 a.m.(A)		
Syrian Vicariate Chaldean St, P.O. Box 19787 Tel: 282657	10.00 a.m.(Sy-A)		
Armenian Patriarchate 3rd Station, P.O. Box 19546 Tel: 284262	9.00 a.m.(Ar.)		
St Saviour's Church 1 St Francis St, P.O. Box 186 Tel: 282868 282354	6.00 a.m.(L) 7.00 a.m.(L) 8.00 a.m.(A) 9.00 a.m.(A) High Mass 10.00 a.m. (L) 11.00 a.m.(A) 5.30 p.m.(L)		5.30–6.30 7.30–8.00 a.m. (L) 5.00 p.m. (A) on Saturday
Cenacle 'Ad Coenaculum' Mount Zion, P.O. Box 14089 Tel: 713597	6.30 a.m.(I)		6.30 a.m. (I)
Dormition Abbey Mount Zion, P.O. Box 22 Tel: 719927	8.00 a.m.(G)		6.45 a.m. (G)
Ecce Homo Via Dolorosa, P.O. Box 19056 Tel: 282445			6.45 a.m. (F) 6.00 p.m. (E)
Flagellation Via Dolorosa, P.O. Box 19424 Tel: 282936	6.00–6.30 a.m. (I) 7.00 a.m.(L+I)		6.00–6.30 a.m. (L+I)
Franciscaines De Marie 9 Nablus Road, P.O. Box 19049 Tel: 282633	9.00 a.m.(F) 11.00 a.m. (S)		7.00 a.m. (F)
French Hospital S. Joseph Sheikh Jarrah, P.O. Box 19224 Tel: 282407	8.30 a.m.(E)		6.30 a.m. (F)

German Hospice S. Charles	6.15 a.m.(G)	6.15 a.m. (G)
12 Lloyd George St	8.00 a.m.(G)	
P.O. Box 8020, Tel: 637737		
Gethsemane – Basilica	6.20, 9.00 a.m. (L)	6.20 a.m. (L)
Mount of Olives	11.30 a.m.(E)	Thurs 4.00 p.m. winter (L)
P.O. Box 186	4.00 p.m.(L)	5.00 p.m. summer (L)
Tel: 283264		except 1st Thurs of
		month: H. Hour
Holy Sepulchre-Calvary	4.30–5.00–5.30 a.m. (L)	4.30–5.00–5.30 a.m. (L)
Old City, P.O. Box 186	6.00–6.30–7.00 a.m. (L)	6.00–6.30–7.00 a.m. (L)
Tel: 284213		
House of Isaiah		
20 Agron St, P.O. Box 1332	6.30 p.m.(H)	6.30 p.m. (H) except on
Tel: 231763		Friday
Notre-Dame Centre	9.00 a.m.(E+A)	6.30 p.m. (E+A)
New Gate, P.O. Box 20531	6.30 p.m.(E)	
Tel: 289723		
Pater Noster (Carmel)	6.45 a.m.(F)	6.45 a.m. (F)
Mount of Olives, P.O. Box 19064		
Tel: 283143		
Pontifical Institute	6.30 a.m.(E)	6.30 a.m. (E)
3 E. Botta St, P.O. Box 497	7.00 p.m.(E)	7.00 p.m. (E)
Tel: 222843		
Ratisbonne Institute	9.00 a.m.(E,F+H)	6.30 p.m. (E,F+H) exc.
26 Sh. Hanaggid St		Friday
P.O. Box 768		7.00 a.m. (E) Mon, Tues,
Tel: 223847		Wed, Thurs
		8.00 a.m. (E) Saturday
St Paul's Chapel	7.30 a.m.(G)	5.50 a.m. (G)
Schmidt College	6.00 p.m.(G)	7.00 a.m. (G)
2 Nablus Road, P.O. Box 19070		
Tel: 283280 – 285927		
Sisters of the Rosary	7.00 a.m.(A)	7.00 a.m. (A)
14 Agron St, Tel: 228529		
St Anne's Church	7.00 a.m.(F)	6.30 a.m. (F)
19 Mujahidin St, P.O. Box 19079		
Tel: 283285		
St James Beit Hanina	9.30 a.m.(A) 10.00 (E)	5.00 p.m. (A+E)
P.O. Box 20089, Tel: 854694	5.00 p.m.(A+E)	on Saturday
St John Ein Karim	7.15 a.m.(F)	7.15 a.m. (F)
P.O. Box 186, Tel: 413639		
Visitation Ein Karim	9.00 a.m.(L)	6.30 a.m. (L)
P.O. Box 186, Tel: 417291		
St Stephen's Church	7.30 a.m.(F)	6.30 a.m. (F)
Nablus Road, Tel: 282213	11.30 a.m.(F)	12.00 noon (F)
Ecole Biblique, P.O. Box 19053		
Terra Sancta	7.00 a.m.(L)	7.00 a.m. (L)
Keren Hayesod St	10.30 a.m.(F)	
P.O. Box 871, Tel 639116	6.30 p.m.(E)	

CHRISTIAN JEWISH AND MUSLIM FEASTS

	1988	1989	1990	1991
CATHOLIC (Gregorian Calendar)				
Holy Mother of God	1 January	1 January	1 January	1 January
Epiphany	6 January	6 January	6 January	6 January
St Joseph	19 March	18 March	19 March	19 March
Annunciation BVM	25 March	18 March	25 March	23 March
EASTER DAY	3 April	26 March	15 April	31 March
Ascension	12 May	4 May	24 May	9 May
Pentecost	22 May	14 May	3 June	19 May
Corpus Christi	2 June	25 May	14 June	30 May
SS Peter and Paul	29 June	29 June	29 June	29 June
Assumption BVM	15 August	15 August	15 August	15 August
All Saints	1 November	1 November	1 November	1 November
Immaculate Conception	8 December	8 December	8 December	8 December
Christmas Day	25 December	25 December	25 December	25 December
ORTHODOX (Julian Calendar)				
Nativity of Our Lord	7 January	7 January	7 January	7 January
Epiphany	19 January	19 January	19 January	19 January
Presentation	15 February	15 February	15 February	15 February
Annunciation BVM	7 April	7 April	7 April	7 April
EASTER DAY	10 April	30 April	15 April	7 April
Ascension	19 May	8 June	24 May	16 May
Pentecost	29 May	18 June	3 June	26 May
Transfiguration	19 August	19 August	19 August	19 August
Assumption BVM	28 August	28 August	28 August	28 August
Exaltation of Cross	27 September	27 September	27 September	27 September
Presentation BVM	4 December	4 December	4 December	4 December
JEWISH				
Purim	4 March	22 March	12 March	1 March
PASSOVER	2–8 April	20–26 April	10–16 April	30–5 Mar/Apr
Pentecost/Shavuot	22 May	9 June	30 May	19 May
Feast of 9th Av	24 July	10 August	31 July	21 July
New Year	12–13 Sept/Oct	30–1 Sept/Oct	20–21 September	9–10 September
Jewish year:	5748/9	5749/50	5750/1	5751/2
Day of Atonement	21 September	9 October	29 September	18 September
Tabernacles	26–2 Sept/Oct	14–20 October	4–10 October	23–29 September
Independence Day	21 April	10 May	30 April	18 April
MUSLIM (dependent upon visibility of the moon)				
Feast of Mirag	14 March	5 March	23 February	12 February
Feast of Ramadam	17 May	7 April	28 March	17 March
Feast of Sacrifice	22 July	14 July	4 July	23 June
New Year – Hegira	13 August	4 August	24 July	13 July
Muslim year:	408/9	409/10	410/11	411/12
Birthday of the Prophet	23 October	13 October	2 October	21 September

EASTER FESTIVALS

YEAR	WESTERN	EASTERN
1988	3 April	10 April
1989	26 March	30 April
1990	15 April	15 April
1991	31 March	7 April
1992	19 April	26 April
1993	11 April	18 April
1994	3 April	1 May
1995	16 April	23 April
1996	7 April	15 April
1997	30 March	27 April
1998	12 April	19 April
1999	4 April	11 April
2000	23 April	30 April
2001	15 April	15 April
2002	31 March	5 May
2003	20 April	27 April
2004	11 April	11 April
2005	27 March	1 May
2006	16 April	23 April
2007	8 April	8 April
2008	23 March	27 April

HOLY WEEK IN JERUSALEM

EASTERN

The forms of worship, of which there are a bewildering variety, yet have a basic similarity which witnesses to their common primitive origins. In all cases, the great act of Christian worship is that instituted by Our Lord himself and called variously the Lord's Supper, the liturgy, the mass, the eucharist. Almost all the ceremonies which a pilgrim is likely to attend have at their centre this great Mystery. Apart from this, the public worship consists mainly in the recitation of the Hours, services of common prayer, suggestive of the ancient synagogue services.

In Holy Week, there are many dramatised forms of worship in which are united the uplifted heart, the spoken word and the outward gesture. The pageantry and novelty of these ceremonies draw many pilgrims and it is necessary to obtain tickets of entrance to the most popular. If the pilgrim's visit covers the Eastern Holy Week, he will have a wider choice of such ceremonies than if he comes for the Western Holy Week. In this case, he will, however, be able to find some of the Eastern rites in the Uniat Churches.

On Palm Sunday, the day begins at about 7 a.m. with the liturgy and processions in each of the Eastern churches: the Orthodox at the Sepulchre and in the Russian cathedral, the Armenians at St James', and the Syrians at St Mark's. On Maundy Thursday, the Orthodox liturgies begin earlier and are followed by 'Feet Washing' (a dramatisation of John 13) beginning about 8 a.m. in the courtyard of the Holy Sepulchre, at 2.30 p.m. at the Armenian Cathedral of St James' where the Gospel is usually read by the Anglican Bishop, and at 4 p.m. in the Syrian Church of John Mark. The Coptic one is during the morning in their Convent of St Anthony, the Abyssinian at noon in their chapel above St Helena's. In each case, the ceremony is a vivid lesson in humility in which the head of each community 'takes the part of' the Christ. In the evening both the Greek and Russian Orthodox enact the ceremony of the Holy Passion – at the Holy Sepulchre and the Russian church in Gethsemane respectively. If the pilgrim cannot stay for the whole service, he should plan to come for the last part.

On Good Friday, the Russians hold the ceremony of the Winding Sheet from about noon, in their cathedral. This is followed by the entombment at 5 p.m. The Greeks enact this ceremony within the Holy Sepulchre, on the actual sites concerned, going in procession first to Calvary, then to the Stone of Anointing and finally into the tomb of Christ. The Armenian entombment at St James' begins at 3 p.m., the Syrian entombment in the Sepulchre at 4 p.m. All these services are vivid portrayals of the burial of Christ.

On Holy Saturday, the central ceremony is the 'Holy Fire', in which the Greek and Armenian patriarchs take part with their Syrian and Coptic equivalents and their processions. The service symbolises the Resurrection, when Christ, the Light of the World, emerged from his tomb. Although the service begins at noon, most of the people will have spent the night in the Holy Sepulchre. The pilgrims will not regret sharing the morning with this excited congregation, in which all branches of the Eastern Churches mingle in a deafening din, penetrated by the ululation of the women and the shouts of the men dancing. The lights are extinguished, the tomb sealed and guarded. At last, after endless processions, the Orthodox patriarch enters the tomb with an Armenian monk – while outside a breathless suspense holds the crowded multitude. Inside, they pray and then thrust out through a 'port hole' on the south side a lighted torch, from which the first candles are lit. Within seconds the whole rotunda is a blaze of moving and waving fire.

Another unique ceremony on the Saturday night is the Abyssinian 'Searching for the Body of Christ', on the roof of St Helena's Chapel at 8 p.m. Here all the colour of the Ethiopians is to be seen in the vestments, umbrellas, symbols and drums of this primitive rite.

The Eastern liturgies then begin, before the tomb of Christ, the Greeks from 11.30 p.m. that night to 2 a.m., the Armenians from 4 a.m. to 7 a.m., while the Russians in their own cathedral have processions, matins and finally liturgy from 1 a.m. to 5 a.m. The pilgrim will do well to begin in the Sepulchre with the Greeks, then go on to the Russian cathedral if he can get there, before returning to the Armenians in the Sepulchre. He should not fail to enjoy the wonderful music of the Russians and the atmosphere of expectancy and triumph within the crowded Sepulchre. Only those who have spent Holy Week in Jerusalem can know the unforgettable thrill of the experience.

NIGHT LIFE OF THE HOLY SEPULCHRE

The hidden and true life of the church is only discovered at night, whether Easter Eve, or any night. At Sundown, the church is shut to the outside world. The Muslim doorkeeper locks the door from the outside, passes a ladder through a square trap to a priest who receives it and locks the church from the inside. As the night begins, there is no light in all the church except for the candles which continually shine before Calvary, the sepulchre and the Stone of Unction. Then, a little before eleven o'clock, lights begin to flicker up. The priests of the various denominations, who have been sleeping about the building in curious dormitories, are coming out for their evening devotions. The Greeks appear on a balcony above the Rock of Calvary; the Franciscans emerge from a tunnel beyond the Latin chapel; the Armenians down an iron staircase above the Stabat Mater. Three bearded sacristans appear and begin to trim the lamps. A sound of door-banging and electric bells is heard. At 11.30 as the ceremonies begin, two vested thurifers appear and proceed around the church incensing every one of the altars.

At midnight the night offices begin, the Latin severe and restrained, the Armenian exuberant and musical. The Latin office is the shortest and when it is completed the Franciscans file off to their tunnel – the Greeks and Armenians sing on. Then begins to permeate through the building the smell of newly baked bread, as the priests of the Eastern rites cook the bread for their morning masses. The Latins, the Greeks and the Armenians say mass every day. The Copts say it on certain days at an altar against the outer wall. The Syrians have a service on Sundays. The Abyssinians perform their liturgy in their homely little church on the roof. The Greeks and Armenians say their masses first. After the Armenians have finished, the Latins say their mass at about 3.30. There is no room within the tomb for more than one priest and his server. Other worshippers kneel outside this claustrophobic little chamber with its single luculus and its antechamber, called the Chapel of the Angels, containing a token of the rolling stone, on which the Angel sat on the first Easter morning.

When all is finished, the ladder is passed out again through the trapdoor, the key handed out to the Muslim doorkeeper and the doors thrown open. The public congregation can come in, for the Latin mass in the sepulchre at 4.30, and other masses follow at all the various altars of Calvary, the Chapel of the Franks and the Latin chapel. At dawn, the worshipper steps out into the street, to be greeted by the cry from the near-by Muslim mosque, 'There is no God but Allah and Muhammad is His Prophet!'

WESTERN HOLY WEEK

The Western Holy Week is less colourful, except perhaps in the Latin ceremonies at the Sepulchre and their processions along the journeys of Our Lord, on Palm Sunday, Maundy Thursday night and Good Friday morning. These routes are also followed by the Anglican 'walks', which are described in detail in the Scriptural Presentations on pages 49–78. These 'processions' or 'walks' offer an opportunity to the pilgrim to share Our Lord's passion and to enter more deeply into the love and purposefulness of this wonderful week, entering with Jesus into the city, passing out in the darkness to Gethsemane, sharing his agony among the olives and following his cross up the cobbled Way of Sorrows to Calvary.

All this, too, is vividly brought home to the pilgrim who attends the Latin ceremonies in the Sepulchre, on Maundy Thursday and Good Friday. On the Thursday, the feet-washing, at which the Latin patriarch officiates, begins at 1.30 p.m. and is followed by the simple and moving service before the tomb, called Tenebrae, because it was originally held at night. There are processions to the Upper Room from St Saviour's Convent at 4 p.m. and to Gethsemane at 7.30 p.m. On Good Friday, the mass of the pre-sanctified, within the Chapel of Calvary, begins at 6.30 a.m. It is usually possible to slip into this, after the Anglican devotions along the Via Dolorosa. The Latin procession along the Via Dolorosa, with an address at each station, begins at 1 p.m. The day closes with the 'Burial Procession' within the Holy Sepulchre once again, with seven sermons at different stations, each in a different language. The climax of the Latin Holy Week is the early pontifical mass before the tomb of Christ on Easter morning.

Finally, neither Eastern nor Western Holy Week is an ideal season for the pilgrim's very first visit to the Holy Land. In fact he will find more peace and less distraction from the basic purpose and pattern of a first pilgrimage at almost *any other* time of the year! But for pilgrims who plan a second visit, Holy Week in Jerusalem – either Eastern or Western – will prove a landmark in their spiritual development.

EASTERN AND WESTERN CALENDARS IN JERUSALEM

The old Julian Calendar, once universal in the Christian Church, is used by the Orthodox Churches today. In the sixteenth century, at the order of Pope Gregory XIII, a new system of reckoning was adopted. This Gregorian Calendar has found acceptance within the Western Churches. Thus, the Orthodox Church, keeping Christmas on their 25 December, actually celebrates on the Western 7 January.

Both East and West observe as Easter the first Sunday after the full moon falling on or after 21 March. As their calendars differ, however, so their dates of 21 March differ and even sometimes, therefore, the moon by which they place their festival. The Eastern Churches still observe the rule of the Council of Nicaea that Easter may never precede or coincide with the Jewish Passover. The West has abandoned this rule long since.

HOLY WEEK AND EASTER IN THE HOLY SEPULCHRE – AS IN 1987

ORTHODOX (ON EASTERN DATES)	CATHOLIC (ON WESTERN DATES)
PALM SUNDAY	
7.30 a.m. Entry of Patriarch in Holy Sepulchre	6.30 a.m. Blessing and Procession of Palms
7.45 a.m. Liturgy in Katholicon	2.30 p.m. Procession of Palms (Bethphage to St Anne's)
10.15 a.m. Procession round Rotunda	4.00 p.m. Daily Procession in Sepulchre
MONDAY	
5.15 p.m. Evening Service in Katholicon	6.00 a.m. Parish Mass on Calvary
	7.00 a.m. Solemn Moss
	4.00 p.m. Daily Procession
TUESDAY	
5.00 p.m. Evening Service in Katholicon	7.00 a.m. Solemn Mass – Holy Sepulchre
	7.30 a.m. Solemn Mass – Chapel of Flagellation
	4.00 p.m. Daily Procession in Sepulchre
WEDNESDAY	
	7.00 a.m. Solemn Mass – Holy Sepulchre
	7.30 a.m. Solemn Mass – Gethsemane
	7.45 a.m. Veneration of Pillar of Flagellation within Holy Sepulchre
	3.00 p.m. Tenebrae in Sepulchre

MAUNDY THURSDAY

5.30 a.m. Liturgy – St James Cathedral

8.00 a.m. Washing of Feet, Parvis of
Holy Sepulchre (Greek)
2.30 p.m. Washing of Feet, St James
Cathedral (Armenian)
4.30 p.m. Washing of Feet, Church
of John Mark (Syrian)

7.00 a.m. Pontifical Mass, Blessing of Oils,
Procession of Blessed Sacrament

2.00 p.m. Washing of Feet
3.00 p.m. Tenebrae & Procession to Cenacle
5.00 p.m. Washing of Feet at Dormition Abbey
8.00 p.m. Holy Hour, in Gethsemane

GOOD FRIDAY

9.20 a.m. Procession to Holy Sepulchre
9.45 a.m. Royal Hours
2.00 p.m. Service in Katholicon
6.00 p.m. Burial Service, Mar Yacoub
7.30 p.m. Procession from Mar Yacoub
10.00 p.m. Burial Service in Katholicon
11.00 p.m. Procession to Edicule

7.00 a.m. Mass of Presanctified, Calvary
10.15 a.m. Way of the Cross from Omariyah
3.00 p.m. Passion Liturgy at Dormition
Tenebrae in Holy Sepulchre
7.00 p.m. Funeral Procession in Sepulchre

HOLY SATURDAY

9.30 a.m. Sepulchre door opened by Armenians
11.00 a.m. Sealing of the Tomb
11.20 a.m. Procession of Banners through
Christian Quarter to Sepulchre
12.00 noon Patriarchal Procession to Sepulchre
12.10 p.m. Armenian, Coptic and Syrian Clergy
attend Orthodox Patriarch in
Katholicon
1.00 p.m. Ceremony of Holy Fire – followed by
Liturgy in Katholicon
8.00 p.m. 'Searching for the Body of Christ',
Ethiopian Convent above St Helena
11.00 p.m. Patriarch enters Basilica of Holy
Sepulchre
12.00 mdnt Procession and Liturgy

6.30 a.m. Blessing of the Holy Fire and
Waters of the Font,
Pontifical mass
5.00 p.m. Solemn Compline in Sepulchre
11.30 p.m. Matins and Lauds in Sepulchre
11.00 p.m. Easter Vigil in Dormition Abbey

EASTER DAY

1.00 a.m. Russian Liturgy – their Cathedral
3.30 a.m. Liturgy of Resurrection ends in
Holy Sepulchre
4.00 a.m. Armenian Liturgy – St James
Cathedral
12.15 p.m. Procession and Solemn Entry of
Patriarch to Holy Sepulchre

8.30 a.m. Solemn Pontifical Mass of Easter
in Holy Sepulchre
4.00 p.m. Daily Procession in Holy Sepulchre
4.30 p.m. Procession to Basilica at
Emmaus (Qubeibe)

EASTER MONDAY

7.00 a.m. Solemn Mass
10.00 a.m. Pontifical Mass, Emmaus, Qubeibe

ST GEORGE'S ANGLICAN CATHEDRAL: Circulates hotels with Holy Week programme, which has included:
Palm Sunday Eucharist with Palms at 11.00 a.m.
Maundy Thursday Devotional Walk from Church of John Mark to Gethsemane from 8.00 p.m.
Good Friday 'Way of the Cross' from First Station, at 6.00 a.m.
Easter Eucharists at 8.00 and 11.00 a.m.
ST ANDREW'S CHURCH OF SCOTLAND:
Easter Sunrise Service 5.00 a.m. and Eucharist 10.00 a.m.
THE GARDEN TOMB:
Sunrise Service, in English at 6.30 a.m., other languages as posted. Otherwise, the Garden may be closed for the rest of the day.

SOME BIBLICAL THEOLOGICAL AND ARCHAEOLOGICAL SCHOOLS WITH COURSES AND FACILITIES IN ENGLISH

ALBRIGHT INSTITUTE OF ARCHAEOLOGY
26 Salah Ed-Din, Jerusalem, P.O. Box 19096   Tel: 02/282131
Language: mainly English
Courses: research students
           academic year and shorter sessions – no courses

AMERICAN INSTITUTE OF HOLY LAND STUDIES
Mount Sion, P.O. Box 1276, Jerusalem   Tel: 02/718628
Language: English, study of Hebrew
Courses: Study and research centre for Bible, archaeology,
           geography, history, etc. Annual programmes, short
           sessions

BEIT ATID CENTRE
2–4 Agron Street, Jerusalem   Tel: 02/226386
Language: English and Hebrew   227463
Courses: Judaic and Biblical studies

BRITISH ARCHAEOLOGICAL SCHOOL
Sheik Jarrah, Jerusalem, P.O. Box 19283   Tel: 02/282901
Language: English
Courses: Institute accepts research students, no courses given

CENTRE BIBLIQUE
Via Dolorosa, Jerusalem, P.O. Box 19056 (Ecce
Homo)   Tel: 02/282445
Language: French and English   282633
Courses: Biblical studies from October to June

ECOLE BIBLIQUE ET ARCHAEOLOGIQUE FRANÇAISE
6 Nablus Road, Jerusalem, P.O. Box 19053   Tel: 02/282213
Language: French, reading Hebrew, Greek, Aramaic
Courses: Annual sessions, seminars, lectures on biblical and
            archaeological subjects (October–June)

ECUMENICAL INSTITUTE FOR THEOLOGICAL RESEARCH: TANTUR
Bethlehem Road, Jerusalem, P.O. Box 19556   Tel: 02/713451
Language: English, French, German
Offerings: Interconfessional, international, theological research
           annual programme: one or two semesters
           summer programme: public lectures

JERUSALEM CENTRE FOR BIBLICAL STUDIES
Damascus Gate, Jerusalem, Spafford Children's
Centre   Tel: 02/285450
Language: English   284875
Courses: Study tours and lectures

SAINT GEORGE'S COLLEGE
31 Salah Ed-Din Street, Jerusalem, P.O. Box 1248   Tel: 02/284372
Language: English
Courses: Biblical, familiarisation with the Holy Land
            (ecumenical) 2-, 3-, 4-week courses from January to
            September;
            10 weeks from September to December

SAINT JOHN'S UNIVERSITY AND CATHOLIC THEOLOGICAL UNION
School of Theology, Collegeville MN 56321, USA Tel: 6123632101
Language: English
Courses: Scripture, history, excursions.
            Programme of 14 weeks (September to December)
Place: Terra Santa Residence,   Tel: 02/419943
            Ain Karim, Jerusalem, P.O. Box 17030

SWEDISH THEOLOGICAL INSTITUTE
58 Prophets Street, Jerusalem, P.O. Box 37   Tel: 02/223822
Language: Swedish, English
Courses: Jewish tradition, biblical studies: annual session, lec-
            tures

JEWISH FESTIVALS AND SYNAGOGUE

FESTIVALS

The festivals are a distinctive feature of Jewish life.
In the Bible six 'appointed seasons' are listed:
The *Shabbat*; The Day of the 'Blowing of the Trumpet'; The Day of Atonement; and The Three Pilgrimage Festivals. Later, other holidays and fast days were added, to reflect occasions of joy and sorrow in Jewish history.

Shabbat
The Bible enjoins the Jewish people to keep the Sabbath as a reminder of the Creation and of the Exodus from Egypt. Not only a day of rest and recreation but a day of joy and spiritual re-creation, the Sabbath is a major influence in Jewish life.

Pesach
Passover, the 'Season of our Freedom', recalls the Exodus. At the *Seder* service, on the eve of Passover the Story of the Exodus is dramatically told. This festival falls in the spring harvest season. On the second day a measure, *omer*, of barley was brought in to the Temple.

Shavuot
The 'Feast of Weeks' – seven weeks after Passover – marks the receiving of the *Torah* and Ten Commandments at Mount Sinai. *Shavuot* is also known as *'Atzeret'* as it marks the 'conclusion' of Passover. In Temple times the summer harvest of first fruits was brought to Jerusalem.

Sukkot
The Festival of Tabernacles is celebrated in temporary huts which recall the booths in which the children of Israel lived whilst journeying through the Wilderness. *Sukkot* sees the ingathering of the autumn harvest, and is celebrated by a procession in the

synagogue bearing the palm branch, the citron, the myrtle and the willow.

Rosh Hashannah
In both character and origin, the Jewish New Year is a purely religious festival. As the traditional birthday of creation, its message is one of judgment. A highlight of the New Year service is the blowing of the *shofar* – the ram's horn – to arouse man to an examination of his deeds.

Yom Kippur
The first ten days of the Jewish New Year are days of Penitence. They conclude with the Day of Atonement, a complete day spent in prayer, spiritual stocktaking, fasting and confession.

Chanukah
'Dedication' is an eight-day festival commemorating the uprising against the Syrian King Antiochus in the year 168 B.C. The victorious Maccabees rekindled the *menorah*, candelabrum, and inaugurated an eight-day dedication of the Temple. In celebration today an eight branched *menorah* is lit.

Purim
'Lots' celebrates the events recorded in the Book of Esther when the Jewish Community in Persia was saved from destruction. In addition to sending gifts to friends and to the poor, the *'Megillah'*, Scroll of the Book of Esther, is read in the synagogue, and, in Israel, there is a national carnival.

Fasts
Three minor fasts in the Jewish calendar are:
The Fast of *Gedaliah*, Third of *Tishri*; the Tenth of *Tevet* and the Seventeenth of *Tammuz*. They are all associated with the end of the Kingdom of Judea. The Ninth of *Av* marks the destruction in the First and Second Temples and, like the Day of Atonement, is a full twenty-five-hour feast.

Lag B'omer
'Thirty-third day' of the *Omer* – barley offering – is a minor festive day occurring in the period of semi-mourning between *Pesach* and *Shavuot*. In Israel it is celebrated by the pilgrimage of many

thousands of people to Mount Meron. Children light bonfires and play outdoor games.

Yom Ha'atzmaut
'Independence Day' recalls the foundation of Israel on the Fifth *Iyar* 5708 – 14 May 1948. In Jewish communities throughout the world special services and celebrations are held. In Israel it is a national holiday.

Tu B'shvat:
The 'Fifteen' of the month 'of Shvat' marks the commencement of spring and is known as the 'New Year for Trees'. On this holiday each school child in Israel goes out to the fields and plants a sapling.

SYNAGOGUE

Holy Ark
The main feature of a synagogue is the Holy Ark, *Aron Hakodesh* or *Tebah*, which contains the Scrolls of the Law, *Sifrei Torah*. It is situated against the eastern wall of the synagogue and is a reminder of the Ark in the Temple which contained the two 'Tablets of Stone'.

Bimah
The platform *Bimah* or *Almemar* is usually placed in the centre of the synagogue. It is from here that the service is read and the 'Reading of the Law' takes place.

The Scroll of the Law
Sefer Torah is a parchment on which the Five Books of Moses have been handwritten by a scribe. Each week on *Shabbat* a portion of the *Torah* is read. There are also special readings for the festivals, fasts and holy days. The *Torah* is covered by an embroidered mantle.

Binder
This is a Binder, *Mappah*, for the Scroll of the Law. In some European communities the wrapper is often decorated with biblical quotations and scenes from Jewish life.

The Bells

Rimmonim, which are fitted to the wooden handles of the *Sefer Torah*, recall the bells which the high priest wore on the hem of his robe to warn the people of his approach. The bells today remind the congregation of this ancient ceremony.

The Pointer

Yad, is used by the Reader of the Scrolls, *Baal Deriah*, to point to each word. He uses it in order not to damage the lettering of the *Torah*.

The Crown

of the Torah, *Keter Torah*, is attached to the Scrolls. It is a fitting ornament to remind the congregation of the majesty of the *Torah*.

The Breastplate

Choshen, hangs in front of the *Sefer Torah* and recalls the breastplate worn by the high priest in Temple times. The little box in the middle contains a plate which indicates the *Shabbat* or festival being celebrated.

THE JEWISH PASSOVER

The Jewish feast of the Passover has for Christians great significance because of its intimate associations with the Last Supper and the Sacrifice of Calvary and it comes about the time of Easter. In origin the feast goes back to the supper eaten by the Children of Israel on the night before their flight from Egypt (Ex. 13 and Deut. 16). Gentiles wishing to witness the domestic celebration of the Passover are often able to do so through the courtesy of Jewish friends, or at Jewish hotels, or by arrangement with the Israeli Government Tourist Department.

The time of the Passover feast is fixed by counting fifteen days from the beginning of the month *Nisan*, making it fall on the night of the full moon. The feast of the Passover lasts seven days from the fifteenth to the twenty-first of Nisan, during the whole of which no leavened bread may be eaten. According to biblical injunction the Passover lamb should be killed on the fifteenth and eaten that evening, since the fifteenth *Nisan* is counted as beginning with sundown.

THE PREPARATION

The home is thoroughly cleaned, and every bit of leaven destroyed, with a special ceremony, on the fourteenth *Nisan*. Tableware and cooking utensils uncontaminated by contact with leaven are brought out for use during the days of unleavened bread.

THE HOME FESTIVAL OR SEDER

On the afternoon of the fourteenth *Nisan*, the Passover table is prepared. The *seder*-dish is placed at the head of the table. On it are placed three large cakes of unleavened bread called *mazzoth*, each wrapped in a cloth. On top of these are placed a boiled egg, symbolic of the daily offering once made in the Temple during the feast; a roasted shank-bone, representing the paschal lamb; the *charoseth* consisting of a mixture of scraped apples, nuts, raisins and cinnamon, said to represent the clay from which the Israelites made bricks; a saucer of salt and water; and the bitter herbs, consisting of horseradish and parsley, which are regarded as signifying the hardship of bondage in Egypt. Each person is provided with wine and a goblet for the four ceremonial winedrinkings, with an additional goblet for the prophet Elijah, should he appear. Large chairs with cushions are prepared for the master of the house, who acts as Celebrant, and for the mistress.

The meal begins with a special blessing *(quiddush)* after which all drink wine and the Celebrant washes his hands. All present are given some parsley and lettuce which is eaten with a blessing. A part of one of the *mazzoth* loaves is broken off and hidden, to be eaten later as the *aficomen* or dessert. The shank-bone and egg are temporarily removed from the *seder*-dish, all take hold of it, lift it, and utter an invitation to all needy persons to share in the feast. The egg and shank-bone are replaced.

The youngest person present then asks why the festival is being kept (cf. Exodus 12: 26), and there follows the ancient story of the Passover supper and the history of Israel, called *Haggadah* or 'telling forth'. This done, the first of the Hallel Psalms, 113 and 114, are recited; a second cup of wine is drunk, and all wash their hands in preparation for the feast. The two cakes of unleavened bread are broken and eaten together with the bitter herbs dipped in the *charoseth*. The meal itself is then eaten, Jewish delicacies being provided according to taste. The *aficomen* which was set aside earlier is now brought forth and eaten. The grace is said and the third cup of wine is taken. This done the doors of the house are opened to allow guests to depart. The fourth cup of wine is poured out, the rest of the Hallel Psalms 115–18, and Psalm 136, are recited and a hymn called the Benediction of Song. The evening ends with popular songs.

THE COLLECTIVE SETTLEMENTS OF ISRAEL

AGRICULTURAL REVIVAL

The return of the Jewish people to Palestine, and the agricultural revival by which it was accompanied, led to a number of interesting social experiments. The Jewish immigrants to Palestine were to an overwhelming extent men and women who had been born and bred in towns. On their arrival they understood that their hope of creating a sound and healthy Jewish national life could not succeed without the formation of a large Jewish farming class. This transformation of the city dweller into a farmer, which would have been difficult in the best of circumstances, was rendered even more complicated by the fact that the soil of Palestine had been neglected for many centuries and that its reclamation involved severe hardship and struggle. The early pioneers realised instinctively that they could not hope to overcome the obstacles in their way – both internal and external – without co-operation in one degree or another. The individual pioneer, working on his own, would have gone under before difficulties which a co-operative group, fortified by a spirit of mutual help, could overcome, granted a sufficient degree of perseverance and devotion.

DEGANYA

This co-operative tendency expressed itself in the first place in the establishment of co-operative workers' restaurants where agricultural labourers were able to get good food at cheap prices and where they could get credit in times of unemployment. From this, there developed the idea of forming co-operative groups for settlement. The first of these groups was formed in 1908 and three years later it established the first workers' collective settlement in Deganya, near the Lake of Galilee.

MOSHAV

The idea of co-operative settlement did not come into existence full-grown. There was a long period of experimentation before two distinct types of settlement crystallised out; the moshav and the kvutza or kibbutz. The moshav is a co-operative smallholders' village in which each family farms its own land on its own account. There is extensive provision for co-operative effort in marketing produce and in buying and distributing commodities which the village cannot produce for itself. There is also a developed system of mutual self-help and in some moshavim there is a system of doing certain types of farming collectively.

KIBBUTZ

The kvutza or kibbutz is a collective village. Land, houses, machinery and livestock – indeed all property – belong to the village as a whole and not to the individual members. The economic position of the individual in the village is governed by the principle 'from each according to his capacity and to each according to his needs'. The kibbutz is a voluntary organisation, every member is free to leave when he chooses, while the act of joining is equally free from any measure of coercion. It is a society based on equality and governed democratically. Today there are 266 such settlements permanently established in Israel, comprising some 132,000 people. The kibbutzim are the focal points in the creation of the new Israel. Theirs is the pioneering role in reclaiming the land, settling not in already fertile places but on the borders of the desert. They form too the front line of Israel's defence.

OPENING HOURS OF CHRISTIAN PLACES *IN* JERUSALEM – AS IN 1987

PLACES	SUMMER	WINTER
Armenian Cathedral of St James Tel: 282331	Mon–Fri 3.00–3.30 p.m. Sat–Sun 2.30–3.15 p.m.	2.00–4.30 p.m. –
Armenian Museum	10.00 a.m.–4.30 p.m. Closed Sunday	–
Bethany St Lazarus Tel: 271706	6.00–11.45 a.m. 2.00–5.30 p.m.	– –
Bethphage, Tel: 284352	7.00–11.45 a.m. 2.00–5.30 p.m.	–
Cenacle-Last Supper room	8.30 a.m.–sundown	–
Cenacle Chapel Tel: 713597	8.00 a.m.–12.00 noon 3.00 p.m.–sundown	– –
Christ Church Office Tel: 282082	8.00–10.00 a.m. 4.30–6.00 p.m.	–
Christian Information Centre Tel: 287647	8.30 a.m.–12.30 p.m. 3.00–6.00 p.m. Closed Sunday	– 2.30–5.00 p.m.
Dominus flevit Tel: 285837	8.00–11.30 a.m. 3.00–5.00 p.m.	–
Dormition Abbey Tel: 719927	7.00 a.m.–12.30 p.m. 2.00–7.00 p.m.	–

Flagellation Tel: 282936	8.00 a.m.–12.00 noon 2.00–6.00 p.m.	– 2.00–5.00 p.m.
Garden Tomb Tel: 283402	8.00 a.m.–12.00 noon 2.30–5.00 p.m. Closed Sunday	9.00 a.m.–12.30 p.m. 2.30–4.30 p.m.
Gethsemane Basilica and Grotto Tel: 283264	8.30 a.m.–12.00 noon 2.30–6.00 p.m.	– 2.30–5.00 p.m.
Holy Sepulchre Tel: 284213	4.30 a.m.–8.00 p.m.	3.00 a.m.–7.00 p.m.
Lithostrotos-Ecce Homo Tel: 282445	8.30 a.m.–12.00 noon 2.30–5.30 p.m. Closed Sunday	8.30 a.m.–4.00 p.m. – –
Lutheran Church of the Redeemer Tel: 282543	9.00 a.m.–1.00 p.m. 2.00–5.00 p.m. Monday 9.00 a.m.–1.00 p.m. Closed Sunday	– – – –
Monastery of Holy Cross Tel: 634442	Irregular. Phone before visiting	–
Paternoster Church Tel: 283143	8.30–11.45 a.m. 3.00–4.30 p.m.	– –
Pilgrims Office Tel: 282621	8.30 a.m.–12.30 p.m. 3.00–6.00 p.m. Closed Sunday	– 3.00–5.30 p.m.
Russian Cathedral Tel: 222565	by appointment	–
Russian Excavations Tel: 284580	9.00 a.m.–1.00 p.m. 3.00–5.00 p.m.; ring bell	– –
St Mary Magdalene Tel: 282897	Irregular. Phone before visiting	–
St Ann's, Bethesda Tel: 283285	8.00 a.m.–12.00 noon 2.30–6.00 p.m. Closed Sunday	– 2.00–5.00 p.m.
Tomb of Mary-Gethsemane	6.30 a.m.–12.00 noon 2.00–5.00 p.m.	– –
St Mark's Syrian Orthodox Tel: 283304	9.00 a.m.–12.00 noon 3.30–6.00 p.m.; ask for key	– –
St Peter in Gallicantu Tel: 283332	8.30–11.45 a.m. 2.00–5.30 p.m. Closed Sunday	– –
St Stephen's Basilica Tel: 282213	7.30 a.m.–1.00 p.m. 3.00–6.00 p.m.	– –

OPENING HOURS OF CHRISTIAN PLACES *OUTSIDE* JERUSALEM – AS IN 1987

PLACES	SUMMER	WINTER
Abu Gosh: Crusader Church Tel: 342798	8.30–11.00 a.m. 2.30–5.00 p.m. Sunday and Thursday closed	– –
Bethlehem: Nativity Church	6.00 a.m.–6.00 p.m.	–
Bethlehem: St Catherine Tel: 742425	8.00 a.m.–12.00 noon 2.30–6.00 p.m.	– –
Bethlehem: Shepherd's Field Tel: 742413	8.00 a.m.–11.30 a.m. 2.00–6.00 p.m.	– 2.00–5.00 p.m.
Cana: Wedding Church Tel: 067/55211	8.30 a.m.–11.45 a.m. 2.30–6.00 p.m.	– 3.00–5.00 p.m.
Capernaum Tel: 067/21059	8.30 a.m.–4.30 p.m.	–
Ein Karem: St John's Tel: 413639	8.00 a.m.–12.00 noon 2.30–6.00 p.m.	– 2.30–5.00 p.m.
Ein Karem: Visitation Tel: 417291	9.00 a.m.–12.00 noon 3.00–6.00 p.m.	– –
Jacob's Well: Nablus	8.00 a.m.–12.00 noon 2.30–5.00 p.m.	– –
Kiriath Jearim Tel: 02/539818	8.30–11.30 a.m. ring the bell	– –
Latrun Monastery Tel: 054/20065	7.30–11.30 a.m. 2.30–5.00 p.m.	– –
Mar Saba Monastery (men only)	with permission of the Greek Orthodox Patriarch	
Mount of Beatitudes Tel: 067/20878	8.00 a.m.–12.00 noon 2.00–5.00 p.m.	–
Mount Carmel: Stella Maris Tel: 04/523460	6.00 a.m.–12.00 noon 3.00–6.00 p.m.	– 3.00–5.00 p.m.
Muhraqa: Sacrifice of Elijah	8.00–11.45 a.m. 1.00–5.00 p.m.	– –
Nazareth: Annunciation and St Joseph's Tel: 065/72501	8.30–11.45 a.m. 2.00–6.00 p.m. Sunday: 2.00–6.00 p.m. only	– 2.00–5.00 p.m. –
Nazareth: Synagogue	8.30 a.m.–5.00 p.m.; ring bell	–
Nazareth: St Gabriel's Well	8.30–11.45 a.m. 2.00–6.00 p.m.	–

Qubeibeh Church Tel: 952495 ext. 4	8.00–11.30 a.m. 2.00–6.00 p.m.	– –
Wadi Kelt: St George's	at any time. Closed Orthodox Easter	–
Bethlehem: St Theodosius Monastery Tel: 742216	8.00 a.m.–12.00 noon 1.00–5.00 p.m.	– –
Tabor: Transfiguration Tel: 067/67489	8.00 a.m.–12.00 noon 2.30–5.00 p.m.	– –
Tabgha: Primacy St Peter Tel: 067/21062 (Mensa Christi)	8.00 a.m.–5.00 p.m.	8.00 a.m.–4.00 p.m.
Tabgha: Loaves and Fishes Tel: 067/21061	8.30 a.m.–5.00 p.m.	
Jericho: Temptation Monastery	8.00 a.m.–11.00 a.m. 3.00–4.00 p.m.	– –

OPENING HOURS OF SHRINES, MUSEUMS, MODELS AND EXCAVATIONS

PLACES	SUMMER	WINTER
Acre: Crusaders' subterranean	9.00 a.m.–6.00 p.m. Friday 9.00 a.m.–1.00 p.m.	9.00 a.m.–5.00 p.m.
Beit Alpha	8.00 a.m.–5.00 p.m.	8.00 a.m.–4.00 p.m.
Beersheba: Abraham's Well	8.00 a.m.–sunset Friday 8.00 a.m.–1.00 p.m. Closed Saturday	– – –
Beersheba: Negev Museum	Mon–Thurs 8 a.m.–2 p.m. 4.30 p.m.–7 p.m. Friday 8.30 a.m.–12.00 noon Saturday 10.00 a.m.–1.00 p.m. free Sunday 8.00 a.m.–2.00 p.m.	– – – –
Biblical Zoo, Jerusalem	8.00 a.m.–sunset Fri., Sat. 8.00 a.m.–3.00 p.m.	8.00 a.m.–6.00 p.m. –
Caesarea Excavations	8.00 a.m.–5.00 p.m.	8.00 a.m.–5.00 p.m.
Citadel, Jerusalem and Museum	8.30 a.m.–4.00 p.m. Fri. 8.30 a.m.–2.00 p.m.	– –
Damascus Gate Excavations	9.00 a.m.–5.00 p.m.	–
David's Tomb, Mount Zion	8.00 a.m.–sundown	–
Dome of the Rock, Mosque	8.00 a.m.–11.00 a.m. 12.15–2.15 p.m.	– –
Al Aqsa and Islamic Museum	Closed Fridays and Muslim holidays	– –

Hadassah, Chagall windows Tel: 446271 or 416333 confirm by phone	8.30 a.m.–3.45 p.m. Friday 9.30–11.30 a.m. Closed Saturday	– – –
Hebron: Tomb of the Patriarchs	7.30 a.m.–11.30 a.m. 1.00 p.m.–1.30 p.m. 4.00 p.m.–5.00 p.m. Closed Friday	– – –
Heikhal Schlomo, Jerusalem Tel: 635212	9.00 a.m.–1.00 p.m. Friday 9.00 a.m.–12.00 noon	– –
Herodium, Bethlehem*	8.00 a.m.–5.00 p.m. Friday 8.00 a.m.–4.00 p.m.	8.00 a.m.–4.00 p.m.
Hisham Palace, Jericho*	8.00 a.m.–5.00 p.m.	8.00 a.m.–4.00 p.m.
Islamic Art Museum, Jerusalem	10.00 a.m.–12.30 p.m. 3.30 p.m.–6.00 p.m. Closed Friday Saturday 10.30 a.m.–1.00 p.m.	– – –
Israel Museum, Jerusalem Tel: 636231 including: Shrine of the Book	Sun–Thurs 10.00 a.m.–5.00 p.m. Tuesday 4.00 p.m.–10.00 p.m. Fri–Sat 10.00 a.m.–2.00 p.m. as above except: Tuesday 10.00 a.m.–10.00 p.m.	– – – –
Jericho, Tel Es-Sultan*	8.00 a.m.–5.00 p.m.	8.00 a.m.–4.00 p.m.
Knesset, Tel: 554111	Sun, Thurs 8.30 a.m.–2.30 p.m. Bring Passport Sitting: Mon–Tues 4.00–9.00 p.m. Wednesday 11.00 a.m.–1.00 p.m.	–
Meggido*	8.00 a.m.–5.00 p.m.	8.00 a.m.–4.00 p.m.
Model of Jerusalem at hotel Holy Land West	8.00 a.m.–5.00 p.m.	8.00 a.m.–4.00 p.m.
Mount Herzl Museum	9.00 a.m.–6.00 p.m. (park) Closed Wednesday Fri., Sat 9.00 a.m.–1.00 p.m.	8.00 a.m.–5.00 p.m. – –
Negev Cities including: Arad, Avdat, Mamshit, Shivta Ophel Archaeological Garden	8.00 a.m.–5.00 p.m. 8.00 a.m.–4.00 p.m. 8.00 a.m.–4.00 p.m.	– – –
Rachel's Tomb, Bethlehem	8.00 a.m.–sundown	–
Rockefeller Museum, Jerusalem	Sun–Thur 10.00 a.m.–5.00 p.m. Fri–Sat 10.00 a.m.–2.00 p.m.	– –
Sanhedrin tombs, Jerusalem	9.00 a.m.–sundown	–
Sebaste, Samaria*	8.30 a.m.–5.00 p.m.	8.30 a.m.–4.00 p.m.
Siloam Pool and Hezekiah's Conduit	8.30 a.m.–3.00 p.m. Friday 8.30 a.m.–1.00 p.m. Friday 10.00 a.m. guided tour Closed Saturday	– –
Solomon's Quarries, Jerusalem	9.00 a.m.–5.00 p.m.	–
Walls of Jerusalem – Walk Damascus to Dung Gate	9.00 a.m.–5.00 p.m.	–

*Friday and Holiday Eve archaeological sites close one hour earlier

PUBLIC TRANSPORT – ARAB AND EGGED BUSES, SHARED TAXI SERVICES

N.B. Egged buses stop on Friday afternoons and resume Saturday sunsets or Sunday mornings. Arab buses run every day.

WITHIN JERUSALEM:

To:	From: JAFFA GATE BUS STATION	From: DAMASCUS GATE ARAB BUS STN	From: EGGED CENTRAL JAFFA STREET
ROUND-CITY	99, stops at major sites – every hour – on the hour		
BIBLICAL ZOO	1 or 15	12 change to 1 or 7	1 or 7
DAMASCUS GATE & ROCKEFELLER (MUSEUM)	1	–	12 or 27
HADASSAH (WINDOWS)	19	27	27
HEIKAL SCHLOMO	19	12 or 27 change to 4, 8, 9, or 31	8, 9 or 31
HOLY LAND HOTEL (MODEL)	21	12 or 27 change to 21	21
ISRAEL MUSEUM	13, 20, 23 change to 9	12 or 27 change to 9	9
JAFFA GATE		21, 22 or 23	13, 20 or 23
MOUNT SCOPUS	2 change to 9 or 28	12 change to 9 or 28	9 or 28
RAILWAY STATION	21, 22 or 23	21, 22 or 23	7, 8, 30, 31 or 38
ISLAMIC MUSEUM	15	12 change to 15	15
JERUSALEM THEATRE			
YAD VASHEM	13, 20 or 23	12 or 27	12, 13, 18, 20 or 23
MT HERTZL			
MEA SHEARIM	2	12 change 2, 35 or 37	35 or 37
SANHEDRIN TOMBS			
EGGED BUS STN	13, 20 or 23	12 or 27	–

OUTSIDE JERUSALEM:

To:	From:	Bus:
BETHLEHEM – (passing Jaffa Gate) –	Arab Bus Station	22
HEBRON – (passing Jaffa Gate)	Damascus/Herod's Gate	23
MT OF OLIVES	Damascus/Herod's Gate	75
BETHANY	Damascus/Herod's Gate	36
JERICHO	Damascus/Herod's Gate	46
SILOAM	Damascus/Herod's Gate	76
EMMAUS-QUBEIBE	Nablus Road opposite Ecole Biblique	45
NEBI SAMUEL	Nablus Road opposite Ecole Biblique	53
RAMALLAH	Nablus Road opposite Ecole Biblique	18
EMMAUS – ABU/GOSH	Egged, Jaffa Road	085 or 086
EMMAUS – LATRUN (½-hourly)	Egged, Jaffa Road	402, 403, 404, 433

LONG DISTANCE FROM JERUSALEM:

To:	From:	Times:	Bus:
ASHDOD	EGGED, Jaffa Road	6.30, 8, 10.30, 12.45 14.45, 16, 18, 20	438
ASHKELON	EGGED, Jaffa Road	6.15, 6.40, 7.10, 7.40 8.30, 9.30, 11, 13.30, 14.30, 16.15, 17.30, 18.30, 19.30	437
BEERSHEBA	EGGED, Jaffa Road	6 to 20.30, every ¾ hour (except 13 and 14)	440 or 443 or 445
BETH SHEMESH	EGGED, Jaffa Road	Every ½ hour	415 or 418
EILAT (book in advance)	EGGED, Jaffa Road	7, 10, 16, 24 (ex. Fri)	444
HAIFA (via Lod)	EGGED, Jaffa Road	6 to 19 every ½ hour	945 or 947
JERICHO	EGGED, Jaffa Road	7, 7.45, 8.20,	961 or 963
TIBERIAS (book in advance)	EGGED, Jaffa Road	9, 11, 12, 13, 14, 14.30, 15, 16.15, 17	
LOD AIRPORT DIRECT (Ben Gurion)	EGGED, Jaffa Road	Express	940
MASADA	EGGED, Jaffa Road	8.30, 9.15, 10.15, 12, 13	486
NAZARETH	EGGED, Jaffa Road	9.30, 13.45 Sundays also 11.15	952 or 955
TIBERIAS, MAGDALA MT OF BEATITUDES HAZOR, KIRIAT SHEMONA (book in advance)	EGGED, Jaffa Road	7, 8.20, 9, 11, 13, 14.30	963

SHARED TAXI SERVICES

To:	From:	Phone in advance:
BETHLEHEM HEBRON JERICHO RAMALLAH ALLENBY BRIDGE GAZA	DAMASCUS GATE	283281 (Abdo)
NABLUS JENIN NAZARETH	3 NABLUS RD	283283
BEERSHEBA EILAT HAIFA ASHKELON	HA RAV KOOK ST	226985
HAIFA	2 SHAMMAI ST	227366 (Aviv) 227967
LOD AIRPORT	CORNER KING GEORGE & BEN YEHUDA ST	227227 (Nesher) 231231

N.B. All information quoted was current at time of writing but may be liable to change. Check in advance.

HISTORY OF THE HOLY LAND
A CHRONOLOGICAL TABLE

EARLY BIBLICAL TIMES

1800–1580 B.C.	Hyksos pharaohs in Egypt, patriarchs in Canaan
1580	New dynasty in Egypt, oppression of Hebrews
1380	Tel El Amarna Tablets begin
1250–1200	Exodus and wanderings in the Wilderness
1200	Invasion of Canaan
1100	Philistine settlements
1000	David: founding of the city
970	Solomon: building of the Temple

DIVISION INTO TWO KINGDOMS

936–722 B.C.	Northern Kingdom of Israel, capital Samaria
936–587	Southern Kingdom of Judea, capital Jerusalem
720–685	Hezekiah
722	Fall of Samaria and Northern Kingdom
701	Sennacherib's invasion and siege of Jerusalem
685–640	Manasseh
587	Destruction of Jerusalem by Nebuchadrezzar
538	First return from exile
538–332	**UNDER THE PERSIANS**
520–516	Rebuilding of the temple of Zerubbabel
444	Rebuilding of the Walls by Nehemiah
332–168	**UNDER THE GREEKS**
332	Alexander the Great
323	The Ptolemids of Egypt
198	The Seleucids of Antioch
168	Desecration of the Temple by Antiochus Epiphanes
168–164	The Maccabees. Independent Jewish kingdom. Dead Sea Scrolls written at Qumran
165	Restoration of the Temple

63 B.C.– A.D. 637	**UNDER THE ROMAN EMPIRE**
63 B.C.	Pompey in Jerusalem
37–4	Herod the Great
20	Rebuilding the Temple
6	The Birth of Jesus
4	Archelaus Ethnarch of Judea
A.D. 6	Judea a Roman Province
14–37	Tiberius, Emperor
26–36	Pontius Pilate, Procurator of Judea
26	Caiaphas, High Priest
30	The Crucifixion
32	Martyrdom of St Stephen
37–41	Caligula, Emperor
37–97	Josephus, Historian
41–4	Herod Agrippa I, king of Judaea. 'Third Wall' built
44	St James the Great is beheaded. St James the Less Bishop of Jerusalem
45	Helena, queen of Adiabene, in Jerusalem. Tombs of kings built
49	Jews expelled from Rome
54–68	Nero, Emperor
64	The Great Fire at Rome
66	The Jewish War
67	Flight of the Church to Pella
70	Destruction of Jerusalem under Titus
70–132	The Legionary Camp in Jerusalem
117–38	Hadrian, Emperor
132	Jewish rebellion under Bar Cochbar
136	Aelia Capitolina founded by Hadrian
185–253	Origen
260–339	Eusebius, historian
313–637	**UNDER BYZANTINE RULE**
306–37	Constantine, Emperor
325	Council of Nicaea
326	St Helena in Jerusalem
333	The Bordeaux pilgrim's visit to Jerusalem
335	Church of the Holy Sepulchre consecrated
346–420	St Jerome. Translation of Vulgate, at Bethlehem
c. 386	Pilgrimage of Paula
408–50	Theodosius II, Emperor

450–61	Eudocia, Empress at Jerusalem
451	Council of Chalcedon. Jerusalem made a patriarchate
527–65	Justinian, Emperor
530	Pilgrimages of Theodosius and Theodorus
570	Birth of Muhammad
610–41	Heraclius, Emperor
614	Sack of Jerusalem by Chosroës, king of Persia
622	The Flight of Muhammad
637	Jerusalem captured by Caliph Omar
637–1099	**UNDER THE ARABS**
661	Umayyad Caliphs make Damascus their capital.
c. 670	Pilgrimage of Arculf, Bishop in Gaul
691	Dome of the Rock built by Abdel Melek
800	Harun er Rashid sends keys of Jerusalem to Charlemagne
870	Pilgrimage of Bernard the Wise
876–939	Eutychius, Patriarch
969	Jerusalem under the Egyptian caliphs, capital Cairo
1010	Destruction of Christian shrines by Caliph el Hakem, including the Tomb of Christ
1048	Restoration by Emperor Constantine Monomachus
1077	Invasion of the Turkomans
1094	Peter the Hermit's visit
1099	First Crusade: Godfrey de Bouillon
1099–1187	**UNDER THE LATINS**
	1099, Godfrey; 1100, Baldwin I; 1118, Baldwin II; 1131, Fulke; 1144, Baldwin III; 1162, Amaury I; 1173, Baldwin IV; 1185, Baldwin V; 1186, Guy de Lusignan
1145–8	Second Crusade: St Bernard and the French
c. 1160	Rebuilding of Church of Holy Sepulchre
1169–93	Saladin, Sultan of Egypt
1187	Battle of Hattin. Jerusalem taken by Saladin
1188–92	Third Crusade: Richard of England
1191	Frederick I, Barbarossa, died
1196	Fourth Crusade: Emperor Henry VI and the Germans
1202	Fifth Crusade: Latin capture of Constantinople

1217	The Sixth Crusade: Andrew of Hungary
1218	St Francis in Egypt
1227	Seventh Crusade
1239	Richard, Earl of Cornwall, and William, Earl of Salisbury, last Christian rulers in Jerusalem
1244–47	The Kharezmian Turkish invasion
1247–1507	**UNDER THE MAMELUKES, CAPITAL CAIRO**
1248–54	Eighth Crusade: St Louis
1260–77	Sultan Beybars
1279–90	Sultan el Mansur Kala'un
1270–2	Ninth Crusade: Edward I of England
1291	Fall of Acre
1453	Capture of Constantinople by the Sultan Muhammad II
1517	Syria and Egypt conquered by Sultan Selim I
1517–1917	**UNDER THE TURKS**
1520–66	Suleiman the Magnificent
1537–42	Building at Jerusalem, including walls of city
1808	Holy Sepulchre destroyed by fire
1832	Jerusalem captured by Muhammad Ali
1841	Anglican bishopric founded
1850	Riots in Jerusalem preceding the Crimean War
1917	Capture of Jerusalem by the British
1917–48	**JERUSALEM UNDER BRITISH RULE**
1917	Balfour Declaration
1923	Britain accepts Mandate of Palestine from League of Nations
1933	Increased Jewish immigration, following Hitler's purge in Germany and East Europe
1939–45	Arab and Jewish units join British forces
1948	Surrender of British Mandate to United Nations. Arab–Jewish War. Declaration of State of Israel
1948–today	**STATE OF ISRAEL**
1949	Israel a member of United Nations
1956	Suez War
1967	Six Day War
1973	Yom Kippur War
1979	Peace Treaty between Israel and Egypt
1983	Israel invades Lebanon. Lebanese Civil War

ARCHAEOLOGICAL PERIODS
IN THE HOLY LAND

Palaeolithic	200,000 B.C. –	14,000 B.C.
Mesolithic	14,000	7000
Neolithic	7000	4000
Chalcolithic	4000	3000
Bronze Age	3000	1200
Iron Age	1200	330
Hellenistic	332	63
Roman	63 B.C.	330 A.D.
Byzantine	330	636
Arab	636	1099
Crusader	1099	1291
Mameluke	1247	1507
Ottoman	1517	1917

RECENT REVELATIONS IN THE OLD CITY OF JERUSALEM

(with thanks to the excavator, Nahman Avigad)

The reconstruction and excavation of the Jewish Quarter has unearthed several important sites and posed various questions. What was the extent of the city at the time of the destruction by the Babylonians in 586 B.C.? Was the city limited to fifteen acres on the ridge of Ophel, or did it extend across the valley and up the Western Hill?

EXCAVATIONS OF THE ISRAELITE PERIOD AND ASSYRIAN SIEGE

In the angle of the Jewish Quarter Street and the Street of the Chain there are two excavations said to prove the extension of the city in the eighth century B.C.

a) *The 'Broad Wall'* of unhewn stones founded on the pink lime-stone rock with eighth century pottery shards, lamps and figurines. Within the wall there were house-walls of undressed stone and plaster, with an inscription 'God, creator of Heaven and Earth'.

b) *A 'Defensive Tower'*, immediately to the north, eight metres high. *Out*side the wall, burned wood remains may be those of siege towers. Also *out*side are Assyrian bronze arrowheads and Persian arrowheads, and Hellenistic arrowheads with tail-shaped fins.

   While *in*side are the iron arrowheads of the Israelites (Isaiah 22: 9–11 & Nehemiah 3: 8 and 12: 38).

EXCAVATIONS OF THE HASMONEAN PERIOD: 164–37 B.C.

These have yet to locate the 'Akra' or citadel, which held out against Judas Maccabeus in 164 B.C. until liberated by Simeon in 141 B.C. Josephus describes it having been within the lower city, and Simeon as 'dominating the Temple'. Certainly the Hasmonean palace must have overlooked the Temple from somewhere on the Western Hill above Wilson's Arch.

EXCAVATIONS OF THE HERODIAN PERIOD: 37 B.C.–A.D. 4

Two residences have been recently excavated.
a) *A Herodian house*, South-East of 'Broad Wall', the north side of Tiferet Israel Street – the short-lived residence of a wealthy family with fine pottery ware.
b) *A palatial mansion*, to the west of and within the Dung Gate, on two floors round a courtyard, with water installations in the basement. A fine fresco on plastered panels and stucco ornamental patterned ceiling in the hall, also a mosaic bathroom.

EXCAVATIONS OF THE FALL OF JERUSALEM: A.D. 70

Titus crucified Jewish prisoners of war along the Mount of Olives, but was reluctant to destroy the Temple or interrupt its sacrifices. He breached the north wall on the fifteenth day of the siege, captured and reduced the Antonia fortress. The Jews razed the buildings between the Antonia and Temple, in order to defend the Temple. During skirmishes in the temple precincts, a Roman soldier flung a burning piece of timber through a door on the North side of sanctuary. Neither Titus nor the Jews were able to quench the flames or restrain the Roman soldiers. All was plundered or burnt.

During a temporary truce and parley, Titus was so angered by the arrogance of the defenders that he gave orders to sack and burn the city. Some 8,400 refugees were then slaughtered by the Zealots in Herod's palace with much looting. With the people slaughtered, the Temple in ashes, the city in flames, little was needed for the Romans to complete the massacre.

'*The Burnt House*' is the name given to a six-roomed house which illustrates the fate of one household in the fire. The piling of the pottery and furnishings of each room in the centre indicates a rapid looting of belongings, before the roof timbers fell in. Several ovens and water vessels seem to suggest its use as a laboratory. The proximity to the Temple suggests spice or incense. An inscription on a weight names the family concerned as 'Kathros', a priestly family infamous for its monopoly of temple trading. Against such was Qumran a protest! A mini 'Son et Lumiere' illustrates the story on the spot.

EXCAVATIONS FROM A.D. 135 TO BYZANTINE TIMES

Following the suppression of the second Jewish revolt against Rome led by Bar Cochba, in the days of Hadrian, the city was again demolished and rebuilt. Belonging to this period and recently excavated are:

a) *The Cardus Maximus*, the colonnaded north south thoroughfare across the city plan in the Madeba mosaic. This was the street leading from the Gate of the Column to the Dung Gate. The Damascus Gate is still called in Arabic 'Bab al Amoud' and part of that monumental second century gate has been excavated below the Damascus Gate. Above the keystone of the eastern arch of the triple gate is a mutilated inscription COL (ONIA) AEL (IA) CAP (ITOLINA) giving the name of the city. Excavations trace the Cardo running south through the Jewish quarter. On to this thoroughfare, in Byzantine times, was built the Church of the Holy Sepulchre and Resurrection, as well as the 'Mother of All Churches' on Mt Zion. In the time of Justinian (527–565) a 'New Church of St Mary' – nicknamed 'The Nea' (in Greek) was also built on to the Cardo, within the wall west of the Dung Gate.

Along the present Habad Street, the Cardo was twenty-two and a half metres wide, bordered on the west by a wall of dressed stones and on the east by an arcade of arches resting on square pillars.

A double row of columns ran the length of the avenue dividing it into three lanes with colonnaded porticoes sheltering the sidewalks. On each side, under the colonnade, ran the drainage channels. The construction is Byzantine on Roman foundations.

b) *The 'Nea' Church.* Built and inaugurated in 543, enclosing a monastery, hostel, hospital and library, as well as the vast church, the 'Nea' is shown clearly on the Madeba mosaic, east of the Cardo and just within the South Gate. Its scale is revealed by the six and a half metre thickness of the perimeter walls. The narthex faced on to the Cardo. The great west door-way, five and a half metres wide, was set back some thirty metres. The south-east corner extends just outside the present sixteenth century wall. The overall length of the Nea complex was 116 metres.

A vast six-vaulted cistern, south of the Nea, complete with plastered walls and pottery pipes, formed a substructure to uphold the complex on the valley side. This accords with a contemporary report on the method of building:

> They threw the foundations out, as far as the limit of the even ground, and then erected a structure which rose as high as the rock . . . They set vaults upon the supporting walls . . . Thus, the church is partly based upon the living rock, and partly carried in the air by a great extension artificially added to the hill.

A large Greek inscription upon the cistern wall reads:

> This is the work which our most pious Emperor Flavius Justinianus carried out with munificence, under the care and devotion of the most holy Constantinus Priest and Hegumen . . .

Abbot Constantine, Hegumen of the Nea is mentioned in patristic literature of the sixth century.

INDEX OF PLACE NAMES
AND PEOPLE

N.B. People's names are shown in italics.